W9-BCE-149

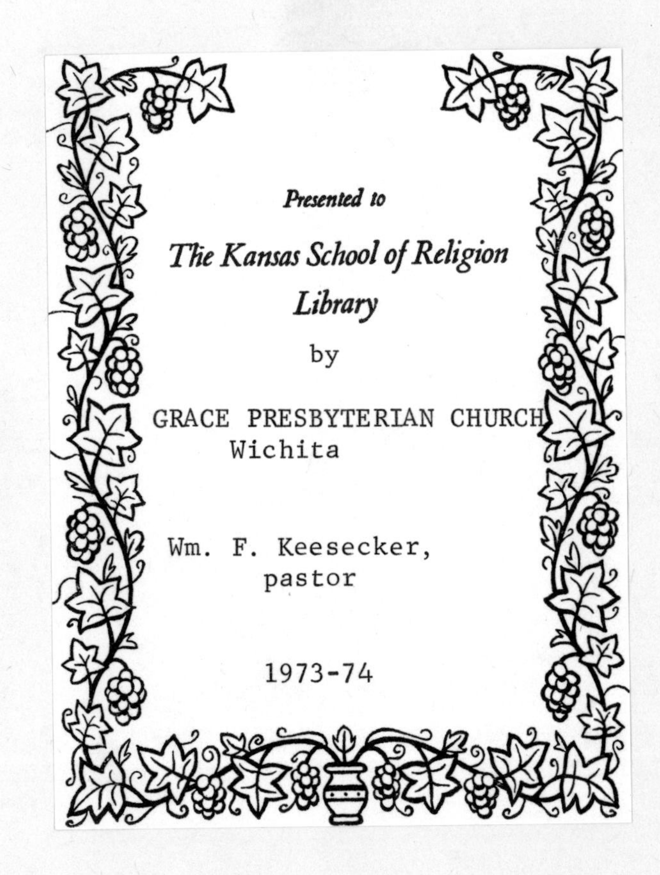
Presented to
The Kansas School of Religion
Library
by
GRACE PRESBYTERIAN CHURCH
Wichita
Wm. F. Keesecker,
pastor
1973-74

STUDENTS RELIGION and the CONTEMPORARY UNIVERSITY

CHARLES E. MINNEMAN *Editor*

EASTERN MICHIGAN UNIVERSITY PRESS 1970

subjects: ① college student - religious life
② universities and colleges - Religion

Ypsilanti, Michigan

Library of Congress Catalog Card Number 70–132320
Printed in the United States of America

ACKNOWLEDGMENTS

Grateful acknowledgment is made to the following publishers and executors for permission to use selections from the works indicated:

AMERICAN ACADEMY OF ARTS AND SCIENCES, Boston: *DAEDALUS,* Journal of the American Academy of Arts and Sciences, Fall 1969, Volume 98, No. 4.

BEACON PRESS, Boston: *ECONOMY AND SOCIETY,* Volume 2, by Max Weber, copyright 1963 by Beacon Press.

COLUMBIA UNIVERSITY PRESS, New York: *CHRISTIANITY AND THE ENCOUNTER OF WORLD RELIGIONS,* by Paul Tillich, copyright 1963 by Columbia University Press.

COMMITTEE OF SOUTHERN CHURCHMEN, Nashville: *KATAL-LAGETE,* Winter 1968–69 issue, Volume 2, No. 1.

NORMA MILLAY ELLIS, Austerlitz, New York: *SONNET CXXXVII* by Edna St. Vincent Millay in *COLLECTED POEMS,* Harper & Row. Copyright 1939, 1967 by Edna St. Vincent Millay and Norma Millay Ellis.

HARPER & ROW, PUBLISHERS, INCORPORATED, New York: "Abraham Lincoln's 'Last Best Hope of Earth'" in *THE LIVELY EX-PERIMENT,* by Sidney E. Mead, copyright 1963 by Harper & Row, Publishers, Incorporated.

LOS ANGELES TIMES, Los Angeles: "Campus Clergy: New Roles in Changing Times," by John Dart, *LOS ANGELES TIMES,* April 1, 1969.

MARC GORDON PRODUCTIONS, INC., For Balloon Music, Inc., Los Angeles: "It's a Great Life", sung by THE FIFTH DIMENSION.

THE UNIVERSITY OF MICHIGAN PRESS, Ann Arbor: *THE POLITICAL IDEAS OF THE ENGLISH ROMANTICISTS,* by Crane Brinton, copyright 1966 by the University of Michigan Press.

ACKNOWLEDGMENTS

THE NEW YORKER, New York: "A New Situation in the World", by Richard Rovere, *NEW YORKER,* February 24, 1968

OXFORD UNIVERSITY PRESS, New York: *A SLEEP OF PRISONERS,* by Christopher Fry, copyright 1951 by Oxford University Press.

SATURDAY REVIEW, New York: *"The Uses of Martyrdom",* by Norman Cousins, April 20, *1968 SATURDAY REVIEW,* copyright 1968 by Saturday Review, Inc.

SOUTHERN ILLINOIS UNIVERSITY PUBLICATIONS, Carbondale: "The Study of Religion: A Quiet Revolution in American Universities" by Robert Michaelsen, in *RELIGIOUS STUDIES IN PUBLIC UNIVERSITIES,* edited by Milton D. McLean, July 1967.

Book design by H. Gralnick Studios

Foreword

The university today is a reverenced place, even when seemingly falling short of honor among its own. Harvard sociologist Daniel Bell recently stated:

> *One of the aspects of modern society is the breakdown of any notion of ritual, a breakdown of a place—call it transcendental place, call it symbolic place—which is meaningful to people and provides some sense of something of importance that goes beyond the immediate self-interest. . . . For most people there are no distinctive places any more; patriotism does not provide you with a sense of identification; religious rites no longer give you that sense of anchorage. To some extent, for a lot of people the university has become, without this being explicated, the transcendental institution in society because it seems to promise the notion of community. It is a place in which people feel an attachment to something beyond themselves—scholarship, learning, books, ideas, the past. The university has some sense of reverence attached to it; it is a place where you have colleagues and engage in activities which are satisfying to you in a very emotional way. (Fall 1969 DAEDALUS, p. 1040)*

Sociologically and religiously the notion of the university as a reverenced place is as fugitive as was Bell's remark in the American Academy of Arts and Sciences' discussion of "The Governance of Universities."

Churchmen, coupling a neighbor-love for the university with something of a selfish regard for their own historic masterworkmanship in the university, are among those who hold the university in such esteem. Today, even the university's secularity is a matter of celebration. "Never on Sunday" is there any large expectation that creed, code and cultus will find extended expression, but rather in the daily round in the college classroom, on the university mall, and in the city streets. As later chapters in this volume will attest, much of the future is seen as residing in "Survival U" with model "university cities" shaped under the ultimate reach of "the City of God."

Students, sometimes leaving the university short of honor, probably provide the best insurance that such a high notion of the university will never reach the point of idolatry. Their critical presence in the university is a constant; yet their quarrelous posture is more like a "lover's quarrel." As later chapters will indicate, even when students think of the university and humankind generally as being without a future, they manage to garner their better hopes for the university. It is seen as, in effect, a launch site for boldly projecting "a grave new world," suffrance in which may require "jail or the translation thereof." Such serious studentship and high regard the university has seldom known.

There is a growing concern among university participants that we not lose this high notion of the university's placement and potential meaning in our society. A concern shared by the sponsoring agent of this volume, the Association for the Coordination of University Religious Affairs (ACURA), this notion of the university as a reverenced place is a watermark on the pages of this volume.

No watermark is without its projecting design. Senator Edmund S. Muskie sets the broad outline of this design: "Religion, the university, and American society are undergoing a common experience—they are all caught up in the turbulence of change." Muskie touches on the fact that no three components in our contemporary situation are being tested or test each other more critically. The survival of each is at stake and is inextricably bound with that of the other. The real test is the critical tolerance of each component and its constructivist posture with respect to the future—*if indeed such be given.*

It is the search for a viable future—more specifically, a viable university future—which constitutes the focus of this volume. Given the occasion of its writing—the tenth anniversary of the Association for the Coordination of University Religious Affairs—one might expect the focus to be on the past. Such a retrospective might concentrate on the developments and constructs marking the coming of age of both religion and the university—a decade of ecumenism in the churches and a ten-year period of university history unparalleled in its design for distinction. In each of these developments ACURA could make some claim as an instrumentality. But as the root term—anniversarius—suggests, an anniversary represents a turning, and given the new challenges posited by this century's closing decades, significant "turnings" become a matter of first interest and import.

Ten original essays follow, honoring the tenth anniversary of ACURA. They represent a collegial attempt to identify and shape "turnings" at points of highest professional challenge. As a unit they constitute a search for a viable university future.

Joseph Shoben introduces Part One—"Soundings Inside the Semesters"—with an in-depth analysis of the current campus sex and violence scenario under the thesis that today's students are the first in history to be unsure that they have a future. Jeopardizing any future just in terms of their *fallout effects* are the immorality of Vietnam, unrelenting racial injustice, poverty in the midst of affluence, the decay of our major cities, and a generalized pattern of depersonalization in our technological, bureaucratic society. Shoben sees the dogmatic existentialism and symbolic politics of student activists as oversimplified and warns that a continued atmosphere of anarchy will only stifle "the very spirit it is our business to nourish and to spread more widely through the world—the spirit of zestful personal life in a proudly humane community." In search of "a new basis for faith in the future" Shoben suggests a reformulation of our contemporary problems "in terms that are congruent to the complicated realities that define our best hopes as well as our gravest dangers." In conclusion he suggests some priority questions for the continuing work agenda of the university.

Viewing the current social impasse as "a spiritual impasse" shared deeply with students, Dan Berrigan and John Smith eschew pure activism and pure withdrawal as "concretely impure." In search of a viable future, the "call to opposite rhythms in our life" is explored. Berrigan moves between the notion of "holy nonchalance, a sitting loose on things," to the search for "a different geography in which to declare a new word" suggesting that "the analogy for these days is jail." Smith holds to playing out a high risk script in the political framework of action. He notes that students in deciding "whether they will resist the draft, whether they oppose the war in Vietnam, and what action they will take relative to the poor and oppressed in the world today" are raising not simply political issues, but spiritual problems as well. Unsure of any future, and essentially cut off from the "blood resources of the tribe" resident in the family, religion, politics and the university, students tend merely to "slap together the latest 'thing' and call it manhood." The result in Berrigan and Smith's view, is "a scrapbook of violence, despair and alienation." For contributing to this situation the university shares responsibility; "The university at one time was a place where . . . new worlds opened up—worlds of meaning and possibility. No longer. The university has simply become another factory, producing its own personnel for industry and business and government."

Because the university "has committed itself to a soul-less technology and neglected the Wisdom dimension," Franklin Littell contends that "the *universitas* is presently programmed for disaster." Radical change is requisite: "the only question is whether there will be sufficient wisdom to provide orderly and reasonable change, or whether the new university will be born in blood." Littell commends student rebels for being "wiser than their elders" in singling out the "fixed positions" requiring change: (1) the university's "subservience to American society's soul-less technology of violence and war"; (2) "mass diplomad mis-education" forged in a "one-generational mold"; (3) the "vested interests" which prevent "codetermination with students in the full gamut of university affairs." Religion's corrective contribution in this situation, states Littell, is "to assist the liberating of higher education through the secularization process, and to advance the inter-personal and inter-religious dialogues which can turn the machine back to the human measure and hold it there."

As the preceding "soundings" indicate, university affairs are now seen as "soul size." In opening Part Two—"Developing the Script of a Profession"—Edwin Bennett interprets this state of affairs as a challenge in religious affairs coordination. He points out that earlier models of coordination, as this involved church-university liaison and the facilitation of existing campus ministries, are generally viewed as marginal to the university's priority agenda. Projecting the model of "initiator" as perhaps more relevant, Bennett sees the coordinator as moving on two fronts—"procedurally, to be a change agent; substantively, to participate in and encourage the dialogue about the religious dimension of the cultural crisis." Working in such a way the coordinator becomes a freed agent in the educational enterprise: "His commitment to human values will make him functional. His need for an identity will be matched as he confronts the need of his institution. His religion, conceptually and existentially, will be coordinate with the reality of these revolutionary times."

One of the assignments traditionally attached to the religious affairs coordinator's office is that of co-curricular programming. Programs about religion in the university's co-curriculum, George Jones indicates, may have as their goal any of several "culturing" thrusts: "(1) the transmission of the religious aspects of the cultural heritage, (2) criticism of the culture or an analysis of current problems from a vantage point of religious positions, and (3) the development of new cultural forms and structures to convey religious meaning and ethical values." Jones describes and evaluates various types of programs: (1) lecture series, art festivals, film series and other forum-type programs; (2) student volunteer service programs; (3) liaison with activist student groups; (4) international programs; and (5) residence hall ministries. Such programs, Jones concludes, assist the university in being "not only a forum for ideas, but also a place where significant search and affirmation of values and meaning can take place."

The coordinator, from time to time, acts in the role of civil celebrant as he participates in events such as Founder's Day, honors convocations, memorial services, and university commencements, all of which still find sanction within the university, even through the celebration tends, at best, to be mere ritual. Students likewise pull off their celebrations—TGs, football busts, the Christmas round, and the "fun and sun" rites of Spring—but without any real university sanction. Suggesting that "we are a culture without the ability to celebrate," Richard Wentz mines for "the sanctions of celebration." Wentz debits our celebrational vacuity to a loss of "appositional power." He defines apposition as "the milieu of meaning that makes it possible for man to live in freedom." Apposition provides three types of sanctions: "sanctions for movement and change, sanctions for participation, sanctions for celebration." These sanctions are provided "insofar as the criteria of meaning, freedom, and hope (respectively) are present." Higher education today, concludes Wentz, is under mandate to "release appositional power for the continuance and well-being of mankind."

Charles Wellborn makes the provocative suggestion that "the coordinator may find some assurance that he is doing his job well if he is occasionally labeled a troublemaker." This the coordinator cannot escape, if he is to act as a morally responsible agent, let alone professionally, within the university as something of a "campus conscience." An even more significant role, in Wellborn's view, is the coordinator's involvement as a "moral counselor," dealing with individual students. He suggests that "university students constitute the code-making (and code-destroying) class in modern American society." Furthermore, the university campus stands as the possible place where the contemporary moral category of "rebellion" might find creative coupling with a parallel search for "therapeutic community"—the search "for somebody who's got the same set of clues so that the clues can be tested and examined." As an educator and moral counselor the coordinator concurs in the classic dictum that "the unexamined life is not worth living."

Against the background of the recently released Danforth Foundation Study of the Campus Ministry, Luther Harshbarger pushes the search for church-university relational models. Viewing education and religion as inextricably related, sometimes heroically, sometimes tragically, in the task of culture transmission-criticism, Harshbarger sees both as currently in "deep trouble." As a counter to "the strident charges of meaninglessness, irrelevance, and even immorality against the university" he sets forth the notion of the university as a "paradigm of the New Technotronic Age" wherein "the soteriological and cognitive converge," valence being given to "the primordial ethic of survival" on one side, and to the "passion for an ordered intellectual vision of the connection of events" on the other. Fittingly "oscillating between the center and periphery" of the university Harshbarger claims a historically precedented, though dramatically shifting, place for religious institutions and their professionals: "If the university is the paradigmatic institution of the socio-technical culture, then the religious professions related to the university are the precursors of the future." The professional precursor is modeled as "one capable of uniting the priestly, pastoral, prophetic, and governing modalities of ministry" so as to permit "discernment of the real occasions in the modern world for thought and action."

Part Three—"Challenges and Prospects"—moves forward along these projective lines. Albert Schaffer suggests that *Techne* has approached a dead end: as "every man a gentleman" becomes reality given the cumulative processes of technological advance, this same technology has also "created the capacity of destroying nations and civilization by nuclear weapons and biological warfare." A compelling "image" of the future is a matter of first priority. Drawing on Weber's analysis of religion, Schaffer notes the crucial role of intellectuals, and especially theologians, in "redefining the 'meaning' of the human condition in the twenty-first century." Exploring such alternatives as the "mobilized polity," the "amusement-entertainment-vacation" style, and the social reforms "quality-of-life" approach, Schaffer sides with a yet undrawn "supranational" ideal concerned with developing global institutions for arms control, universal rule of law, and peaceful conflict resolution—"an international community of man under God." In developing the institutional framework for such an "international, pluralistic society," Schaffer states that the "transcendental beliefs and ethos of the Judaic-

Christian creed, with its universalistic commitment to the brotherhood of man would seem to be prerequisite."

In the attempt of the concluding essay to anticipate or project "the future—if any— of the nation" and "those peculiar American twins, the city and the university," Hubert Locke notes the historic role of religion in their development. He also notes the shift of "the ancient question of 'what has Athens to do with Jerusalem' " to the more pressing one of "what has Athens or Jerusalem to do with Detroit, Chicago, Houston, San Francisco or a dozen other symbols of burgeoning technopolitan complexes." Locke further commends the "indelicate but extremely pertinent questions" of today's students "about the structure, nature, purpose and direction of American society in the second half of the 20th century" as "profoundly religious questions." Locke suggests that "universities can best assure that society will reach the year 2000, and that life in that new epoch will be worth anticipating and living, if they become primarily centers of diligent, rigorous, politically and economically uncommitted, intellectual endeavor." At the same time religion "must cease to be a consecrator of, and become instead a critic of, that culture of which it is part, in the name of and for the sake of . . . the ultimate concerns and questions which man and society face in every age." Together Athens and Jerusalem "may save Megalopolis from itself and for a far brighter future." To demonstrate in the present the shape and style of this future Locke suggests that church and university look on the city "as the social-environmental model of the future," also working "to transform the present dynamics of their institutional life into representations of what that future setting should be—to make, indeed, university cities symbols of the city of God."

One does not move into the publication of a volume of this sort without the assist of many. Serving as co-projectionists of this anniversary volume were two ACURA colleagues, George Jones of Ball State University and Lloyd Putnam of the University of Michigan. The title suggests the next line of assistants. Students immediately involved as kind of confrontationist mentors were Bryan Brown, Helen Malvitz, Barbara Thomas Brown, Phil Butcher and Jerry Whitlock. Religious associates whose tutelage has persisted with me through the years are Charles Sandrock of St. Paul Lutheran Church in Grosse Pointe Farms, Luther Harshbarger of Penn State, the late H. Richard Niebuhr and James Gustafson of Yale. University associates giving encouragement in this project were Dean Susan B. Hill, Vice President Robert Zumwinkle and President Harold E. Sponberg, all of Eastern. A particular debt is owed to my near and dear colleague, Mrs. Gladys Erikson, who has served me and the University so faithfully in the first decade of my professional career at Eastern. Guiding this work to its completion was the director of the University Press, Mr. Curtis Stadtfeld. To all, including the writers, both published and unpublished, one can only say, "Thanx muchly!"

Charles E. Minneman

Contents

Part Three
CHALLENGES AND PROSPECTS

STUDENTS RELIGION and the CONTEMPORARY UNIVERSITY

Introduction

Religion, the University and the Future of American Society

Religion, the university, and American society are undergoing a common experience—they are all caught up in the turbulence of change. Traditional concepts of belief, authority, justice and even the basic premise of our democratic process, are being questioned by our young people as never before.

This is the standard equation of history—the challenge of the young against the old; the emergence of new ideas and new technologies to break down old myths; the development of a younger leadership to challenge the old establishments and doctrines. If this is a standard equation, so is the reaction to it. And the reaction is perhaps increased by the dimension of the challenge. Those of us who are older may shudder at the demands of youth, and become angered by the methods they use to dramatize their concern. I know that there is a growing feeling of resentment at what we feel is the ingratitude of the young; there is astonishment at their reaction, and there is on the part of many of us who are older a feeling of helplessness and even fear.

These feelings are understandable as we do not see our own lives with the same sense of failure as the young people see them. We tend to look back over our younger years with a sense of accomplishment. After all, we pulled ourselves out of a catastrophic economic depression; we mobilized a nation to fight a world war, and we won; we built up a stable post-war economy; we went on to develop a defense and military capability second to that of no other nation; and we have maintained the longest period of prosperity in the country's history.

We may, however, have allowed ourselves to rest too comfortably on these achievements. Perhaps we have not fully understood the meaning of our past as seen in the minds of young people, and we are too eager to reject what they are trying to tell us today. After all, many young people are not concerned with what is to us recent history, but is to them ancient history. As Professor George Wald put it recently, the young are "strangers afraid in a world they never made." In that fear, they are quick to observe our faults, to question our system of values and to challenge our order of priorities for the future. It is, after all, their future too.

That future is marred by many things that they do not like. They see a country committed to a policy of technological suicide—in the production of atomic bombs and missiles, chemical and biological warfare devices, and military space equipment, rather than committed to a real policy of international peace, a de-escalation of armament, and a major program of peaceful assistance to underdeveloped nations. They see a jungle war being waged without end; they know that war is thousands of miles from our shores, that it is costing more than $30 billion and 35,000 American lives a year, and they know that they will have to fight in that war or suffer the shock of jail or exile; and they reject the war.

They are constantly reminded that we are an affluent society; that our gross national product is skyrocketing; and that unemployment is at an all-time low. Yet they walk through the streets of our cities and rural communities, and they see 22 million Americans living under conditions of hunger, poverty, rat-infested and dilapidated housing, disease, pollution, crime and fear.

Young people, whatever their color, economic background, or schooling, are constantly being reminded of freedom and equality of opportunity; the right to a good education, individual respect; a chance to work and have a meaningful part of our political process. Yet they learn from one national report after another that the nation is moving toward greater isolation between black and white, rich and poor; young and old; the suburbs and the city, and war and peace. They know from their own experiences that participation in political affairs is not effective because they cannot vote during those important years from 18 to 21; and because there is no viable policy to involve them in our political structure—either in government, or in our political parties.

Thus, the world that much of youth observes today seems to be one of hypocrisy, unfulfilled promises, broken dreams, and despair. The result is a festering anger and frustration which has broken into violence from the ghettos of the great cities to the ivy covered halls of Harvard University. And there are no signs of its stopping. Other young people have found an alternative by dropping out of life, by using drugs, or by strange rituals and habits that older generations cannot—or will not—possibly understand. Either way, striking out in violent dissent or withdrawal, places a basic mark on those involved.

The real tragedy is that many young people are exaggerating the deficiencies in our American society and the forces opposed to social change. Their emotions and frustrations have conjured up visions of conspiracies against them so great as to blind them to reason. Their despair and anger makes them suspicious of any authority—even those in our institutions who honestly want to help them in their efforts to reform society.

I am worried about this trend, for it is a movement involving more and more young people, not just in universities and colleges, but in high schools and even junior high schools as well. It is a trend we cannot possibly sweep under the rug—it must be considered in every public forum.

THE ROLE OF RELIGION

Religious organizations can help in providing new approaches toward reaching out to our young people. Our faiths are beginning to learn that old doctrines, old texts, and old attitudes about religion and human values need reassessment in a technological age. The young are seeking answers in pragmatic terms; not in pious generalizations. The ecumenical movement in this country is being tested not so much by clerics relating to each other in a common bond of respect for their methods of worship, but in their ability to combine—suburb and city—to reach out to the people who need help. And the greatest need is in the center city. This is the place to concentrate that movement.

Young people desperately need centers where they can talk out their fears, express their grievances, seek individual encouragement and counseling. They need to get their minds off their problems, and on to creative things outside themselves. Sports, the arts, job training, reading, social and religious work—all can make a tremendous therapeutic contribution.

Federal, state and local governments have not moved fast enough and in sufficient degree to provide these necessary alternatives to the idleness and indifference affecting much of our youth today. Even given the great social programs of the past eight years, we have only tapped the top of an iceberg. Despite Constitutional implications, there is a real place for religious institutions working with government to provide the space and the staffing to communicate with young people, and provide a method for explaining to them, and convincing them, of the importance of their individual growth in the years ahead.

THE UNIVERSITY

Like religion, the university in America has developed its own traditions and blindness to the developing frustrations of youth. Perhaps its greatest fault is that it has chosen to be an island for the repose of its students, rather than a center of learning and growth for the entire community in which it resides. In too many instances, the constituencies of the university have been the alumni, the business world and other financial benefactors, including the Federal, State and local governments. Its real constituency—and we must never forget this—is the students and the people who surround the university complex and are affected by its presence in their community.

Much of the unrest on campuses across the nation has related to issues outside the university—international, national, and the immediate urban area. This is extremely significant. Colleges and universities have a responsibility to the nation to cool down their students, and deal with their increasing demonstrations and grievances in a more effective and humane way.

This is not to say that I condone extremism that flouts law and order. It is to say that there are steps, which if carefully taken, may defuse the extremists, and at the same time improve the morale of the university, faculty and students. More than communication, the lines of personal contact between administration, faculty and students should be intensified. Student participation in the decisions of the university should be encouraged. The students know what they don't like about university policy, courses, and campus services. The more rapidly positive reforms can be put into effect—even though it may mean admitting mistakes or breaking with tradition—the more the majority of students will understand that the university really cares.

Panic and overreaction by administration and faculty, and particularly a premature over-saturation of police on the campus, is precisely what the radical leaders seek. The majority of students are not in favor of violence, but when they see unfair sanctions and physical injury inflicted on their friends and associates, they become swept up in the confrontation. Overreaction and massive force can only exacerbate the situation.

Finally, our colleges and universities must begin now to review completely their policies in the light of what appear to be student grievances on a national scale. Waiting for a campus riot to happen is an invitation to disaster. This may mean a de-escalation of military research and greater concern for urban development. It may mean a substitution of a Peace Corps Program for the ROTC. It could mean the single expedient of establishing student faculty advisory boards to develop new curricula bearing more closely on immediate domestic and international issues.

Education is everyone's business and everyone's right. It knows no class, color, or environment. Higher education can no longer be considered a privilege, but rather an essential ingredient of our national development for all citizens who want to become involved in it, and want it to become involved in the building of their nation.

THE FUTURE OF AMERICAN SOCIETY

Young people are right to speak out, to demand a new society, new approaches to life, art and politics. But they must understand that the future of American society is dependent upon the orderly way in which we achieve changes in our social and political institutions and in ourselves.

We are a nation under technological acceleration. We have learned more and invented more in the past five generations than in all the years since the beginning of man. What happens during the next thirty years will be critical to the future of the world.

We must not forget the lessons of man's experience as we seek to build this future.

Intolerance is not the road to justice

Violence is not the road to peace.

Intransigence is not the instrument of reason.

Solving problems is something more than just recognizing them.

No institution or man is endowed with a guarantee against mistakes.

Our challenge—particularly the challenge of youth—is to move with reason, order and logic, not with a tyranny of fear, frustration and disorder.

EDMUND S. MUSKIE
UNITED STATES SENATOR

Part One

SOUNDINGS INSIDE THE SEMESTERS

Edward Joseph Shoben, Jr., widely published specialist in higher education and past director of the Commission on Academic Affairs in the American Council on Education, serves as executive vice president of the Evergreen State College in Olympia, Washington.

The Futureless Generation: Value-Conflicts in the Campus Community

Edward Joseph Shoben, Jr.

As puzzled and disturbed as the rest of us are by the restless and hostile discontent that currently pervades our colleges, George Wald, a Nobel laureate in biology, recently furnished[1] us with a fundamental hypothesis: The present generation of students, he said, is the first in history to be unsure that it has a future. His reference, of course, was to the ironic legacy of the atomic age—ironic because the greatest feat of human creativity yet recorded, the unlocking of the atom's trove of power, has put all the earth's people under the dark shadow of a genocidal weapon. The heritage of youth is a world threatened by its own capacity for global destruction.

That ugly and ultimate danger is reinforced and made more powerfully compelling by the plight of the modern world and harrowing contradictions in American society. Shrunken to a tiny ball by our recently and rapidly developed technologies of transportation and communication, our planet trembles whenever serious troubles break out at any point on its surface. When no place on earth is more than a day's jet travel from any other place, when television signals bounced off man-made satellites can make men in Kyoto or Keokuk simultaneous eye-witnesses to occurrences in Caracas or Copenhagen, then no war is merely of brushfire proportions, no misery simply of local significance, no reallocation of power purely a circumscribed phenomenon. From places once exotic and harmlessly remote, but now functionally close at hand and potentially determinative of our most intimate lives, juggernauts of information roll regularly over us about man's inhumanity to man, about his greedy shortsightedness, and about his lack or loss of reverence and respect for the natural environment in which he lives.

ISSUES IN STUDENT UNREST

In the United States, we are harried and turned a little desperate by two complex issues that defy the constructive imaginations of many of us. One revolves about the American posture in Southeast Asia. The other centers in our patterns of racial injustice, which have come into sharp and inescapable focus as they have become entangled with the degenerative elements in the processes of urbanization and the decay and primitivism that have metastasized throughout our major cities.

In Vietnam, we are fighting the longest, least popular, most incomprehensible, and most inconclusive war in our history. For many of us, but especially for our youth in general and for students in particular, that war represents something close to precisely the brands of imperialism that we have learned to despise in the records of other western nations. It suggests a paranoid style in the conduct of our foreign policy and an almost pathological persistence in anachronistic and wrong-headed interpretations of communist energies in both China and the Soviet Union. In a number of ways, our venture in Vietnam presents an image of a powerful authority figure attempting to impose his will on a weaker and less advantaged member of a community (in this case, the community of nations), simply because it appears to be in his most immediate and self-serving interests to do so. The war diverts resources in both money and men from domestic difficulties of far greater human significance. There is the disturbing racist component of the white man's burden being carried against the stirring "Yellow Peril," and there is the widespread popular—and sometimes official—opposition to our Vietnamese involvement in countries that traditionally have been our allies. And although wars are always and inevitably brutal and brutalizing affairs, one still must shudder with shame at the statistics on bombing density and the volume of explosives and ammunition used, at the employment of napalm and other weapons of a comparable kind, and at such rationalizations as the necessity of destroying the city of Hue in order to save it.

With concerns of this sort agonizingly in circulation, it is not hard to understand the disaffection among young people, who are the ones primarily called upon to fight in such a war, for their country and its principles. There is little that puzzles in the angry resistance of youth to the draft, which is perceived not as a legitimate form of national service for the nation's general benefit, but as a piece of machinery for feeding the guns in Vietnam. And because the course of our action in Southeast Asia has gone on for so long, and been so massively intransigent to change, peace talks in Paris and discussions in Washington of a possible American withdrawal do little to soften among the young the hopeless sense that the outrage and the humiliating immorality of Vietnam are their destiny, and they feel that only a miracle or a destructive revolution will save them from futures that are nasty, brutish, and short.

At home, students, like the rest of us, confront a polarization in race relations some 15 long years after the *Brown* decision and in spite of some genuinely enlightened and humane federal legislation. Domestic violence and pervasive fear underscore an animosity between black and white about which huge numbers of people in both ethnic categories feel helpless and impotent. The signs and symptoms of white backlash, rationalized in the great names of law and order, sometimes seem to be too closely bound up with right-wing extremism in politics and social policy, and they entail, on occasion, the rhetoric of a more sophisticated Ku Klux Klan. The difficulties of extending *de facto* opportunities to Negroes in education, in housing, and in employment after a century of oppressive denial often seem quite intractable. As some elements in the black community become more separatist, whatever the advantages may be, the chance for the races to develop a more harmonious understanding and a more congenial set of relationships, may be lessened; and the dynamics of racism, regardless of its object or of its determinants, remain destructive and a source of anxiety. Similarly, as Negroes grow understandably more militant and demanding, sectors of white society respond more repressively; and on the principle that violence begets violence, the social fabric is torn by erupting mistrust and uneasiness, by an increasing crime rate, and by more frequent civil tensions of a highly upsetting and ominous kind.

Although it is undoubtedly true that more progress toward racial justice has been achieved in the past decade than in any previous period ten times as long, the pace of progress, relative to the expectancies that have been generated, is frustrating. If impatience, a characteristic that typifies more than youth, is not very helpful in this context, neither is it hard to comprehend. And as is the case with Vietnam, so it is with America's blistering racial troubles: for informed young people like students, although hardly exclusively for them, these inhumane and frightening sources of distress often seem to have been with us always and to give little sign of ever abating. What future there may be takes on the shape of a nightmare from which there is no waking.

But if the monstrous complexities in Vietnam and in our racial crisis feed our doubts about tomorrow, there are even more profound and subtler currents in our culture that erode our capacity to imagine and our will to invest ourselves in visions of a brighter day's dawning. Although college students (and many others) find it difficult to articulate their worries about these matters, they are nevertheless deeply disturbed by them, and the trends developing in our larger ways of life echo influentially on our campuses.

There is, for example, the tempo of social change. More massive, more intimate, and more rapid than ever before, the processes of change have made our era virtually discontinuous with our previous history.[2] Since 1910, men have extracted from the earth about the same amount of metal that was mined throughout the existence of the human species before that very recent date. The entire record of aviation, from the Wright Brothers' first tentative moments aloft to the jets that are now a commonplace in our experience and to our fantastic explorations of space, is compressed into the lifetime of a man just ready for retirement. Television was invented only in 1928 and became commercially available only after the end of the Second World War. In less than three decades, man has released the energy of the atom, broken the hold of the earth's gravity, basically solved the riddle of the genetic code, created and made widely available the computer, and worked out ways of transplanting natural organs from one person to another and of subsituting mechanical and electronic devices, (like the artificial kidney and the cardiac pacemaker), for living tissues that no longer function adequately. Within the memories of many of us, various types of environmental control have come into widespread and easy use—air conditioning, the management of insects and other pests, transistorized radios and household appliances, servomechanisms and automatic lathes, and a variety of inexpensive and sure contraceptive devices.

Although the benefits of this incredibly rapid and radical transformation of our world are obvious, they are, in some respects, terrifying. Population data, for instance, convey horror in their cold numbers. Due primarily to advances in medicine and the technology of public health, about one-quarter of all the people who have ever lived are alive at the present moment. By 1977, we can expect something like four *billion* persons to be roaming the globe, representing a doubling in only 40 years. In the United States, our present population of about 200 million will swell to 230 million by 1975 and probably to 250 million by 1980. As Garrett Hardin has recently made clear,[3] such a density of people defines a problem for which there is no technical solution. Neither the development of synthetic foods nor the exploitation of the resources of the oceans is likely to save us from virulent famines; the colonization of other planets as a means of relieving our desperate crowding is little more than a pipe-dream, and notions about the enforced resettlement of people in remaining open areas runs afoul of not only predictable reluctance and overt opposition, but also of a startling possibility, based on mathematical computations: By about the year 2000, there will average only about one square yard of the earth's surface, counting the slopes of the Himalayas and the atolls of the Pacific for each living human being.[4]

The relationship of overpopulation to hunger, poverty, and strife is too well known to require documentation here. But increments in population also account in major ways for other difficulties. The sheer pressure of people explains much of our increasing loss of wilderness and recreation areas. The pollution of air and water is a direct result of fecundity facilitated by technology. Barry Commoner has argued that our environment is under stress to the point of collapse and that "this planet is approaching a crisis which may destroy its suitability as a place for human society." Similarly, Lamont Cole has suggested that even the continued availability of the earth's oxygen supply is threatened by such factors as the increasing volume of jet traffic and the release of industrial wastes and auto exhausts into the atmosphere; the world's population, in his view, may "be already beyond what the earth can support on a continuous basis."[5] For many who are young (and for a not inconsiderable number well over thirty), these interrelated tendencies to reject population controls, to foul the natural nest, and to deplete our global resources reflect a system that is rife with myopic and self-righteous belief in a "progress" that is defined almost wholly in materialistic and power-centered terms of immediate gain. Such an inference is significantly supported by the prevalence of conceptions like that of built-in obsolescence in consumer goods, by the creation through advertising of an endless variety of human wants to support an industrial complex that can thrive only with limitless opportunities for expansion, and by the inevitability of increasing bureaucratization in commercial establishments, in labor organizations, and in government as they grow ever more gigantic. One need not be a prophet of doom to question the future: The decades ahead may indeed be crowded, dirty beyond belief, and as synthetic and ugly, regardless of their potential affluence, as dystopian novelists warn that they may be. And the trends described all imply a manipulation and demeaning of the individual, a progressive removal of the person from the seats of crucial decision-making.

This pattern of depersonalization, which underlies and is deeply enmeshed with what we discuss as the current crisis in personal identity, is also hastened by developments in automation, which may make unemployment a necessary way of life for unprecedented numbers of people in the United States, especially in the categories of semi-skilled and skilled labor and middle management. Within the next 30 years, whole families of jobs are almost sure to vanish before the superior efficiency of servomechanisms, making work far less than the central thing it now is for literally several million people.[6] Such a possibility is so novel that it must be faced with virtually no guidelines to be sketched from past human experience. Our growing knowledge of how to manipulate the genetic code may create heavy pressure to regulate procreation according to some eugenic scheme based on national manpower needs. The progressive refinement of chemopsychic drugs and psychological conditioning processes may extend markedly the controls over conduct that those in positions of authority can exercise. Highly rationalized techniques of systems engineering, applied to industrial and governmental administration, have already produced impressively stringent results in a number of places in the management of organizational affairs. Under all these conditions, the individual, whose distinctiveness has been our traditional touchstone of value, is subordinated to a search for those regularities and consistencies that make for orderliness, predictability, and efficiency. It is not only students that can cite experiences consistent with the idea that this reduction of individuality is already a serious reality. If there is good ground for doubting that the tones of a Cassandra are completely appropriate, there can be no doubt that anxieties of the kind sketched here are certainly relevant to those vague but dark and troubled uncertainties about the future of which Dr. Wald spoke.

FROM EXISTENTIALISM TO ANARCHY

It may be that observations of the kind so briefly sketched here go far toward explaining the existential emphasis of contemporary youth on the present, on that omnipresent *now* that so denies our culture's central and historic orientation toward the future.[7] To be oriented toward the future means putting a premium on reason and foresight as the means for realizing a safer and richer time for one's self and one's family. It means an exaltation of prudence and self-control in the panoply of virtues because they prevent the mortgaging of tomorrow's security against today's pleasures. And it means looking to tradition and history for authority because the future is conceived as the projection of past themes improved by planned variations, not as a radical transformation of what men already know and are familiar with.

When the future commands little faith, however—when its very occurrence can be questioned, or when it is viewed either bleakly or with a hostile apprehensiveness—then it follows that the present acquires a new and more powerful valence. Feeling and affect tend to outweigh cognition by virtue of their sheer immediacy. If there are no anticipations of adequate rewards, then self-control becomes essentially pointless; and if there is too little to look forward to with relish, then prudence becomes unnecessary. Authenticity, directness, and engagement become major values and the catchwords of a very different ethic. Similarly, the logic of tradition and history—the logic of a continuous unrolling of the human scenario—loses place to a logic of experience and involvement. One's operative *Weltanschauung* derives from one's transactions with a series of present moments, from one's interchanges with the current situation, rather than from a sense of history or a bred-in-the-bone belief in either the constancies in human nature over historical time or the recurrent nature of major human difficulties. When a man must choose a "reasonable" course of action or justify his position, he looks not to precedent, which represents the authority of the past, but to the condition of his own heart and the nature of his present passions, which summarize the outcome of his own experiential involvements.

This rise of a rough and loose but powerful form of existentialism, opposing the varied but comprehensive essentialism of our basic tradition, cuts in at least two important directions. In generally defining a philosophical stance, it quite properly feeds upon the notion that the essence of barbarism lies in an imbalance among the inherent qualities of humanity. There can be barbarians of the emotions and of the spirit, as well as of the intellect, and all are threats to civilized and humane ways of life. In our time, one can at least make a case for cultural developments that have enhanced the intellect at the expense of the spirit and to the impoverishment of the affects. A concept of science as the only genuine way of knowing and the rise of scientific positivism as the dominant *motif* in our thoughtways provide the foundation for such an argument. The speculations then lead, quite reasonably, to the manner in which science, translated into technology, has transmuted our entire society into levels of technical and managerial complexity such that ordinary men, far removed from the levers of power, feel helpless and alienated in their roles as citizens and in the degree to which they are captains of their own destiny. One somewhat desperate result is the need to assert their identity as a way of finding it, to upset the workings of what is perceived as an insensate machine as a means of proving their individuality, their strength as persons, and the hegemony of their humanity. The alternative, it is felt, is a full surrender of the spirit and the emotions to the intellect-*cum*-machine, to the learned barbarians of a technological New Germanica.

Whatever the moral implications and merits of these ideas and reactions, they have a certain psychological importance and tenability; they are founded firmly in the theme of man versus the machine that has plagued our culture since the beginnings of the industrial revolution, and they are allied with a number of movements[8] that take as their fundamental point of departure the same basic proposition: In our education as in our communal life, we have exalted intellectual efficiency over emotional development and the cultivation of the resources of the human spirit; to preserve man as man, this excess must be sharply corrected.

The other road down which the existential rationale of today's dissenters takes us leads to a distinction between the dissidence of the 1960s and that of, say, the 1930s. The earlier revolts were rooted in or strongly influenced by the ideology of communism. Marx as interpreted by Stalin contributed the ideas and the rhetoric of Depression radicalism. The Marxist of the time conceived of himself as a "worker," meaning that he had no quarrel with the ethic of work as embodied in capitalism, only with capitalism's economic context. Thinking in terms of an eventual struggle for power between sharply discriminated proletarian and bourgeois factions, he willingly subjected himself to Party discipline or to a discipline modeled roughly after it; he took his tactical cues from an internationally planned and directed strategy, and he kept his eyes fixed steadily on the vision of a post-revolutionary world in which quite specific inequities, cruelties, and injustices would be no more. Toward the arts, his attitudes were deeply conservative, deriving essentially from matters of content with little regard to form or to affective subtleties. Morally, he leaned toward the prudish in all but some approved sexual liberalities; sheer self-indulgence or the muddling of the mind with liquor or drugs was, in his eyes, precisely the kind of thing that capitalism encouraged, using more than religion as an opiate of the people.

The existentially oriented New Left is marked by almost none of these attributes, even when, as is the case with the Maoist Progressive Labor Party, it takes some interpretation of Marx as its formal point of ideological departure. In those who have been radicalized by a sense of having no future, the ethic of work is severely challenged; the difference between proletarian and bourgeois is much less important than the difference between opponents and proponents of "the System," and a subjugation of self to something like Party discipline is almost unthinkable. The tactics of choice are those of confrontation and direct action, especially when they can be combined with spontaneity and conducted under an overflow of powerful emotions; and statements of revolutionary objectives rarely go beyond the specification of what is to be destroyed, seldom attending to the kinds of society or to the sorts of institutions that should replace today's anathemas. Although well aware of the global setting of modern unrest, the contemporary radical fixes primarily on local interests and aims—the humiliation of a university, the overthrow of a ghetto landlord, the embarrassment of a draft board, the harassing of the police in a particular precinct, etc. Aesthetically, he pays almost no attention to content and a great deal to form and the novelties of experience that unusual forms can produce. In personal morality, he argues that no limits can appropriately be imposed on his engagements with sex, with his ways of presenting or expressing himself, with alcohol, or with drugs. In short, although the radical—especially the youthful radical—of the late 1960s may assume many guises, ranging from the dropout flower child to the thug, his basic common denominator is anarchy; his modal style is that of activism and confrontational politics, and his heroes are romantic leaders of guerillas rather than disciplined ideologists and strategists of revolution. Che Guevara is a little reminiscent of the Garibaldi who so stirred British liberals a hundred years ago, and the Ho Chi Minh of radical esteem was more the tactician of jungle warfare than the incredibly patient, persistent, and intellectually ingenious statesman and politician of a unified and independent Vietnam.

Three difficult and complicated points must be made clear in this context. First, the anarchistic impulse that we have been discussing is rooted far more deeply in the social psychology of our time and in the experience of a segment of our population, particularly our youth, than it is in ideology or any intellectual tradition of revolution. Kropotkin and Bakunin are virtually unread among the leaders of student dissent; the trial of Sacco and Vanzetti is not invoked as a part of today's radical rhetoric, and the assassinated Carlo Tresca occupies not even a minor niche in the nihilist hall of fame. We are dealing, it would appear, to a significant degree (a phrase which is *not* a synonym for "totally" or "exclusively") not so much with a revolutionary program based on revolutionary ideas, but with an intense and bitter *reac-*

tion—a reaction that takes *ad hoc* forms, depending primarily on tactical considerations of the moment, in its enraged assault on the perceived Establishment. These observations are entirely consistent, of course, with expectancies generated by Wald's hypothesis of the present generation's sense of being without a future.

Second, our discussion here, like the issues around which campus confrontations characteristically center, is focused more on the problems that sear our society, and on the relationship of the university to the larger social order of which it is inevitably a part, than it is on questions of educational reform. It can be cogently argued that higher education is shockingly poor[9] —almost deliberately inattentive to the difficulties of personal development that beset undergraduates, much too frequently far removed from the problems that buffet students outside the college's boundaries, overly preoccupied with the strategies of an increasingly specialized and professionalized scholarship while quite unimaginative with respect to the processes of learning and teaching, and inclined to present only the model of the don as an image of adult life against which students can react in defining their own identity and their own style. Moreover, for many thoughtful and concerned critics of the university scene, the reformist ideas of students often seem more constructive and more insightful than do the occasional tinkerings of faculty with instructional or curricular affairs. With respect to grading policies, curricular structures, the relationship of instructional devices to the improvement of learning, and the ways in which habits of reflection can be more tightly bound to an enlarging reservoir of experience, the student voice has typically been informed, reasoned, and questing, in marked contrast to the disinterested recalcitrance with which a large number of educational elders reply. Why, then, are we not concentrating more sharply on these questions of educational change?

The answer lies in what may be the sheer fact that the contemporary anarchist, whatever his distinctive stripe, is minimally, if at all, interested in educational reform *per se.* Indeed, he may regularly subvert efforts in such a direction. In part, he may regard improving the quality of educational experience as irrelevant to his more all-consuming concerns and as too tame an objective in which to invest his passions; probably more importantly, he looks upon an institution that genuinely tries to provide, in imaginative and flexible ways, an effective and meaningful education for its students as a barrier to his own task of radicalizing his fellows. After all, the university is a part of the system that has produced his agony. As we have seen, that agony is not without warrant. Should the university then prove itself both kind and challenging, both attentive to developmental needs and responsive to the great issues that now tear the basic tissues of our culture, both a humane place to live and a stimulating place in which to learn how to reflect on one's experience, then the extremist leader will find a reduced base of disaffection and disappointment on which to build his own constituency. On campus after campus that has been rocked by destructive demonstrations, one finds little evidence of educational change, and the opportunities for reform have typically been derided by student leaders, always ignored by them so far as positive action has been concerned, and usually closed by the repeated raising of competing issues that siphon off the energies that must be steadily and responsibly invested to transform a university into an educationally productive and exciting enterprise. Those in whom the anarchistic impulse works, then, must be discriminated from those who yearn for academic reforms, and this distinction is simply one of many that must be firmly kept in mind when one tries to think one's way through the thickets of contemporary unrest. Today's campus radicals, dissenters, and reformers are anything but a homogeneous group, and one may be guilty of injustice as well as error if one succumbs to the temptation of regarding them as cut essentially from the same cloth.

Third, those who fit in some significant fashion the anarchist mold certainly represent a minority of students but a minority the size of which is difficult to estimate. The cadres of revolutionary leadership at large universities rarely exceed 30 or 40, and the number of students whose full loyalty they command is ordinarily no more than two to three hundred. The rallies and mass meetings at which they legitimate their decisions and actions by voting are, with few but possibly increasing exceptions, attended by no more than six percent of the student body. At Berkeley and Columbia, polls taken during the peaks of crisis showed a maximum support for the FSM and SDS that was a little shy of one-fifth of the students enrolled. Although these figures are far from negligible, they clearly make the point that the extremist faction is a small one that claims what often would be regarded as only inconsequential support from the balance of the college population. What, if such is the case, gives this group its apocalyptic power?

Answers here must be tentative, amounting to only a little more than reasonably educated guesswork; but the possibilities that seem most plausible bear directly on the question of whether there is or can be a meaningful collegial community. In all those universities that have been severely battered by student revolts, recognized student governments, typically not at all of the playpen variety, have been the first parts of the institutional apparatus to crumble. Without enforcement mechanisms, neither their legislative nor their judicial powers have proved viable. From within the student bodies at large, two responses among those opposed to disruption have been modal: One has been an impulse to counter-violence, most publicly symbolized by the so-called "jocks" at Columbia. The other and much larger reaction has been one of anxious regret coupled with a refusal to become actively involved. Whatever else it may entail, that refusal seems built upon a profound and often poignant sense that one's integrity as a student will be somehow compromised or damaged if one interferes with or bears witness against other students, regardless of how much one disapproves of the actions taken or looks upon them as flagrant and unjustified violations of acceptable rules or laws. Those who counsel counterviolence raise the spectre of control by vigilantes and define an additional problem with which harried administrative officers must deal. But those who feel that their integrity as students is threatened by any effort to protect the institution represent a still more monstrous fear and put at hazard all notions of community.

Fundamental to the meaning of a community is the implication of a group that is self-regulating and that has the clear capacity, although it may have to exercise it only infrequently, to preserve its own dynamic character against destructive forces that may develop within it. If self-government is to be more than a shibboleth, this kind of resource must be available. When men become gods and their societies heavens, then the necessity for enforcement mechanisms may vanish; until that time, they are one of the harsher realities that derive from the imperfections that inherently characterize the tragic animal that we call man. Usually the preferred and sufficient enforcement device in universities is public opinion and a shared adherence to the processes of civility. In the case and in the climate that we have been discussing, public opinion and the norms of civility have broken down as vehicles of social control; as a result, minorities of no more than 20 percent have disrupted and intimidated large campuses. What may make this peculiar and unsavory situation possible is an unfamiliar and troubling generational element in current patterns of student revolt and in the general student temper.[10]

SINGLE-GENERATIONAL POLITICS

Generational conflict is, of course, a natural and healthy business. In all dynamic socieites, youth makes its cultural inheritance its own by altering it and by departing from it in significant ways. By setting its special stamp on the flow of culture, each generation makes its distinctive contribution to the race's experience and properly defines its particular character in history. If this necessary process usually entails some discomfort and a sense of struggle across society's age gradations, it also occurs ordinarily in a context of generational balance and, with only individualized exceptions, intergenerational respect and even affection.

What confronts us now may be quite different. Complexly compounded of several different tendencies, the contours of student turbulence may presently represent an upsetting of that essential equipoise among generations and a symptom of serious social disorganization. If such should be the case, then it less implies a hopeful quest for solutions suitable to the great problems that hang ominously over all of us, than it describes an additional source of difficulty that interacts with the other issues before us in ways that make them more intense and more perilous. Facing up to this unattractive possibility requires that we explore some of its dimensions.[11]

To begin with, in an age of anxiety like our own, the impulse toward scapegoating becomes a strong one. If our fears, insecurities, and guilt can be loaded, even symbolically, on some source of blame, and if that source of assumed culpability can then be destroyed, the resulting sense of relief, no matter how illusory, is powerfully reinforcing. Not only can we feel absolved from responsibility ourselves from the circumstances that threaten us, but we can escape, at least for a time, the awareness of our impotence and powerlessness through the act of successfully aggressing against some accessible person, group, or institution. Under current conditions, there is a degree of psychological plausibility in the argument that those who are chargeable for the terrifying flaws in contemporary culture are the members of the generation in power—those over, say, 40 years of age. Through the hostile and active condemnation of the elders, young people can both express their disturbed frustration over the nature of so much of modern life and establish themselves as morally superior to those in authority. Because the university is readily accessible and an institution symbolic of the older generation's dominance, it becomes a particularly inviting scapegoat, made all the more so by its vulnerability and its lack of retaliatory power. Even some faculty members can join in scapegoating the university, thereby asserting their youthfulness (and therefore their innocence) and reducing their own anxiety by actively participating in the crippling of an institutional symbol of the Establishment. Among students, it is only in the tiniest fraction of our student bodies that the impulse to scapegoat is so compelling that it amounts to a belief in voodoo: If we stick a pin in Columbia or Oberlin, Harvard or Berkeley, San Francisco State or Michigan, then the war in Vietnam will die or the patterns of racial injustice at home will wither. But among the large numbers who are thoroughly disenchanted with extremist postures and tactics, similar dynamic processes may still be operative. Their disagreement with their peers seems tolerable only if they conform to the norms of generational hostility. In consequence, whatever their opposition to anarchist leaders, they are still prevented from making common cause with professors or administrative officers on behalf of the institution for fear of that ultimate rebuke, "administrative lackey" or "faculty boy." Despite sharp differences within the age group, identification by generation outweighs identification by common ideas or common values.

Second, the stance of extremist leaders implies a generational logic: Because we are students, we are the elite of youth; and because we are a youthful elite, we know best how the world should be shaped. The arrogance here, although it is striking, need not detain us. What is important is the denial of either wisdom or authority to any other age grouping. It follows that the acceptability to the radical core of any older figure is a function of his agreement with them on any particular issue, and such seems to be very much the condition that presently obtains in many universities. The extent to which a faculty member is listened to by the anarchistically inclined depends essentially on the degree to which he supports, articulates, or intellectually legitimizes their own feelings and their own aspirations. For many other students of quite different persuasions, professors represent objects of greater or lesser ambivalence. To be too attentive to their ideas or to them as potential sources of intergenerational friendship risks peer group ridicule or punishments like ostracism; to ignore them or to respond to them positively only when they are on some radically favored list makes a mockery of educational opportunity. One result is that a number of students appear to use faculty members as if they were slot machines out of which information, certain kinds of advice, letters of recommendation, etc., can be extracted, but to be extremely wary of relating to them as people. In any event, the age-grounded generational logic introduces a new and cacophonous note of uneasiness into student-faculty relationships and widens the so-called generational gap.

Third, if today's campus discontent finds its sources in the understandable frustrations, anxieties, and feelings of powerlessness born of a sense of being without a future, its forms of expression seem to entail a constant search for issues to which these affects can become attached. Contemporary student militance contrasts markedly, for example, with labor militance. When an industrial or trade union strikes, it does so for higher wages, shorter hours, improved conditions of work, more rewarding fringe benefits, greater attention to safety features in plant or mine, or for some other goal that is more or less indigenous to the inherent concerns of working men. Similarly, in the long history of earlier student revolts in the United States, a great many of the particular episodes have aimed at educational reforms or at improvements in the qualities of college life that have been quite consonant with the interests of developing young people. The difference in the current situation shows up in the changing nature of the demands presented to administrative officers, in the non-negotiability of those demands, and in the concentration on general political and social issues rather than on the character of the educational experience. In moving from civil rights to Vietnam, to the power of the military-industrial complex, to the presumed deficiencies of capitalism and its culture, student dissent has seemed to become not more intellectually sophisticated, but more intensely concerned with fusing a sense of generational identity with the great issues of our age. If such an effort provides much to admire, it also provides a basis for doubt: To what extent is it oriented toward resolving some of our world's great and distressing tensions, and to what extent is it oriented simply toward giving visibility and vitality to a "movement"? To what degree is its function that of defining a theatre in which particular students can play out their essentially private dramas, heedless of the distinction that C. Wright Mills urged[12] between personal problems and public issues? And do those private dramas, related to, if not rooted in the ugly pressures that our fractured culture exerts, find in significant ways both allies and antagonists for each self-styled hero in generational discriminations? There are times, at least, when it looks as if the good guys and the bad guys are cast far more on the basis of age than on that of outlook or commitment, and when it appears that the task of the hero is more that of radicalizing his fellows (*i. e.,* creating allies from the same age grade) than that of achieving substantive goals.

Fourth, there is a peculiar interaction of the doctrinaire with the oversimplified that seems bound up with student status and the growing power of the youth culture. On the one hand, if students are sufficiently radical they can do no wrong; therefore, they can commit unlawful acts with full expectation of amnesty. On the other hand, because their hearts and aspirations are pure,[13] they need not attend to the complexity of the issues on which they fasten; therefore, they can insist upon simple and immediate answers to profoundly complicated questions. When the notion that the end justifies the means[14] is coupled with the concept that social righteousness is instantly attainable, the seeds of fanaticism have begun to sprout. The occupancy of buildings, the invasion of files, the destruction of facilities, and the threatening of both other students and some faculty members are all tactics employed in the morally idealistic effort to enlist the university in the elimination of war, racism, and poverty. If the interests of others—in getting on with their education, in pursuing a long established line of scholarship, in developing the material resources of the institution or in furthering its capabilities as an educational and investigative enterprise—are interfered with, it is of no account because they are so clearly subordinate to the great purposes to which the tactics are dedicated. Regardless, then, of damages done or inconveniences inflicted, police must not be called; punitive measures must not be invoked, and the membership of the offenders in the academy cannot be called into question. Such a pattern is a long way from the heroic tradition of civil disobedience in which a law is broken and the penalties for doing so are insisted upon precisely to demonstrate the regulation's immorality, to increase public awareness of its injustice, and to mobilize decent people to change it.

More substantively, one illustration makes the point. One of the issues around which dissent has crystallized is that of campus ROTC units. The move to oust these endeavors from college programs is presumably calculated to weaken militarist tendencies within American society, an aim that commands the support of many. Whether the removal of ROTC from the campus will actually achieve this goal, however, is a question rarely considered in any depth among those ostensibly outraged by the power of the military. Will such a change in training facilities spawn a large number of West Points? Does ROTC actually inject a civilian leaven into the officer corps and therefore represent an arrangement more consonant with the avowed goal than would the demanded ouster? Is ROTC so crucial to the military services that they are likely to be seriously discomfited or in any way weakened by its detachment from an academic context? Is an interest in a professional military career among some students so thoroughly illegitimate that its frustration through moving ROTC off campus is completely justified? Or is the fight to get rid of ROTC not an anti-militaristic matter at all, but an exercise in purely symbolic generational politics? These questions are not easy ones, but they are uncomplicated relative to those raised by issues bearing on institutional research policies covering projects financed by such governmental agencies as the Department of Defense, on the rate at which disadvantaged students can be admitted to universities ill prepared to provide them with relevant and meaningful educational experiences, on the involvement of colleges in the construction of low-cost housing in their neighborhoods, or on the investment policies and patterns of relationships with legislatures by which universities attempt to keep afloat in their turbulent financial waters. On none of these topics is one likely to hear a discussion in a student setting that is broadly informed, rational, and oriented toward the identifying of important problems and the finding of alternative solutions to them. One hears many in which wealth is equated with evil, in which academic involvements with either corporations or certain branches of government are *ipso facto* self-condemnatory, and in which the uses to which knowledge may conceivably be put are the sole criterion for judging either the intellectual suitability or the moral acceptability of scholarship. There are indeed grave problems in these realms of concern; it is dubious that there are wise answers in the simplistic value-assumptions that are sometimes brought to their consideration. In such patterns of over-simplification in young people who have demonstrated in other contexts their capacity to deal effectively with complexity, we are brought back to Professor Wald's hypothesis that the angry discontent of present-day students stems from their all too reasonable doubt that they have a future.

TOWARD A FAITH IN THE FUTURE

As previously indicated, Wald's humane formulation is a deeply insightful and diagnostically useful one. What is his prescription? "We have got to get rid of those nuclear weapons . . . Our business is with life, not death . . . This has become one world, a world for all men. It is only such a world that can now offer us life, and the chance to go on." All men of good will can only applaud these sentiments, but are they more than sentiments? To be released from the dark shadow of atomic weaponry is certainly a consummation devoutly to be wished, but is such a consummation at all probable?

If there is a sense in which ours is inevitably one world, the shrunken character of our globe has not yet eliminated the reality of separate nations whose relationships are touched at best with uneasiness and at worst with intense hostility. Among those nations, the United States, the Soviet Union, England, France, and China all possess the bomb. The prospects of their simultaneously defusing their warheads and destroying their stockpiles are simply not visible. Although there may be a route to the scrapping of nuclear weapons, it is sure to be a long one, leading through the jungles of very different national interests, entailing compromises that must be negotiated with great delicacy and patience, and leading to agreements that are virtually certain to arouse the anxiety and displeasure of many. If good will is essential to the task, a creative and persistent rationality is even more requisite to its successful resolution.

But the problems are even more difficult. As is well known, the expertise for the manufacture of atomic bombs and their delivery systems is widely and ever more broadly distributed throughout the world's industrialized and industrializing nations. Theodore Taylor recently documented the grim proposition that,

> *The knowledge required for the construction of relatively crude fission explosives . . . light enough to be carried in an automobile, is easily available in unclassified books and documents and is known to thousands of people throughout the world . . . such explosives could be designed and built in six months or less by a dozen or fewer people without extraordinary technical experience, using materials and facilities that are commonplace, at costs that many private individuals could afford.*[15]

In short, these dread devices may very soon become a part of the arsenal of criminal or terrorist organizations. The dimension of private intimidation has been added to that of international warfare in the definition of our difficulties: and to the resources of humane sentiment, men must add a disciplined imagination and a great deal of hard-headed thinking if they are to escape a new range of horrors.

This point, of course, is that the new range of horrors endangers all of us, not just one generation. And yet our problem is basically a very ancient one. The myth of Eden is not the only reminder that knowledge can be used for human good or human ill; and the great ethical issue, lying at the very heart of the human condition, is that of how to apply knowledge in ways that maximize man's growth and finest aspirations and that minimize his propensities for evil. That issue assumes social and political forms of immense importance, but it also has personal implications for each of us that demand that we search our souls with some care before we act on the basis of sentiments alone or before we employ techniques of violence in order to achieve what our understandable desperation defines for us as desirable ends.

With the basic knowledge available, the horrible and complex threat of nuclear aggression from a variety of sources illustrates the shortcomings in Professor Wald's hypothesis. The fear of being without a future plagues all of us. Although it may explain much of our shared vision of the apocalypse and the instigations that all of us sometimes feel to scapegoat and to behave violently to relieve our anxiety and frustration, it neither legitimizes those impulses nor provides pointers toward constructive action. In fact, it has in it an element of a self-fulfilling prophecy[18] that is both destructive and self-defeating. If we are convinced that, unless we "get rid of those bombs," we are doomed, then we are quite likely, being men and therefore the heirs of folly as well as wisdom, to give full vent to our emotions and our appetites and to insure by our conduct the fate that we fear. None of us is so far removed from our primitive beginnings that we can honestly deny this possibility. A neo-Luddite assault on the bombs in any one nation, improbable as it is, stems primarily from such a dangerous desperation, but the fact that it is being thought of forces us to face the implications of ideas that have gained a peculiar currency. If we leave aside, for example, the moot question of the extent to which a unilateral scrapping of weapons would leave the country taking such a step at the potential mercy of any other nation that has or generates its own atomic arsenal, we must still consider the likelihood of tension-ridden if not actually bloody conflict between factions in the society that have very different notions about how best to cope with the profound perils defined by these engines of destruction. Even more importantly, an attack on the bombs would almost surely escalate into an attack on their makers and quite probably on science itself. As was the case in the nineteenth century, a revival of Luddite energies would imply an upsurge of anti-intellectualism and a movement toward censorship and thought-control. History is reasonably clear about such situations: Once this kind of suppression of information and ideas is begun, it tends to generalize massively; not only does an elaborate network of inquisitorial power expand and envelop a culture, but its jurisdiction broadens until only a few and innocuous ideas are free of the test of official sanctions. But most of all, the get-rid-of-the-bombs prescription begs the central and inescapable issue in the human condition: How do we become men whose morality matches our creativity and whose forms of social organization facilitate our generosity toward each other while controlling and disciplining our acknowledged hostile impulses?

Here is the great task of education. The route to its accomplishment must be discovered by informed, persistent, and cooperative intellectual searching combined with the humane pluralism that is so tragically violated by our position in Vietnam and that is so well exemplified in Dr. Wald's conception of one world. If "democracy" is more than a shibboleth, then efforts as thoughtful as they are vigorous must be bent toward understanding more deeply and realizing more fully its two most fundamental implications—a respect for personal differences, and a pattern of social arrangements that is capacious enough to allow the widest possible expression of the varied constructive potentials in man. Basic to both is a richly developed awareness in all of us, being men and not angels, of the barriers to our undertaking such a quest. A taste for excitement and the thrill of power occasionally overwhelm in most of us a dedication to justice and decency; a yearning for freedom and the rhetoric of liberty sometimes merely rationalize the venting of the aggressiveness that inherently mars our human make-up,[17] and a sense of self-righteousness not infrequently narrows our minds and foreshortens our vision in ugly ways. There is a good deal of relevance here in the image of Oliver Cromwell, ordinarily thought of as the archetype of the fanatic. Worried before the battle of Shrewsbury that his troops might loot and ravage the city, he rode through his army shouting, "I beg ye in the bowels of Christ, be mindful that ye may be wrong."

As Albert Szent-Gyorgyi,[18] another Nobel laureate has put it, the crisis of our age may lie less in our immediate problems, gigantic and frightening though they are, than in the question of whether man as a species, evolved to meet the conditions of life 10,000 years ago, has the intellectual capacity and the moral and psychological resources of courage, self-control, and cooperativeness to sustain and humanize the world he has created. Universally and primitively endowed with the emergency reactions of "flight or fight,"[19] men must now deal with the issue of how these fundamental affects can be constructively employed in societies that are densely crowded and in which a decent distribution of food, peace, and personal fulfillment is dependent on the dynamics of a moral management of technology and highly complex patterns of social organization. Educationally, this state of affairs demands, among many other things, two intensively cultivated lines of development. One is ancient in its formulation but has been attended to in only the most cavalierly shallow fashion—the Greek concept of self-knowledge. If the Socratic injunction of *gnothe seauton* is finally to be fulfilled, it must include a functional sense of the tragic features in man, of the destructive forces that work powerfully in all of us, and of how each of us may use the loftiest language to justify releasing the most primitive energies of hate and hostility. In this informed acknowledgement and acceptance of personal responsibility for dangerous imperfections in our essential characters lies the psychological basis for the one world that Dr. Wald envisions. The second requirement is that of dramatically increasing the technical comprehension and competence necessary to understand societies that are increasingly technical, managerial, and organizational. These trends, set in motion by human inventiveness and founded in the human propensity to create or discover new knowledge, are unlikely to be reversed. They can serve decent goals or vicious ones. Which they serve is in large part a function of how widely they are understood and how fully they are subjected to foresightful and rational evaluation and control by people educated to long-range moral concerns. Such a view does not entail an end to disagreements or sharp conflicts of value; it does suggest a more cooperative spirit in the ways in which differences can be resolved and social decisions made, and it bluntly condemns as inhumanely inappropriate such current movements as the Japanese Soka Gakkai, a compound of primitive religion preaching the primacy of "experience" and equally primitive politics based on an ethic of "sincerity."

If it is true that the future of man is in genuine jeopardy, then it is a condition that affects an age, not just a generation. Although the desperation it evokes may be dynamically comprehensible, responses born of that desperation are not likely to be constructive. If we merely react to the condition of our time—in neo-Luddite, in dogmatically existential, or in other oversimplified ways—we may momentarily relieve our feelings of anxiety and anger; we shall not be creating a new basis for faith in the future. That task requires our resolving our problems by transcending them, by reformulating them in terms that are congruent to the complicated realities that define our best hopes as well as our gravest dangers. Instant escape from fear is improbable, but we may find a far better prescription with which to answer Professor Wald's diagnosis if we bend our energies more fully to the questions that lie at the root of our trouble: How can men effectively couple long-range moral concern with the vigor of technical thought? How can human beings provide the necessary outlets for their inherent destructive impulses while harnessing the force of their emotional resources to the search for social forms that enhance and facilitate individual dignity and interpersonal generosity? How, in crowded and technical societies, can the political process be shaped and controlled so that the decisions of government reflect as fully as possible the spirit of one world in both domestic and international affairs? In dealing with such crucial issues, no single generation can lay claim to special wisdom; the thrills of symbolic politics are of dubious relevance, and an atmosphere of anarchy will soon prove stifling to the very spirit it is our business to nourish and to spread more widely through the world—the spirit of zestful personal life in a proudly humane community.

NOTES
THE FUTURELESS GENERATION: VALUE-CONFLICTS IN THE CAMPUS COMMUNITY

*Adapted from addresses given at St. Louis University, Vanderbilt University, and Ball State University during the spring of 1969.

1. Given on March 4, 1969, at a special convocation of scientists at the Massachusetts Institute of Technology, Dr. Wald's speech has been widely reproduced in the press. It is perhaps most readily available in *The New Yorker* magazine for March 22, 1969.
2. See, for example, "Toward the Year 2,000: Work in Progress," the special issue of *Daedalus,* 1967 (Summer), *96* (No. 3); Kenneth Boulding's *The Meaning of the 20th Century.* New York: Harper Colophon, 1965; Lewis Mumford's *The Transformations of Man.* New York: Collier Books, 1962, and the two volumes edited by Nigel Calder, *The World in 1984.* Baltimore: Pelican Books, 1965.
3. Hardin's article repays careful reading on a number of counts. See "The Tragedy of the Commons," *Science,* 1968 (13 Dec.), vol. *162* pp. 1243–1248.
4. H. von Foerster, Patricia Mora, and L. A. Aminot. "Doomsday: Friday 13 November, A. D. 2026." *Science,* 1960 (4 November), vol. *132* pp. 1291–1295.

5. These statements were made by Commoner and Cole at the annual meeting of the American Association for the Advancement of Science in December, 1967. Easily available expressions of their informed concern are available in Barry Commoner, *Science and Survival.* New York: Viking-Compass, 1967, and LaMont C. Cole, "Can the World Be Saved?" *New York Times Magazine,* 31 March, 1968, pp. 35ff.
6. See, for example, D. N. Michael's discussion of "The Next Twenty Years" in W. C. Jones (Ed.) *Higher Education for All?* Corvallis, Ore.: Oregon State Univ. Press, 1965.
7. I have dealt in somewhat more detail with the existentialist impulse among students and the youth culture in "Toward Remedies for Restlessness: Issues in Student Unrest," *Liberal Education,* 1968 (May), *54* (No. 2), pp. 221–230.
8. Such enterprises include efforts as varied as the derivatives from group dynamics, A. S. Neil's Summerhill School in England, and a variety of experiments in communal living. See, for instance, such works as W. Schutz's *Joy.* New York: Grove Press, 1968; G. B. Leonard's *Education and Ecstasy.* New York: Delacorte Press, 1968, and—much more academic—W. G. Bennis, E. H. Schein, D. E. Berlew, and F. I. Steele, *Interpersonal Dynamics.* Homewood, Illinois: Dorsey Press, 1964.
9. See my "Means, Ends, and the Liberties of Education," *J. Higher Educ.,* 1968 (Feb.), *39* (No. 2), p. 61–68; C. Jencks and D. Riesman, *The Academic Revolution,* Garden City, N. Y.: Doubleday, 1968, and the quite different book edited by Theodore Roszak as *The Dissenting Academy.* New York: Vintage, 1968.
10. I have tried elsewhere to record my very considerable sympathy and support for a great deal of student discontent and for a large number of the efforts by students to improve the quality of their educational experience. See "Academic Freedom for Students," *Journal of the National Association of Student Personnel Administrators,* 1967 (July), *5* (No. 1), pp. 25–30; "Demonstrations, Confrontations, and Academic Business as Usual," *Western Humanities Review,* 1969 (Winter), *23* (No. 1), pp. 63–72, and "The Climate of Revolt" in D. Long and J. Foster (Eds.) *Students in Revolt.* New York: Morrow, 1969.
11. This section was written before I became familiar with Lewis Feuer's learned if bitter, useful if ominous, *The Conflict of Generations.* New York: Basic Books, 1969, which I later reviewed for *Change Magazine,* 1969 (July–August), *1* (No. 4).
12. In conversation, Mills used this distinction in a variety of provocative ways. For illustrations, see "Plain Talk on Fancy Sex" and "The Big City: Private Troubles and Public Issues" in his *Power, Politics, and People.* New York: Ballantine Books, 1962.
13. The whole question of the "purity" of one's motives, intentions, and aspirations needs psychological and philosophical exploration in this context. For two provocative and helpful treatments, see Robert Penn

Warren's "On Pure and Impure Poetry" in his *Selected Essays*. New York: Vintage, 1942, and D. K. Price's presidential address to the American Association for the Advancement of Science, "Purists and Politicans," *Science,* 1969 (3 Jan.), vol. *163* pp. 25–31.

14. Aldous Huxley's all but forgotten *Ends and Means* (New York: Harper, 1937) is enormously instructive here.
15. Quoted in Richard Rovere's important essay, "A New Situation in the World," in *The New Yorker* for February 24, 1968.
16. R. Merton, *Social Theory and Social Structure*. Glencoe, Ill.: Free Press, 1957.
17. There is a considerable body of helpful and provocative, if somewhat inconclusive, literature on this point that well repays serious examination. For example, see R. Ardrey, *African Genesis*. New York: Atheneum, 1961; P. Bohannan (Ed.) *Law and Warfare*. Garden City, N.Y.: Natural History Press, 1967; K. Lorenz, *On Aggression*. New York: Harcourt, Brace and World, 1966; and J. P. Scott, *Aggression*. Chicago: Univ. of Chicago Press, 1958.
18. In an address at Bard College, Annandale-on-Hudson, N Y., on January 25, 1967.
19. The phrase is W. B. Cannon's classic one. See his *The Wisdom of the Body*. New York: Norton, 1942.

Catholic and Protestant colleagues, respectively, in the Cornell United Religious Work, Daniel Berrigan and John Lee Smith are associate directors on Cornell University's Anabel Taylor Hall staff. Their headline anti-war, black empowerment, and other educator-advocacy activities in Cornell, church, civil and professional arenas represent an advance attempt to style the prophetic mode of campus ministry with a governance weld.

In Search of Soul

A Dialogue between Daniel Berrigan and John Lee Smith

BERRIGAN: As a point of departure, I'd like to discuss a movie I saw recently here at Cornell. It was a ten-minute film that was supposed to be a basis for discussion on a topic similar to the one before us; where we are, where we are going. The metaphor was a well-dressed, middle-class white businessman type who was manipulating a pair of mechanical hands, the kind of mechanism that is used to pick up radium behind a lead-shielded wall. And at the end of his hands there was a world globe, cut into segments and scattered around the floor. Our star sits about ten feet away from it, trying to manipulate the pieces back into position with these hands. And obviously getting nowhere, though he is well dressed and his face wears an expression of achievement. The film keeps cutting away into the real world, as contrasted with the segments he is trying to put together at a distance; into scenes we are all familiar with: starvation in Biafra, the riots on the campuses, poverty in America, the exploitive landlord. Finally, he comes to a decision. (This is supposed to be the denouement, the solution.) He realizes that his fumbling at a distance from reality is getting nowhere. He sweeps aside the tools, stands up, takes off his coat, goes in and starts putting things together by hand. By human hand.

The fellow that made the film wanted a critique on it. I said I thought technically it was very beautiful, and showed considerable savvy. But I said that historically it was back with the Kennedy days, with the kind of philosophy that was emerging then. The white people who had made it could help others by "getting in there." But when one thinks of what has happened since, what we have had to learn since the Kennedys, that idea is about 400 years gone. If you want to keep the metaphor of the movie, the idea isn't that this fellow takes his coat off as though he were going out to manicure his lawn. The current metaphor is that he strips naked, strips out of his skin, admits that he cannot bring any change and still keep everything he has. That was the old Peace Corps philosophy; we can transplant ourselves anywhere and bring change and keep everything. I think that is dead. And the first sign of the death is the death of the Kennedys. I mourn for them, but I am trying to recognize what is finished. Well, I tried to suggest this to the film maker; if he wanted me in on any future work that was where I was and where I had to start talking. My views included what I took to be a much more radical biblical response to social change than the film was willing to admit. If he wanted to circulate his film in the suburbs, that was all right with me. But he wasn't to count me in on that metaphor.

I think the word of Jeremiah is the word for the times. It is not the time to build justice, it is the time to confront injustice. It is the time to say No to death. And what is going to be built is still very obscure. But I don't think there are any shortcuts. And that was what I thought was wrong about that film. It was a liberal panacea, an assurance to the man who had "made it." "Making it" is still something that you can impose on the world to get the world put together again according to those norms. And I just don't believe that.

SMITH: My experiences recently with the class in City Planning have been very revealing to me. I often think that the kind of students to whom we can speak very readily, tend to be primarily out of humanities, or literature or history. And in City Planning you seem to get a different breed of student of whom I was a little wary at first. It becomes progressively clearer to me that the great majority of the students in that course, average age around 23, 24, 25 years old, have become extremely cynical, certainly saddened, by what they consider to be a kind of irreversible trend in a society over which they have little or no control. We read for this past week's session Jacques Ellul's *Technological Society,*[1] which devastated many of them. The question that was being raised was why in hell are we in City Planning with the sort of future that we can anticipate: control of a technological, bureaucratic society becomes progressively more impressive each year; little gestures and efforts on the part of people with passion and moral sensitivity are simply small eddies in a fast stream. The curious thing is that they all share in the sentiments expressed by the Ellul book; but they were not willing to buy as legitimate, a kind of miraculous change in modern society. So they were really raising, you might say, a very existential question, "Why am I working on a Ph.D. in City Planning when perhaps this is pure bravado and has nothing to do with the real world?"

A SPIRITUAL IMPASSE

BERRIGAN: The social impasse I take to be a spiritual impasse; it is one which we share with the students, very deeply and obscurely. Here is an interesting quote from the magazine, *Katallagete* (Be Reconciled), its March '69 issue, mourning the death of Karl Barth and Thomas Merton. The editor is recalling the beginnings of the magazine; "Thomas Merton, in his first article for this journal almost three years ago, observed that 'Bonhoeffer himself said it was an 'Anglo-Saxon failing' to imagine that the church was supposed to have a ready answer for every social problem.' The point of Merton's observation was given in a later issue when John Howard Griffin recalled that good Trappist's answer to the perennial question of oppressor to victim: 'What can we, as Christians, do to help?' 'Before you do a damned thing,' Tom would reply, 'just *be* what you say you are, a Christian; then no one will have to tell you what to do. You'll know.' "[2]

I thought there is something there for us; the posing of that question is a kind of instinctive response to the fact that our noses are up against the wall. "What can we do to help?" And the editor comments, "That's the perennial question of the oppressor to the victim." That immediately puts the relationship right where it is. If you want to step away from that relationship you step away from the question. And that seems to be what Merton has done. He refuses to admit the validity of the question as a statement of where his life is. He realizes that there is nothing that can be done if you are not going to be a slave master. Now I think that it is worthwhile lingering over that. Merton, it could be objected, is telling the Christians to join the general impasse, as a sign of Christianity. That is to say, "Be what you are, a Christian, and no one will have to tell you what to do, you'll know." Is he saying that there are just two simple steps: 1) go through the boot camp of Christianity, and 2) then you will have the social answer?

I think this elemental observation is also a release from obsession that one must prove something by his life. That one must be "relevant" with his life. I think you just go down a different drain if that is the ruling passion of life. Whereas I think from Camus back to Christ and forward to Merton we have a very different view of things. And it is perilously close to what the contemptuous liberal would call a cop-out. That is to say; one deliberately chooses not to prove anything, because life is not interested in proving anything; it is interested in life—itself. If one's life is obsessed with proving anything then life has been assimilated to a machine; because the machine is a non-organism that has to prove by producing.

SMITH: I think that one of the key questions especially with students, one of their gut feelings, is that they have been co-opted by an efficient, highly organized, logically oriented machine. In its service they find justification, by virtue of producing efficiently. The humanity and existence of students as being authentic is jeopardizing the question itself. This is what I sense when I return to the group of students in City Planning. They feel that the groanings of the spirit are being clearly heard. And rather than questions of meaning, purpose and existence which we raised in the '50's, I think that today the virtue and issues that are evoking the spirit are those that relate to one's vocation, how one is going to live out his life in society.

BERRIGAN: It seems to me that the times pose a unique challenge for the Christian—the challenge to effect change, yet not to get ground up for any better reason than to maintain the same old machine. Stringfellow had a beautiful little thing in *Christianity and Crisis* a few weeks ago.[3] He said it was good for Christians to remind themselves now and then that Judas was a social revolutionary. He was inflamed with evident passion for change; he wanted it rapidly, and radically; moreover, he wanted to be a factor in bringing it about. He wanted to be a hero. And it is instructive that he ends up, according to tradition, in the same old dustbin. He didn't quite make it as a human being. Somewhere along the line priority reversed; the questions of discipleship and of the person before one yielded to the question of "the cause." And he began the trend that I think dead-ends with modern man; the idea that the concrete presence of another human being is less important than the abstract principle, when the chips are down. And therefore betrayal is a preferable choice to other choices.

SMITH: I think that a number of students find this kind of talk very convincing. Yet at the same time they are acutely aware of the power of social organization and technique, which determine not simply the external condition of our existence but the internal appropriation of the human condition. And they wonder about living out one's life in the way that you suggest; refusing causes, refusing movements, refusing abstractions, believing in some ways that life today is a real cop-out. I think that this is where the agonizing issues are being raised. Many of these students would say that they much prefer to live on a desert, wanting to herd sheep in New Zealand; but they feel a kind of irresponsibility in that. You see what I am trying to say?

THE CALL TO OPPOSITE RHYTHMS

BERRIGAN: I do. And in a way I am turning in the same gyre; I sound like a stranger to myself when I talk this way. I think what I am trying to lead toward is a growing conviction that our call includes the call to opposite rhythms in our life. A man can no more be called to pure activism than he can be called to pure withdrawal. The abstractly pure is concretely impure. And the question of keeping open the alternatives of life is a grievous one in the long run, a wearing one. As is quite clear, there is going to be no return to normalcy. And we have to find in the small space between the millstones a new way of living and of dying. And that is going to demand of us, I think, a new relationship to the students; to help them to find breathing space, to see a little further than the crushing hour that they are in.

I was struck by this so much the other night on a trip to Connecticut. There we were, seven beings in this little yellow submarine, going through the rainy night to a grievous hour for a young fellow student, trying to understand it with one another, knowing the horror that lay ahead, trying to shore him up, trying to shore ourselves up (because it was harder for us in some ways) and trying to see a little beyond it for all of us. Because obviously our lives were not going to stop there, neither his nor ours.

Well, what I am trying to get at is this—I have felt lately that the question is one of rhythms, it is an effort to gain breathing space. To be enabled to see that nothing is changing as far as pure politics are concerned; purely political interpretations, purely religious interpretations. But we are required to look at that "beyond" that Bonhoeffer speaks of, the beyond that is really very close but unapprehended; it has not yet entered into consciousness. One can be very quiet, very inward about the crisis at the same time that he is trying to meet it. But if he tries to meet it only as a political animal, he is lost. That is the position I am objecting to, the fact that religion is tempted to become politics. Whereas it seems to me that religion's calling is to creation, it is a call to become a new man, it is a call to be born again. That is what we are talking about. And if someone wants to be so daring as to call that politics, I will have no quarrel with him. I believe that might be a way of putting a 'new testament' into politics. But I want to be precise about what we are going to do, and call it like it is.

SMITH: Yes, but again I think the question the secular student is raising, in contrast to those of us who have been reared in the Christian faith and basically share in its hope and confidence, doesn't presuppose some strange notion that there are forces operative in history and in the universe beyond that of man. That if one remains faithful and obedient and courageous in the faith, in the face of persecution, somehow there is always a resurrection beyond the cross. On the contrary, I think students today don't have any such hope or any such confidence. And this is why I think the whole press to "do your own thing," to respond to persons as persons and "do the thing that in some way is really satisfying to yourself" is in some way really to sacrifice the ballgame. Because what seems to be required is that if we are going to win a battle, we have to become just as abstract, just as Machiavellian, just as cunning as the opposition, in order to create a different kind of a future. That is the issue which the whole anomaly of religion and politics has posed for a lot of people.

BERRIGAN: This idea of what the Christian adds to the general scene of course is one way of putting our quandary, our continuing debate. I was struck recently in a seminar, when we were talking in a mixed group about Bonhoeffer's *Letters and Papers From Prison.*[4] The students who may not share his transcendent hope are still forced to respect him because of his geography. Anybody who writes from prison is worth being heard from. I think they are close enough to this to realize Bonhoeffer's worth. And a silence settles over them when we start reading the text of those letters. We spent two hours on the first session and got through about eight key words of Bonhoeffer in about a page and a half of the text. It was like an intense diving into a page of the Bible. And they had trouble surfacing because there was so much there. Starting with Bonhoeffer's analysis of eight key attitudes of life by eight different Germans we saw him demolishing all of them, and then coming up with something as classical as the Nicene Creed; to believe in death and resurrection as a force for new power, new energy, in the breech. And the interesting thing was that I had to end this like the *Perils of Pauline* because we never got to his eighth way. We were so concentrating upon his analysis of modern man without the transcendent of modern man without God, and man's insufficiency, that we never got to the question of faith. But we decided at the end of the class that we were going to continue with Bonhoeffer; which was interesting because we had only assigned one class for him. I found the whole thing by way of analogy quite devastating. And I pushed the discussion deliberately into their experience, because I don't think that this was a question of a German soul. It was a question of the American soul. And that is what they were feeling. For instance, his analysis of the free man, the dutiful man, the man of conscience. None of this was working . . . none of this was enough. I think that Bonhoeffer would grant that it was enough for normal times, for traditional times, for another society, for anything up to the 19th Century. But he was saying that it wasn't enough for the lives we are called to, the lives we are stuck with. His analysis was totally from the point of view of the dramatic crisis.

And the question that he put was, "What kind of man makes it in the crisis?" And "makes it" in a way that is not just another accumulation of selfishness, or murder, or racism, a qualitatively new way. And he comes back to that great tradition, back to Jesus Christ, and His death and victory. The man who finds staying power becomes a man of his times. I don't know yet whether they are going to find that a bathos or are going to attack it, whether they are going merely to be puzzled by it, or are going to find it uninteresting. Maybe a little of everything.

SMITH: I think that is a good example after reading Kenneth Hamilton's little book, *Life in One's Stride:* A Study of Dietrich Bonhoeffer.[5] His basic thesis is that a lot of secular "death of God" theologians have taken some of those passages out of *Letters and Papers From Prison* and have concocted a kind of theology that is inappropriate to Bonhoeffer's basic attitude and faith. And Bonhoeffer, as he contemplates his execution, says that his life is now ending but life is just beginning. In effect he is clearly living in a deep faith and confidence in an after life or resurrected life. And I was trying to compare that to the position of most students relative to their thinking on meaning and hope.

I was recalling, while we were discussing Bonhoeffer, the movie, *La Dolce Vita,* and the part played by Steiner. He wants to play the organ, gets permission from the priest to play the church organ. Here is a world in which he can respond clearly, even though it is a world that no longer is.

Maybe God is eclipsed or is absent for a while, but he has confidence that all the fundamental affirmations of the Christian faith are true. But we are facing something far more radical; we are not playing little games with symbols or myths, we face a brand new world in which there is no ultimate hope. The world of Camus, or the world of Sartre, this is where I think we like to play fast and loose with the theological distinctions. We want to convince ourselves, or convince other people, that there is no real difference between Bonhoeffer and Camus, there is no difference between Dostoevski and Steiner. You know there is. There are some big differences. And this is where I think the majority of the students that I talk to happen to be. They do not even have any nostalgia for that other world.

BERRIGAN: No. The cutoff is complete, brutally complete, a cutting of an umbilical. We are at the point where we can become a little more specific about this burning question, what it is to be a student, how the students see themselves, how we see our lives in relation to theirs. I would like to suggest something that has struck me deeply in trying to evaluate the year and a half since I came here. I have an obscure sense that life at Cornell is paradoxically an ideal climate in which a Christian can thrive. Here I find new ways, new understanding of what it is to be a Christian.

It seems to me that I have noted this even as the storm rose, the "winds of contrary doctrine" grow more violent and chaotic. The students are waging a long war of attrition to become men. They are also more and more seriously tempted to accept forms of non-manhood in the course of their struggle—violence, chaos as methods. I find that to be Christian on this campus is constantly to reassert, not verbally but by one's silence, by one's style, by one's listening attitude, by one's presence, that he is not being bought. The game which is being played on either side is closely scrutinized; one is not buying the next automatic response of the student movement because it is a student response, any more than he buys the game of corrupt power.

A SCRAPBOOK OF VIOLENCE

To be concrete, one notes in the last few weeks* a disturbing tendency toward violence, a giving up of the idea that social change can come about except through violence. That places one in a minority position, not only with regard to the whole situation, but with regard to the movement itself. So one comes continually to deeper self-knowledge, to scrutinizing one's own soul.

Which brings us once more to Bonhoeffer, by way of analogy. Conflict is exactly the condition in which one's fiber is tested even against one's will.

*Reference is to the weeks just preceding the black student "take-over" and armed occupation of Willard Straight Hall, Cornell's student union building, in April 1969.—Editor's note.

Because one would like to believe that an atmosphere of normalcy and peace that induces human growth, that the best climate of soul in which to decide how to be a man, is one of what those in power like to call rational discourse. But that is simply not granted to us.

By standing within the chaos of contrary human passion and having the resources to scrutinize, to penetrate rhetoric, to say No where No should be said, that seems to me to be the clue to what it is to be a Christian, in the midst of others who are not drawing upon our tradition, who have no real connection with it, who as you said, do not have even a nostalgia for it. Such men, I would submit, are almost entirely at the mercy of the same winds that are blowing down the old power. I think that I am trying so say that I discern in the students a very different mode of concentration than I discern in myself. And this is because we draw on two radically different traditions, two ways of being a man in a world. In many ways, their concentration I take to be no more than a distraction. Thereby I risk evading the issue, of course. Observe, for example, the shifting position of some activist leaders who place a great deal in the breach, who face the courts and even jail, and who then began to say No this is not important enough to go to jail, this is not important enough to face the courts; one must find a way of delaying the consequences, if necessary even of renouncing one's original gesture. Perhaps it is having destroyed a draft card. One may send for the card again, announce that he is going into the Army, and go do his thing there. Or, contrary wise, one may stay out and help organize those forms of violence that are going to be most useful, in light of what we are really facing.

That, it seems to me, is to sell out to the passions of the moment. Such activity has nothing to do with the process of manhood, the work needed to forge the alternatives we have always persuaded ourselves we were offering. I call such acts a form of amnesia and distraction in the sense T. S. Eliot speaks of. That is, a man is no longer capable of possessing his soul, of declaring for himself what his form of life is going to be. Rather, from here and there, from whatever current is loud and persuasive at the moment; he slaps together the latest "thing" and calls it manhood. The forms of alienation around him are forming what he would like to call his consciousness. But such a life is nothing more, I submit, than a scrapbook of violence, despair and alienation. And since the project has been slapped together in an hour, it isn't going to last much more than the hour.

SMITH: Do you think this kind of development is taking place in the resistance?

BERRIGAN: In my more discouraged moments that is the way I see it now; amnesia. And I think this has a serious biblical connotation. In the Bible we are told that the ability to remember is equivalently the ability to be a man in a certain way. It is to be a man of tradition It is to be a man in command of what Niebuhr would call the blood resources of the tribe. We could almost be literal and say that if man can re-remember he can "put himself together." That is, he can put his limbs and organs together again, after they were scattered by non-life or by violence.

I have been haunted for many years by that phrase in the New Testament. The Lord advises Christians as a central act of worship to remember Him. "When you do these things remember me." The opposite of this kind of man is the amnesiac, that is to say, the man who acts out of the resources of this or that moment because he has nothing to draw on, toward real action or crisis. And I feel that this is a great clue; what do we mean when we speak of the alienation of young people? Perhaps that their resources are cut off in almost every direction; family, religion, trust in the forms of secular authority, trust in the university as a vehicle of human development. You may ask, why are these resources cut off? Is this something that the person has done himself, or the family has done, or the society? Is this what is meant by the generation gap?

I like to refer to a statement by a Nobel Laureate, Dr. George Wald, Professor of Biology at Harvard, during the Massachusetts Institute of Technology research "strike" on March 4, 1969.[6] What he said was received with an enormous ovation; evidently he spoke from the heart. He felt that the deepest meaning of student alienation was a number of cutoffs, in which the person was no longer capable of remembering his past or his future. He says that the nuclear build-up has been the most spectacular occasion of disbelief in any future by our youth. The world as they now know is threatened with momentary destruction. And so youth is forced back to the intensity and validity of the moment they are living through; they can't stretch themselves and say, "I have space in which to walk into tomorrow." There may in fact be no tomorrow to walk into. Young people see the most spectacular of all the cutoffs that have occurred and, a tragic and powerful symbol of all other alienation. The nuclear occurrence signifies something that is occurring spiritually. The family has ceased to be the vehicle of nurtured, protected, gradualist, social change in which a young person emerges organically from the nest into the world. The church is stalemated along the same lines; so is the university.

I think the implication of this is that the first cut-out was not on the part of the young; the young person is clearly trying to say something about the truth of a situation that already exists. That is to say, these institutions which once sheltered and encouraged human life have ceased occupying that position. They have first given up on the young person. That is the first fact. The young person as a result has decided to give up on them: church, university, politics, all of them.

SMITH: I want to comment on a couple of points you made. One was the importance of remembering, in possessing the past in such a way that he may also have a future. I once saw an NET show that I think was to my point. The subject was hypnotized by a psychiatrist; it was suggested at certain points that he assume certain assumptions about his life. Then he was asked for example, to assume that there was no tomorrow. Then he was asked to comment; how did it feel to have no future? He was casual, nonchalant, almost giddy, about any basic attitude toward any serious question. And the final question he was asked by the psychiatrist was, "Now assume that there is no past before this moment. Come out, begin to talk." But the fellow could not; he was in a catatonic trance. He refused, or was unable to speak.

And this was being done on the scene; it was a live broadcast. Suddenly the psychiatrist realized that he was in trouble; he had the man in a hypnotic trance, he could not communicate with him. There was a flurry of activity, he was calling an assistant to try to get the subject out of the trance. And then there was a long, involved routine, gradually getting the subject back into the world. And once they got him back they asked him, "Did you hear me?" And he said, "Yes, I heard you." "Well why didn't you answer?" "Why should I answer?" And then it continued; "If a man has no past, no present and no future. . . ."

And I thought it was from an empirical, clinical point of view, an extremely good illustration of this whole business of remembering. If one has no recollection or rememberance of anything before, he has neither a present or a future.

And the second point I wanted to mention has to do with the loss of faith or of any kind of meaning within the given structure of the family, of government, the economy. There I find a greater cynicism and disaffection on the part of young people; at this point they find in these institutions no genuine support for a grappling with spiritual issues. The university at one time was a place where one was enlightened, one was confronted with great ideas, where one met convictional models, where new worlds opened up, new worlds of meaning and possibility. This may no longer be true. The university has simply become another factory, producing its own personnel for industry and business and government. This is why you, John, recommended that the Cornell United Religious Work become a Center for religious and cultural affairs, or a center for advocacy, is it not?

SMITH: Exactly. I think the university, by some historical accident, ceased to be a genuine community in which, spiritually, questions and concerns are adequately supported or dealt with. University people are very cynical about this. And the same thing is true of the family. Even if the son looks upon his father as some kind of convictional model, someone whom he would engage in an honest and open grappling with the spiritual questions of vocation, sex, the meaning of life, we know what families are today. No real dialogue takes place within the family. And then the church! In some way we still have all this bric-a-brac of religiosity present on campus: worship services, fellowship groups, denominational programs. I would be willing to venture they are not providing, any better than the family or university, the kind of context where one's spiritual groanings and agonies can find honest exposure or confrontation. I think of the students who come to Sage Chapel. Are they really grappling with the basic spiritual, moral, social and human questions? Or are they fraternity and sorority types who come because it is the thing to do on Sunday morning at 11 o'clock?

APPROACHING THE POLITICAL

What precisely are the experiences that students are having today in which questions of the spirit are being evoked? I would suggest that it is at the point where students make a decision regarding their involvement in politics—whether they will resist the draft, whether they oppose the war in Vietnam, and what action they will take relative to the poor and the oppressed in the world today—it is at these points that not only political issues are being faced, but spiritual problems as well. And in some way it is our task to discern the groanings of the spirit precisely within these situations, and not to dismiss them in the kind of blasé fashion that I find religious people so often do. They say, well that's politics, or that has to do with social action; as if such questions were utterly irrelevant to the basic theological or religious questions that are being raised in our time. But I think it is precisely at that point that a man is beginning to grapple with himself, beginning to find out who he is, what he is going to do; and not primarily in the traditional mold that has found meaning in the past.

BERRIGAN: I would like to lead up to a response to that by recalling a visit we shared a few weeks ago when Michael Novak was here. I am not referring so much to his sermon as to that discussion afterward. As you may recall, there were a couple of students here from Milwaukee associated with the *Milwaukee 14.** Their response to Novak was a very important one, I think. You remember the discussion. A great deal of it centered around the new experiment at Old Westbury, and what I took to be a certain disaffection on Novak's part in regard to the students that they have brought into that experimental college situation. This Milwaukee pair listened without responding; as usual, when students disagree with some official figure, they clam up.

Later we were to learn that their response to Novak was explosive. They spoke of the "segregationist" tactics at Old Westbury; taking 60 or 70 vital young people, their juices running hard and fast, and bringing them into a country area for some special educational experience. They agreed this was asking for trouble, asking for a kind of inbred distress and unhappiness, and dislocating students from real political issues that the city would actually bring to a head. Their feeling was that such an educational experi-

*Michael Novak is a member of the faculty of State University College, Old Westbury, Long Island; his most recent book is THEOLOGY FOR RADICAL POLITICS (Herder & Herder). The Milwaukee Fourteen is a group of Christian activists like the Baltimore Four and the Catonsville Nine (numbering Father Berrigan himself), who raided Selective Service offices in Milwaukee and destroyed 1 A draft files in protest against the war in Vietnam and the conscription system.—Editor's note.

ence meant absolutely nothing. They found Novak very much off the track. If that was his way of inducing political relevance in young people, his way of inviting them into the human, he was denying his own postulate by what he was doing.

Now I have no difficulty with the idea that a Christian is called to deal with and to resolve these political questions. As long as one is serious, this may even be a preliminary to personal conversion. I feel though that in most cases we are actually accepting the American definition of politics and the political animal, and are more or less trying to discover Christianity within that definition. That is to say that we are accepting the perennial American supposition that our system is good, that it needs only a certain upgrading, a certain kind of adjustment, in order to be of benefit, to make possible the good life for most of our people. That, I take it, is not so much accepting politics as a form of Christian life; it is denying Christian life in the name of a very inferior kind of secularism. And into that kind of co-option, I submit, most of our Christian liberals soon disappear. They began by identifying with the Kennedy hopes; they can now hire out to the White House and find that this new acceptance of the latest "lesser evil" is entirely in accord with their conception of Christian life today. So the question "After Nixon, what?", after this adjustment what comes next?—this question doesn't seem to trouble us anymore, because they have built into our moral mechanism an endless capacity for such adjustment.

I think indeed that at some point one must decide that his public responsibility is going to have to cut off from current forms of power and assumptions of authority and get very modest, even go underground. One must undergo some risk in order to say no to an assumption about politics that is no longer tolerable. On the other hand I see nothing in political "adjustment" except the disappearance of anything new on the scene at all. And I think that the rejection of Christianity by students is being verified as a realistic judgment, in the light of some kinds of "Christian" activity. I have to say students are right if that is all Christians have to offer; a continual political adjustment to whatever comes along.

SMITH: What did you say earlier? Even if one doesn't know what to put in its place, he is called to stand against an evil?

BERRIGAN: I think it was the radical thing that I was drawing from Jeremiah. God's first word to him was to uproot, to pull down and destroy; it is only afterward, he is called to *plant* or build. But this utterly destructive work preceeds it.

SMITH: Are you saying that you think there is too much confidence in political solutions and that man may have to put himself on the line without making accommodation to the political?

BERRIGAN: No, I am refusing the current American definition of the political animal. And I am saying that for a Christian to be political today in any worthwhile sense, is to be a biblical man. This implies a curt refusal to shortcut attempts to be relevant to current Republican politics. I am saying that to be a political man in the definition of the Bible is to step back and to say No to such forms of power as oppress men at home and wage useless wasting wars abroad. As Tom Wicker wrote in the *New York Times* today, "we have gone to the polls twice to elect a new kind of leadership; we are back where we started, deeper in, further from an out."[7] I find that interesting from the point of view of a Christian. We are called, I take it, to refuse alignment with such power, to begin in a new direction.

SMITH: Let me raise a question relative to the whole business of confronting. It occurs to me that if you follow out the logic of what you are saying, even to oppose or to offer an alternative position is to fall into the same trap. Let me give you an example. The Colgate Rochester take-over by the blacks* has been very much on my mind. It was curious to me that I found at Colgate a microcosm, a pathology that you alluded to in the existing institutions. Not only were the administration and faculty bewildered as to how to respond; they lacked imagination, and failed in nerve. But more to the point, the demands made on the administration by the black caucus were as misguided and irrelevant as the response of the administration. It was a completely quixotic engagement.

Now what was required, was opting out of the whole struggle. For example, Dick Shaull is planning as soon as he can get free of his contractual relationships to Princeton, to move to Philadelphia and begin a new grassroots kind of teaching with no guaranteed salary. He thinks that if one is going to do any effective theology, he cannot do it in the seminary. Any kind of reformist, revolutionary action in the seminary is doomed at the outset. Whether this is planting or tearing down, I'm not sure. But he feels that the way to move is to move outside the existent structures, no matter how benign they appear on the surface. The assumption being, I presume, that theology flows out of this kind of wrestling with the spirit, this kind of engagement that goes on in the real world.

JAIL OR THE TRANSLATION THEREOF

BERRIGAN: I would like to hear you re-state, in light of this, what the restless believer is in search of today? When we say that he is in search of soul, what does that mean?

SMITH: I think he is in search of life. He is in search of some kind of human satisfaction.

BERRIGAN: But not of answers.

*Reference is to the 18-day "lock-in" (March 1969) of a 19-member Black Caucus of seminarians at Colgate Rochester Divinity School. The lock-in, behind nailed doors of Colgate Rochester's main building, dramatized demands for more black representation in all phases of the school's operations.—Editor's note.

SMITH: Jacques Ellul, which we have been reading in a course on City Planning, has an extremely powerful passage toward the end of his book *The Technological Society.*[11] He talks about the average man who is caught up in this whole productive process, who sees himself as a link, a cog in a large machine, whose existence is justified only in terms of his productivity and efficiency. The man finishes his day in which nothing has really happened, in which no life has really been expressed. He goes home and in search of nothing more than amusement, primarily amusement with television, or he goes out to a movie; but even his diversions simply dig a deeper hole in which the big questions about life and creativity and his own identity, are further buried. Even the amusement industry serves to dull man to the fundamental questions without whose posing man is incomplete, unsatisfied. There is something natural, instinctive, about raising these questions; I don't know what you call it. You might say man's brain structure itself demands the kind of satisfaction offered by such questions.

BERRIGAN: Are these intellectual satisfactions?

SMITH: It is difficult in these days to give a clear definition. The satisfaction has something to do with the urge to talk with people, to be with people. A man wants in some way to have his life taken seriously, to have its value independent of any function he might perform. He wants to make decisions that have import. He knows the kinds of thing he is usually involved in don't mean a damn thing; all the organizations, that pass all the resolutions; they don't mean anything as far as the future is concerned. A man wants to feel that his life counts for something. And the whole society is geared in such a way that he doesn't count for anything, it tries to obliterate any kind of consciousness that life counts for something. And I think this is a response to your question, where are the issues being raised. They feel them viscerally. They lose hope because they can't articulate the problem. A lot of the oppression and the brain washing is on a subliminal level.

BERRIGAN: Somebody asked Charles Starkweather, who killed 11 people seemingly for no reason, why he did it. And he said, "I just wanted to *be* somebody." Now that is one way of wanting your life to count for something but, what does *that* count for? That is the question. Are students looking for some kind of satisfaction, like the boy who came into the room bent on suicide. He was sent to me by another chaplain, and was suicidal because his own desires weren't being filled. The things he wanted he wasn't getting. The people he wanted to be with didn't want to be with him, and the people he didn't want to be with, wanted to be with him. What is life worth? What is it all about? Now, he was seriously contemplating self destruction. What I am asking is, how do we meet the question of Jacques Ellul? Maybe, a kind of holy nonchalance, a sitting loose on things, maybe that is part of what has to happen.

SMITH: That is where I disagreed with you earlier. You see, I'm not really satisfied that being nonchalant, letting society go its own way, do its own thing, without investing one's own creativity and imagination, that this offers any light. I want to make a difference not simply to what is happening inside me, but to what is happening in the social level, the conditions of given existence. I am not sure that we are not kidding ourselves. I think a lot of this short circuit happens in students who find drugs, or sex, immediately satisfying. They have broken loose from the conformist pattern. They are able to snub their nose at conformist society. Yet they find that, strangely and ironically, as they move into this sub-culture, it is simply another variant on the same basic theme. That is scary!

BERRIGAN: This is interesting to me, but not as interesting as your earlier declaration, that black student demands don't seem to offer anything new. Would you talk about that?

SMITH: Ellul talks about the phantom in our midst. That we refuse to recognize or cannot recognize the phantom that is calling man to assume responsibility for his life, to be free and humane. I think the Blacks at Colgate-Rochester were caught up in the game that is being played on them. They decided in consequence that the solution to their deep feelings of dissatisfaction, indignity, powerlessness, was to play the game the way that the establishment plays the game. So the solution to their problem of spiritual malaise and impotence was to demand twelve Black trustees and three Black faculty members. In sum—preposterous. They did not translate their deep, legitimate feeling of being robbed and cheated and oppressed, into meaningful and tangible programs. And the administration did them a double injustice by taking the Black demands seriously and meeting them one-to-one. By giving them twelve Black trustees they think they have created a Black presence at Colgate Rochester. Which is absurd. Now that is the sort of thing I am worried about. And I have these two feelings, that maybe the battle is not worth fighting, and yet on the other hand I am ambivalent, because if you don't fight the battle you can't win.

BERRIGAN: This reminds me of another remark that Stringfellow made in his article in *Christianity and Crisis.*[9] He believes that the Black movement is going to prove historically uninteresting. It isn't bringing to bear upon society the newness, the quality of change, the sacrifice, the sense that we are at the end of something and could start a new beginning, the newness that we really require and that we learn of from the Bible. He finds the Blacks not biblical enough; which is very interesting. In their own loud way and by their own rhetoric, they are asking for more of the same old stale pie. And the question is whether the pie shouldn't be tossed out.

SMITH: But there was a time, it seems to me, in those halcyon days of civil rights movement, when new things were happening. In Mississippi and Alabama, for example, a few voices were being heard. But such activities were repudiated because they did not establish as top priorities the rapid social changes that I think we are all geared for. We are talking, I think, again about a biblical understanding of man.

BERRIGAN: Being rather harsh toward these young people, white and black, is a way of coming back again to ourselves. As far as I can see this is a way of trying to face ourselves, trying to understand what difference our form of life can make in their regard. And I find myself increasingly horrified by the Christian obsession to be relevant to the scene. And that is why I believe that my brother's analysis is proving correct over the long haul. You search out a different geography in which to declare a new word. And the analogy for these days, from Bonhoeffer to ourselves, is jail or the translation thereof. Which is interesting because one is no longer asking about relevance because one doesn't like the taste of that pie.

SMITH: What do you mean by the translation thereof?

BERRIGAN: Let's say, an equivalent geography from which to declare what might be a new word. And the analogy is jail.

SMITH: One other comment that comes to mind, what it means to be a Christian in this age, and the obsession with relevance. In regard to the Colgate-Rochester flap, everybody was asking what the Christian thing was, which put extreme pressure on the board of trustees, who wouldn't be caught dead not being Christian. And I thought to myself, why is it that Christians always live before some kind of imputation. It is a bit like going to shave in the morning. One has posted some kind of little aphorism over your mirror, to remind you who you are. Now, if I have problems with my children do I ask myself what is the fatherly thing to do? When I have difficulty with my wife do I ask myself what is the husbandly thing to do? I wonder about Marxists; do they ask on this or that occasion what is the Marxist thing to do? If you really are a Christian you don't need to raise that kind of question. And so with Jews and Buddhists and all men who claim to connect with a tradition. It just comes naturally.

NOTES
IN SEARCH OF SOUL

1. Ellul, Jacques, *The Technological Society,* Alfred A. Knopf Publishers (1964).
2. *Katallagete* (Be Reconciled), Winter 1968–69, Vol. 2, No. 1—Quote from an editorial by James Y. Holloway (Editor).
3. *Christianity and Crisis,* Vol. XXIX, No. 3, March, 1969. "The Shadow of Judas" by William Stringfellow (page 40).
4. *Letters and Papers from Prison,* Dietrich Bonhoeffer, Macmillan Co., Revised Editions (Hard cover and Paperback) 1967.
5. *Life in One's Stride:* A Study of Dietrich Bonhoeffer, Kenneth Hamilton, Eerdmans Publishers, (1968).
6. Speech given by Dr. George Wald on March 4, 1969 during the M.I.T. Research Strike (Excerpts appeared in the *Bulletin of the Atomic Scientists,* May 1969, "March 4, the Movement, and M.I.T." by Roger Salloch.)

7. *The New York Times* column by Tom Wicker, March 21, 1969, page 42
8. Ellul, Jacques, *The Technological Society,* Alfred A. Knopf Publishers (1964)
9. *Christianity and Crisis,* Vol. XXIX, No. 3, March 3, 1969, "The Shadow of Judas" by William Stringfellow, page 40

Franklin H. Littell, one of the founders of ACURA and consultant on religion and higher education in the staff of the National Conference of Christians and Jews, currently serves as professor in the department of religion at Temple University. Dr. Littell has written nine books and over ninety major articles, many dealing with religion and higher education.

Secularity in Higher Education

Franklin H. Littell

When even the President of the United States feels called upon to speak to the crisis of the campus, one is inclined to reflect that "When Gabriel blows his horn, it is later than you think." What a calm and critical appraisal of the current campus situation lacks in sense of urgency will be brought home to us in tomorrow's newspapers. As regards the future direction and style of higher education, the mood is almost apocalyptic.

I must confess frankly, at least as an honest preface to this discourse, that I share the sense of impending tragedy. I believe that we shall see in the next decade more agony and conflict, violence and civil war, on our campuses than in the ghettos of our cities—on which more attention has been recently focused. My reasons for this belief are two-fold. After World War II, I participated in the rebuilding of a destroyed society, with 25% of its population expellees and displaced persons, and saw it reconstructed in less than a decade. The problem of the inner city is, technically speaking, comparatively simple: when black power and poor people's power has been mobilized, the politicians will respond. The crisis of the campus is far more complex, however, involving conflicting goals and structures in the society itself. The problem of colonialism, whether abroad or at home, is acute, but the moral issue is generally recognized for what it is. The future of the "academy" is in doubt, however, and even wise and good men differ greatly as to the direction we must go. I shall feel free to state bluntly some of my own views, since this occasion deserves more than polite palaver, but I shall do so counting on the reader's common sense awareness that I am not blind to the ambiguities and genuine conflicts of values in which all educators are caught up.

STUDENT REBELLION

The crisis on campus is worldwide, involving universities in every country as well as church-related and independent and state institutions here in America. I have just received a letter from a colleague at Marburg who recently returned from a semester of teaching as Distinguished Visiting Professor in one of our universities. Having enjoyed for thirty years the status of professor in a German university, he has reacted in a predictable way to social revolution led by students:

> *I found Marburg very much confused by the terrorism of some students. Directors of our universities are helpless. They even refuse to accept the proposal of the Minister of the Interior to cancel the very high stipends of all such students who have committed criminal acts during the different terror acts in the university buildings. So our criminals continue to destroy our university on the costs of state salaries.*

The parallel to our own most critical situation is noteworthy, and if a campus has descended to the state of anarchy the responsible administrator has no options left but to rely upon police power. The secret of statesmanship is, however, to provide leadership for orderly change in time to forestall such polarization. In what directions must such orderly change move? I am convinced that, unless we are content to have the campus become the battlefield for civil conflict of increasing intensity, we must move on two fronts: first, to establish the inter-personal relations and structured procedures on campus which today mark a society of persons of culture and education; second, to relate the campus—secure in its own integrity, liberty, and self-government—actively and responsibly to ministering to the needs of the larger society. Neither of these aims can be fulfilled without a measure of secularization, both in the internal organization of the university and in the commitment to accept involvement in the affairs of the world. "Secularization" is in fact proceeding apace: the question is whether it can be mastered and directed, or shall remain something undergone, something passively accepted.

We should not forget that American students have played significant roles in American social history before. The modern movement of home and foreign missions was launched by students at Williams and Andover. Students played a large part in the Abolitionist movement, of which the role of Theodore Dwight Weld and his friends in the founding of Oberlin is but one sign. Student movements launched the modern ecumenical movement and were instrumental in the international conferences which led to the founding of the League of Nations and other instruments of international conciliation. Up to a century ago, however, higher education in America was a preserve of the elite; only a dozen or so colleges a century ago had more than 500 students. Today, nearly half of our youth go on to college, and the frustrations and alienations, demonstrations and riots on campus affect fundamentally the future of our country. No society can afford to break off communication, to proletarianize its youth, without facing frankly the fact that it is creating the conditions which make orderly change and continuity impossible. We are, at our present gait, guaranteeing revolution—although whether Left Wing extremism, symbolized by the rapid growth of Maoist ideology and discipline, or Right Wing extremism, symbolized by reversion to fascist and police-state measure, will win out is certainly not clear.

If communication is to be maintained, we must ask what the campus rebels are trying to say, even if sometimes poorly said. An analysis of 81 major confrontations between the fall of 1965 and the spring of 1968 has shown that 78 of them centered on the two most serious moral crises confronting America: racial injustice and the war in Vietnam. In both cases, mobilized "student power" and "black power" charged that our society, dominated by a mindless technology serving violence and war, lacked "soul."[1] The charge that our educational system, both secondary and higher, is ignoring the Wisdom dimension (*Logos*) to concentrate on artifice and invention (*Techne*) is not without merit. If the misuse of our GNP is any index, the highest achievement of American technology to date has been violence and war. The present disproportionate allocations of our budgets, the present commitments of our investments, the present fealty of our colleges and universities to the programs and the direction of government and industry—all proclaim the same truth: the American way of life is violence and war. Student power and black power arouse the most savage demands for suppression precisely because they have attacked the most precious Maginot Lines and fixed positions in our society: first, the false goal orientation of the society itself which gives vested priority to war and violence; second, the archaic educational patterns which let these false goals go largely unthreatened; third, those imbalances of authority in college and university which reduce faculty to employees and students to serfs. There should be no mistake about it: when student voices raise the demand for a voice in helping to make the decisions which govern their present and future, they are not just expressing a classical demand of all who love liberty and self-government. They mean that they disagree with the direction society is moving, and that they are disenchanted with the way in which the campus is subordinate to the goals of that society. I believe that the students have been more perceptive in perceiving the basic issues than their teachers have been intelligent to understand how the style and nature of the "academy" is itself challenged to reassert its integrity and re-establish its essential mission.

A BUILT-IN CONFLICT

In a recent Position Paper on "The University Crisis," three professors from Pennsylvania, Temple and Swarthmore have brilliantly summarized the conflict developing on the campus, which, as they say, "flows directly from the ambiguous nature of the university as an institution and from the dual, contradictory role the university plays in society." As they state it,

> *The unique role of the university is the systematic refinement, expansion, and transmission of culture. In this role, the university, unlike other institutions, is explicitly required to challenge present human knowledge and understanding by a continuous review in the search for further knowledge and deeper understanding. Thus the university stands for non-conformity to the status quo and acts as a critic of contemporary institutions which are based on our present state of knowledge.*
>
> *In sharp contrast to this role, the university is also explicitly charged with training the leadership needed for the complex of social, political, and economic institutions concerned with applying current knowledge to the ordering and control of contemporary society. This role extends to the training of special leadership expected to provide the ideology and the rationale of the status quo. To discharge this obligation, the university must, in effect, negate its critical role and educate, instead, for conformity, dependability, and willingness to accept the values of contemporary society . . .*

Refining their basic analysis, the three professors go on to ask how the present degradation of the university may be reversed and a new direction emerge, and they conclude:

> *The essential ingredient in all this is power, not student power or faculty power. That is, the university must have power over its own life as an institution if it is to exercise full control over its roles and functions.*
>
> *Just as the university is dependent on the establishment for its financial support, so the establishment is totally dependent on the university for unique training, research and service functions which are vital to the governance and operation of modern society. The academic community must insist that these vital functions can best be discharged by independent universities which are representative of all components of the academic community, and in which the establishment can be represented but not dominant . . .*[2]

This puts the prophetic challenge precisely where it belongs and indicates the extent to which substantial change is necessary. It is the students who have forced the issue, not in most cases the faculty or administrators and trustees.

FIXED POSITIONS REQUIRING CHANGE

Change is pressing, and student rebels have singled out the fixed positions. The university's best defense becomes an offensive geared to radical change. Three fixed positions require such change: (1) the educational establishment's subservience to American society's soul-less technology of violence and war with the consequent neglect of more humanistic concerns; (2) mass diplomad mis-education forced in a one-generational mold outside any "community of teachers and students" requisite for the maturing of wise persons and for building a high culture of continuity; (3) the vested interests of professional educators, administrators and trustees preventing co-determination with students in the full gamut of university affairs.

First, although the false practices and goals of the general society cannot now be discussed in total, it may be worth noting that the students are not alone in challenging an educational system which submissively serves violence and war. This is precisely the conflict—a minor one but symbolically significant—between the Amish and the public school authorities in several states.[3] The Amish are strangers in the land, who once found in America, the land of liberty, the freedom to go their own peaceful and law-abiding and upright way without interference. The recent charge that they are opposed to education is false. Their ancestors, in fact, provided universal education for the young three centuries before the practice was introduced by any government. They are wholeheartedly committed to the Wisdom dimension, with careful cultivation of the oral tradition (fundamental to a vital dialogue with the past), and to repudiation of the technology of violence and war. Since the Gaither Report's effect on secondary and even elementary education has tilted the public schools overwhelmingly toward technology, and Departments of Public Instruction increasingly toward devotion to the training of technicians which the modern society demands (Russian and Chinese and Spanish as well as American), a number of pre-totalitarian attacks on the Amish education system have been made. The hatred of innocence which is so evident in the attacks on the Amish is the same—and often advanced by the same people!—as the hatred which demands savage suppression of the student rebels' plea for "soul" in the education machine. Even Christian educators seem hesitant to utter the obvious truth that a society, and the educational system which serves it so uncritically, which has nothing better for its young than violence and war, has lost the right to expect the confidence and the support of its students and its churches (those, at least, which remain Christian in some sense). As Mr. Justice Jackson—commenting on Hitler's university men—said at Nürnberg, the most awful figure of the 20th century is the technically competent barbarian.

Out of my experience as a board member of the National Committee for Amish Religious Freedom let me say quite frankly that in Iowa and Kansas, at least, the kind of devotion to a mindless and soul-less technology which some of us had identified with fascist and communist power systems has made large and cruel inroads into the public school systems. And dangerous to the American experiment in liberty and self-government, and to any educational system which cherishes Wisdom as well as *Techne,* is the widening rift between the public schools and those colleges or universities which try to maintain a residuum of concern for the human person and the human measure. The Amish will retreat into their social fossil, confirmed in their Biblical belief that the ways of the world are sin, corruption, and violence. The young adults come to us, however, filled with resentment against the close control and demeaning procedures they have endured in many high schools, and ready to organize and attack "the establishment" at the first opportunity. Werner Richter, in his fine study entitled *Re-Educating Germany,*[4] dwelt at length on the way the Nazis successfully exploited the rift between the common schools and their methods-oriented administrators *(Techne!)* and the professors of Humanistic commitment in the university. I would like to suggest that there is nothing this Association could do more useful than to institute a study of a rift of similar proportions and dangerous import which is evident in our own secondary and higher education situation.

It has been popularly commented by popular columnists to popular acclaim that the trouble at Columbia and Berkeley and elsewhere has not come from the engineers and chemists and medical students, but from the "radical" students in Humanities and Social Science and—horror of horrors!—Theology. Of course those students who go on from a technologically-exclusive base to a technologically-financed job without once asking the meaning of life will cause no trouble! They can fit in equally well in Communist Russia or China or Cuba, or fascist South Africa or Spain or Egypt or Greece. But aren't those students right who cry out that social goals, life commitment, and meaningful personal relations are also a fundamental part of education? The split does not lie any more, as it did three hundred years ago, between the physical sciences and the humanities. It lies between the single-minded concentration on *Techne/Wissenschaft* ("cool," supported by the necessary ideology) and "Soul." Most of us are, when we stop to think, agreed that we want to live with both Science and Wisdom. And some of us feel that in the raging dialogue about the future both the Amish and the student rebels have something important to say. The Amishman and his buggy, even if he doesn't vote or hold office, will be a good deal safer and more edifying neighbor in the years ahead than the technically competent barbarian.

Second, the educational patterns which are still dominant are archaic—both in terms of the liberty and dignity and integrity of the human person, and in terms of the sociology of knowledge. Again, technically competent individuals can be turned out of the assembly line, with even a maximum use of teaching machines. But wisdom can only be imparted within that "dialogue of fathers and sons," that *universitas magistrorum ac scolarium,* which was once the very definition of the modern "Academy." Such interaction must today, however, be entered by contract: i.e., it must be based on full respect between the faculty and students. Here, I am sorry to say, the church is almost always on the wrong side. The church college has its own misunderstandings of self and history which run parallel to those of the assembly-line procedures in the massing situation. Far too readily it thinks of tiself as both church and college, with compulsory chapel and patriarchal *Gemeinschaft* rather than structures, and retards the maturing process of students. In its own way it denies the emancipation of God's creature, the *universitas,* from Christian colonialism and close control, and it tends to smother young citizens as effectively as the massing process destroys them by neglect and its own authoritarian structures. In the massing situation, the abuse of Teaching Assistants as a slave caste and other procedures have created a one-generation culture without continuity across the generations and without deep awareness of tradition. Dormitories, cafeterias, registration lines, arbitrary controls both written and unwritten, de-personalize and dehumanize. To put it in blunt language: American universities have built up the best graduate and professional instruction in the world by cheating undergraduates. In both small college and university the present directions must be reversed: toward the dignity of the person, toward the liberty and self-determination and integrity of the human person which—as good Pope John XXIII proclaimed so splendidly in "Mater et Magistra"— is the most encouraging aspect of the world social revoltuion. The student is learning his social responses right now: he is not being trained for future responses. The notion that the teachers are there to teach and the students to learn is false: they are there to learn together.

We are led inevitably to the *third* boundary-line which must be moved, and perhaps the most difficult. I have observed that educators who are most ready to be critical of the goals of the society are sometimes hopelessly defensive when it comes to altering the power structure of the classroom or the campus itself. And I have also learned in the last three years something else important: that enlightened trustees, men active in business and industry, are well aware that "the name of the game is change." The time has come to cut the students into the decision-making process at all levels: development, business affairs, educational policy. Those institutions which effect this change in time will—as radical as it now seems to some—ten years from now be found to have acted in the wisest conservative way. And those which resist, where the professors continue their paternalistic self-image and the administrators reflect only a franchise limited to the owners of the property, will be racked from stem to stern. There are not enough policemen, National Guardsmen, and Army troops—as yet—who have lost sight of what America is all about to permanently occupy our campuses and keep young citizens not in uniform from sharing in making the decisions which govern their present and future. A wise conservatism will effect orderly change and forestall the fatal polarization between ideologically tainted and disciplined extremists which is becoming the curse in more and more crisis situations.

The third and most important change, in terms of educating for effective and loyal citizenship, is to establish a new pattern of co-determination on campus. As the three professors earlier quoted at length pointed out, the integrity of the institution can only be regained by a new structuring of the stakes of students, faculty, and trustees. Wise trustees, who are used to re-tooling their businesses and industries every two or three years, know that any concern which remains fixed in its basic patterns will fail; at least, if I may say so without chauvinism, I have found it so in effecting a new Trustees' Charter, a new Faculty Constitution, a new Student Constitution, and a new curricular and co-curricular program and staffing at Iowa Wesleyan. I believe that if, resistant to change, the college or university—one of the most magnificent achievements of civilization to date—is destroyed, it will be primarily the fault of the professional educators themselves.

There is a false notion that the students cannot be involved in making real decisions—and therefore the patent fraud of most "student governments" is excused!—because they are so mobile. But the truth is that the faculty are mobile, having their basic loyalties defined along disciplinary lines and by extra-campus associations, while the students have made a life commitment. The degree which they carry brands them for life; the quality of the institution affects them for life; the Alumni Department will pursue them for life for financial support. Moreover, our students are older and more sophisticated. Studies have shown that the point of biological maturity has been reached by American youth at a time declining an average of six months per decade since 1880. Students come to campus with from 4 to 6 years longer experience of physical maturity, of the self-identity crisis, of awareness of self-history apart from general history, etc. than did their grandparents. Young citizens of the TV generation, many of whom have fought in Vietnam, registered voters in Mississippi, demonstrated in our cities for decent schools or housing, are sick to death of a protective custody operation which is both pretentious and demeaning. (I recently saw a Student Handbook for a university of 17,000 students which included the rule: "There must be at least one adult present at every student function"!) From the seriousness of the issues which they have raised, from the stake which they have put in with their lives and their money, and for the sake of a society which at its best features participatory democracy, the time has come to cut the students into a piece of the action. Nothing which we shall read in the next magazine which has been done by trustees, regents, state legislators or the Congress, professors or administrators, will be so awesome in its wisdom that student leaders such as we have on every campus cannot do just as well. Every argument against co-determination for students is an argument against liberty and self-government itself; there are such arguments, but they ring more hollowly with every passing year.

THE SOCIAL COMMITMENT OF HIGHER EDUCATION

The first duty of our colleges and universities, then, is to maintain the integrity and liberty and dignity of the Republic of Learning. This they cannot do in bondage, whether it be the bondage of a mindless technology or the bondage of a smothering church or legislature. Inherent in that integrity is the realization that the campus is a model *Gesellschaft,*[5] a rational community whose members are learning good citizenship or bad citizenship through the power-structures which operate in the institution itself. It is useless to talk about ecumenical dialogue in a religiously monochromatic campus. It is senseless to talk about eliminating second-class citizenship in a racially homogeneous college. It is a playful charade to study *The Federalist* and the Constitution and Bill of Rights where 90% of those involved have no effective representation in the governance of their affairs. There was a time when the modern Academy, emerging out of the monastic and cathedral schools, admitted novices to submit to older teachers who were spiritual directors as well as instructors. That time is past; there now exists a contract, overt or inherent, between entities/"persons" whose different roles and traditional status should not obscure the fact that a constitutional order is involved if simple justice is to obtain. If students are concerned about absentee professors, for example, the question of the special consultancy arrangements enjoyed by the instructor with industry and government should not be guarded behind a Chinese wall of professional prerogative. If the students are concerned about trustee conflict of interest and servility of the university to military R & D, the old corporate tradition that the franchise is restricted to those who own the property should not silence the discussion. We are still a long way from "One man, one vote," in higher education. But we are at least beginning to perceive the wisdom in Colonel Rainboro's rejoinder to Colonel Ireton in the Putney debates in the New Model Army. Ireton argued that decision should rest with those who owned the property, paid the taxes, and lived with the mistakes as well as the gains. Said Rainboro: "I verily believe that the poorest he that is in England hath a life to live as the richest he."

The second duty to social responsibility, expressive of the Wisdom dimension of the dialectic, is to encourage students in participatory democracy off campus. They need to learn with their professors the way in which power is organized and operates in a society which at its best maximizes full, free, and informed discussion; which rests upon a base of liberty and self-discipline. A police-state does not want educated persons who know how to organize power: it wants technicians who will do efficiently—if necessary, ruthlessly—what they have learned. But the American experiment cannot survive the withholding of responsible participation by those of status and decision in the society. The answer of the free society to the totalitarian is not anarchy: it is the volunteering, the self-discipline, of free men.

Some few colleges and universities are beginning to develop academic credit programs which place service experiences squarely within the framework of the educational process. An example is Iowa Wesleyan College. All students at Wesleyan, unless they have already performed military service or served in the Peace Corps or on the mission field, are required to spend an intensive period of time in a service project and submit a report on same for faculty approval. Building up to this service experience are between-semester "Interims." During the Freshman year the Interim of 7 weeks is dedicated to "American Self-Identity"; the existential question is, "Who am I as a citizen?" During the Sophomore year the Interim concentrates on Social Pathology (totalitarian ideologies, parties, and systems); the personal query is, "Who are the enemies of liberty?" During the Junior year the question is centered in Communications: Theory and Practice. The Senior service Interim is the capstone of the Wisdom dimension and is based in the conviction that no one is truly educated until he has learned the importance of service for others.

Under this plan, during the two 14-week semesters the emphasis is cast on achieving technical competence in a chosen field, *Techne*. During the Interim, with altruism the highest expression of it, the emphasis is on the Wisdom dimension. It is felt that this approach is more likely to implant a life-long tension than two years of general study followed by a major, and that it will implant the fundamental truth: to be educated means to mature into a full and a whole man or woman. To this all material during the college years, as in life itself, is relevant: the only question is whether it can be turned into a learning event in an imaginative effort of learning. The campus is viewed as no ivory tower, no encampment training students in preparation for life; rather it is seen as a significant, sometimes determinative, part of life itself for ever-increasing numbers of American youth.

SECULARIZATION AS AN HISTORICAL PROCESS

What we are seeing in the present struggle on campus is an effort of this "creature," the *universitas*, to free itself from an earlier pattern of colonialism in which close control was exercised by the church or the legislature or a "company of adventurers" (in the language of the Harvard College charter) usually called "Trustees." In this, its battle for integrity is part of the larger process of entering what Dietrich Bonhoeffer called—in a moment of ecstatic utterance—"a world come of age."[6]

As we emerge out of the centuries during which the civilizing of the tribes called for the enforcement of Christianity as an ideology ("Christendom") and the close control of key social institutions by ecclesiastics or their delegates, a number of "creatures" (theologically speaking) are struggling to achieve their liberty and dignity and integrity. One is government: under the rubric "Religious liberty" we are beginning to understand that the best kind of government is "secular" (i.e., modest, unpretentious, eschewing "God-talk" and control of conscience, theologically speaking—"creaturely") just as the best kind of religious covenants are voluntary. Another, now in hot dispute, is the family. The historical wrong of the encyclical on birth control, *Humanae Vitae,* is not that the population explosion threatens human life (which it does), nor that the encyclical was defective because it did not truly represent a *consensus fidelium* (although that is true), but that a husband and wife are today far better able to decide such matters of conscience than any company of bachelor ecclesiastics outside the family. The integrity and true function of the college and university, which can be destroyed by such retrogressive controls as exercised lately at Drew University (Methodist) and St. John's University of New York (Roman Catholic), can only be secured by directing the line of march into the new historical age of pluralism and dialogue. The ancient bondage of government, family and *universitas* in a sacral society must be broken.

There is a false "secularization," in which institutions of higher education simply slide into a new bondage—to industrial society, to nationalistic goals, to Marxism or facism. (The latter ideologies, however, introduce a re-sacralization rather than a true secularization process.) For the liberating process to hold to the right course the gyroscope of Dialogue is required. And that Dialogue must involve in a full way all those—students and faculty, as well as trustees—who have a legitimate stake in the decisions of this present and this future of the *universitas.*

THE THREE DIALOGUES

The first dialogue is the dialogue with the past. Represented by the "fellowship of teachers and students," the dialogue with those who have gone before ("History") provides a vital appropriation of the heritage and the traditions. The most spiritually impoverished persons are those who have only contemporary resources to draw upon.

The second dialogue is the dialogue with the world, the created order. This is primarily represented by the "hard sciences," where in the laboratory the world of Nature is "put to the question" (as Francis Bacon said). In the long haul this can only be constructive if men respect the good earth and see themselves as stewards of its riches.

The third dialogue is the inter-personal, especially the inter-religious. The old order of close control, "Christendom," required the enforcement of a uniform religious ideology—through compulsory chapel, uniform public liturgy, standardized creeds. The great contribution of ACURA to "dialogue on campus" has been to help free the campuses from their monochromatic and monolithic commitment and to train students and staffs in the benefits to be derived from open-faced, full, free, and informed inter-religious dialogue. America is struggling to become something far more significant than an appendage to European Christendom: a World City, in which equally "entitled" citizens of the most varied cultural and racial and religious backgrounds learn to live together as whole human persons. The student stake in campus governance prepares him for full participation in the American experiment in liberty and self-government.

Some universities have not yet recovered sufficiently from the shock of freeing themselves from churchly imperialism to introduce the Offices of Religious Affairs and Departments of Religious Studies which can build the gyroscopes to hold them on the course of serving the human measure. Others have slipped into the posture of a cast-iron secularist ideology which is as anti-humanistic and anti-dialogical as the old churchly inquisitions. But for those that value the pursuit of Wisdom the line of march is clear. And the educational imperative is clear, too: no student graduates as a truly educated citizen unless he has learned to practice the three dialogues. Of these, the third—the inter-religious—is the most imperative and the most widely neglected.

CONCLUSIONS

The campuses require radical change, both internally and in their ties to society at large, if they are to serve persons with integrity in the new age. Change is pressing: the only question is whether there will be sufficient wisdom to provide orderly and reasonable change, or whether the new university will be born in blood. To date, the student rebels have been wiser than their elders to perceive the need and to single out the pressure points.

The *universitas* is presently programmed for disaster because it has committed itself to a soul-less technology and neglected the Wisdom dimension.

The contribution of Religion to the campus, rightly conceived, is to assist the liberating of higher education through the secularization process, and to advance the inter-personal and inter-religious dialogues which can turn the machine back to the human measure and hold it there.

NOTES
SECULARITY IN HIGHER EDUCATION

1. cf. "Students in Search of 'Soul'," VI *Journal* of the Division of Higher Education, United Church of Christ (September, 1968) 11:2–9.
2. XLVIII *The Temple News* (Temple University, 1969) 80:lff.

3. cf. "Sectarian Protestantism and the Pursuit of Wisdom: Must Technological Objectives Prevail?", Ch. III in Erickson, Donald, ed., *Public Controls for Non-public Schools* (Chicago: University of Chicago Press, 1969), pp. 61–82.
4. Richter, Werner, *Re-Educating Germany* (Chicago: University of Chicago Press, 1945), pp. 23–24.
5. Readers will recognize the writer's indebtedness to the Fr. Tönnies typology distinguishing *Gemeinschaft* from *Gesellschaft.* The problem of small colleges and many universities is that they have not disengaged themselves from the familial self-image and matured into institutional, rational orders.
6. Bonhoeffer, Dietrich, *Prisoner for God* (New York: Macmillan Co., 1957), p. 157.

Part Two

DEVELOPING THE SCRIPT OF A PROFESSION

Edwin de F. Bennett is coordinator of religious and leadership activities in the student life division of the University of Houston and executive board member of the Association for the Coordination of University Religious Affairs.

Coordinating University Religious Affairs

Edwin de F. Bennett

Now that the religious dimension in higher education is coming into its own, the coordinator's role is more uncertain than ever before, and also more challenging. There is little question that contemporary university affairs are now "soul size." Witness the hard questions being asked concerning the university's mission, direction, goals, even its future; these are questions of the university's being or non-being basically—generic religious questions. It can be said that the crisis underlying the turbulence, the confusion and, in many places now, the violence taking place on the campus is essentially a religious crisis. For the coordinator this new situation contrasts sharply with the formative years of his profession in the quieter 50's. There is now a whole new action-set, at minimum calling for a rethinking and reformulation of the coordinator's role and responsibilities. The changes could even mean the demise of the role, depending on how the university as a whole responds to the crisis in higher education.

Our concern is to make the most of the current crises—the educational, the cultural as well as the religious. Poisitions may come and go, roles and jobs change. But if institutions of higher education are to fulfill themselves, those responsible for their shape and order must recognize the pain and hope and vision lying behind the crises. Our stance is optimistic—not sanguine in the sense that eventually all will work out well—but optimistic in the sense that opportunities for creative response to the crises are present, awaiting effective action by those sensitive to the possibilities. It does appear that new coalitions are developing, and that commitments are focusing on change designed to put more humanistic clothing on our functional institutions.

The question is always open as to whether we will win the race between civilization and chaos. The tools for planned change through the application of knowledge to the crises facing America are emerging from all fields. The purpose of this chapter is to analyze the place and function of religion on campus, with particular reference to one mode of higher education's response: the position of coordinator of university religious affairs. We approach this positively, convinced that we human beings can and will move creatively in response, once the challenge is clarified. Our mood is well articulated in the words of Christopher Fry in *The Sleep of Prisoners.*

> The human heart can go the lengths of God.
> Dark and cold we may be, but this
> Is no winter now. The frozen misery
> of centuries breaks, cracks, begins to move,
> The thunder is the thunder of the floes,
> The thaw, the flood, the upstart Spring.
> Thank God our time is now when wrong
> Comes up to face us everywhere,
> Never to leave us till we take
> The longest stride of soul men ever took.
> Affairs are now soul size.
> The enterprise
> Is exploration into God.
> Where are you going? It takes
> So many thousand years to wake,
> But will you wake, for pity's sake,
> Pete's sake, Dave or one of you,
> Wake up, will you?

EVENTS AND IMPLICATIONS: A CAPSULED HISTORY

As indicated, this chapter will seek to examine the role and function of a coordinator of university religious affairs within the context of the crises in higher education. We will note, first of all, how this position came into existence and developed in the fifties and early sixties. We will then seek to understand how it may function in these times of awakening and reordering. Our hope is that by such analysis the reader may project new and relevant designs for dealing with the religious dimensions of cultural change as they affect higher education.

As happens usually in changing situations, the efforts of certain key people led to the initiation of the position of religious affairs coordinator in the 50's. This found its most widespread expression in the Big Ten schools, especially Minnesota and the University of Michigan. The names of Henry Allen, DeWitt Baldwin and Franklin Littell stand out. Cornell University and the Cornell United Religious Work, centered in Anabel Taylor Hall, holds similar meaning. As is generally true today, the position of coordinator was located in the Student Affairs or Student Life area. It was, therefore, viewed as extra-curricular and peripheral, as were allied departments within the student affairs area. Granted, there were and are cases where some coordinators both administer and teach. Examples of this are found at the University of Kansas, University of Minnesota, Ohio State, and Florida State. In some cases coordinators hold faculty rank. Generally speaking, however, this is not because religion is understood as essential to the educational process, but because the person hired as coordinator has a competence academically certifiable. Sometimes, it becomes a convenient way to categorize an administrative task that is bothersome to what is perceived as the real business of the institution, yet necessary to keep the peons satisfied.

Many within the ranks of the profession of coordination feel that the orientation should be, essentially, academic. Others, while not rejecting the academic, understand the role of higher education in broader terms. This creates a real tension within the profession. This tension mirrors one of the basic crises within higher education, the ill defined relationship between cognitive and affective learning. And this in turn points to a dimension of the cultural crisis, namely, the yearning for a new image of what it means to be human. The syntheses of the past emphasizing man as spiritual being, and man as rational being, no longer provide a complete response. A new myth, a new symbol, adequate to the changes of the post-industrial era, is overdue. The crisis within the profession of coordination is part of this broader crisis within higher education and within culture.

It is interesting to note that in several instances the coordinator's portfolio has been one of several held by an assistant or associate dean. And in some cases, for a variety of reasons, this has been the extent of the institution's open recognition of the importance of religion. It has been a convenient way to provide a service to the representatives of local religious institutions desiring to establish a ministry on campus, while avoiding confrontation with Church/State issues. Many universities have dealt with the problem in stages. A beginning is made by assigning the liaison function to someone whose primary work lies elsewhere. Then, steps are taken to move toward a full-time staff position. Sometimes directly related to this move, sometimes parallel to it, course offerings, or programs, or even departments in religious studies develop.

Crucial to such a progression is an open, honest and forthright confrontation with all the issues inherent in the American concept of separation of Church and State. Underlying this functional outgrowth of the American experience is both past encounter with repression growing out of alliances between Church and State, and an anthropology that split men down the middle, projecting an image of being human that separated the human body and the human mind. This image, or myth or symbol, no longer holds, and not only because traditional ways of picturing the transcendent dimension of living no longer fit. But, much more positively, it is now too restrictive because men and women are discovering a broader sense of themselves, without a false dependence on an authoritarian deity.

A strange, wondrous paradox emerges: even as the weight of religion, in one sense, diminishes and so makes concern with Church/State issues irrelevant, so a recovery of a thrust toward wholeness brings religion to the forefront. The new strength is not a threat to human freedom and dignity, nor anathema to the freedom of thought and expression essential to the academic process, but a resource for insight and action in the necessary process of reshaping the educational institutions.

In some institutions the initiation of the role of coordinator has been the beginning point for the establishment of a significantly deep and broad Department of Religious Affairs with a wide-ranging outreach and a skilled staff. Illustrative of this progression is the University of Michigan development. From a risky, tentative beginning through the framework of the YMCA, a department developed within the Student Affairs area staffed not only to facilitate the work of religious professionals from off-campus, but staffed to take initiative to meet and deal with the religious dimension of issues emerging on campus. These may bear little resemblance, superficially and in the formal sense, to what traditionally is termed religion. They deal, however, with such basic concerns as academic reform and the involvement of all members of the institution in the governance of the institution.

Although younger by far in this enterprise, the University of Houston approach exhibits innovative design. There, within the Student Life Division, the coordinator's role combines responsibility for religious activities and student leadership development. This approach includes, but moves beyond, concern with facilitating what outside institutions offer to the campus. It moves on to include initiatives in preparing students, faculty and administrators to implement their value commitments, including that to religion, by reassessing present modes of university life both inside and outside the classroom, and continues by designing methods for changing systems and procedures so that they may become more congruent with values seeking to maximize human potential. The basic assumption is that religion is fundamental to being human, and that humans can reshape their environment to serve the quest for wholeness. The conviction is that the direction of change is possible, given the insight and training that comes from religion and knowledge.

Like other Departments within a university's Student Affairs Division, Departments of Religious Affairs have been seen as auxiliary services. Universities seek to respond to the needs of their clientele. Consequently, when this position was initiated, its operation was largely seen as making the services of established religious institutions available to their membership in the University community. A certain amount of control was also exercised in this approach because religion was perceived as potentially threatening to the academic enterprise. Because its expression through institutional forms has all too frequently stymied, if not harassed and subverted, the search for truth, a safe way to deal with religion was to avoid presenting it directly to the campus, yet make it available through limited channels. Thus, the coordinator's job, in this type of situation, was to serve as liaison for religious representatives as they dealt with the need of on-campus folk. In some instances and at certain times in every institution, this type of response was seen as adequately "taking care of religion." To be just, it must be realized that the desire was not so much to keep religion in a box as to prevent religion from boxing in the free flow of ideas, essential to the task of truth-seeking that makes a University worthy of the name.

The forties and fifties saw the blossoming of the foundation movement with its development of student clubs through which the churches and synagogues sought to minister to the campus. There was the Wesley Foundation, Hillel, Canterbury, Newman, and many others. The coordinator came on the scene, and sought to be the man to open doors for their activity. His primary function was facilitating their work, and wherever possible, working to develop patterns for joint projects.

ISSUES AND CHALLENGES

The emphasis of the coordinating function was facilitation of existing approaches to campus ministry. The focus was on students, and the context was extra-curricular activities. The coordinator was a broker between the campus bureaucracy and the churches, and between the various representatives of institutionalized religion established on Main Street and transplanted to the campus. In some instances the person fulfilling this role took significant initiatives in the area of academics by encouraging development of religious studies programs; in social action by encouraging summer workshops, and projects such as tutorial programs; in personal development by mobilizing resources to offer human relations laboratories.

It should by now be clear that it is impossible to generalize about how the coordinator functions. On no single campus is the approach the same as on any other. But the common denominator is the institution's desire to regularize and manage the forces that desire to exercise their ministry on campus. Two great difficulties confront the coordinator: one is the diversity among the religious entities seeking to work on campus, and the other is the lack of acceptance by the institutions themselves of the religious dimension of education. On the one hand, there stand those committed to focusing on human religious needs; and on the other, there is the institution that tolerates the peculiarities of religious expression, but sees such concerns as secondary to the educational enterprise. The possibility of productive response to this situation emerges from the creativity and concern of the professionals assigned to campuses by religious entities, and from the insight and understanding of key faculty and administrators.

It is most difficult to typify the present status and role of the coordinator, but it is even more difficult to establish a normative framework definitive for this role. The coordinator may hunger for amnesty, but if the role is to be alive, the person filling it will face, and immerse himself in, the ambiguities and tension-producing movements on campus. He may yearn for a transcendent order as much as any other citizen of the academy. Yet, if he is to share in the rebirth and reordering process, his own identity needs must be faced as realistically as he might wish the institution to face its own. He is caught up in the flux of these times. It has been said over and over again that "a new era is upon us. . . . a new society is emerging." But it is one thing to sense this and rejoice in the possibilities for reshaping things, and it is another to chart a path through the radical ambiguity that exists.

Is there a special role needed in these times that we can symbolize by the term "coordinator of religious affairs"? A way to get hold of this question is to begin by focusing on our cultural crisis, rather than by reviewing and describing all that has been done and is underway within the structural factors of formal university bureaucracies. It is the thesis of these remarks that the cultural crisis is a religious crisis, and that by immersing ourselves in the task of understanding the place of religion within the cultural crisis, clues will emerge for tentative steps in reshaping the function of religious coordination. Our concern is essentially functional, and is not that of considering only, or primarily, the position of coordinator as a "slot" within the university bureaucracy. Positions come and go, "captains and kings depart," but the shaping and developing of systems, procedures and institutions relevant to human beings and adequate to the tensions necessary to life, such as freedom and order, call us to act.

FRAMEWORK FOR UNDERSTANDING

We have stated that "religion is coming into its own," and that this could mean fresh possibilities for the coordinator of religious affairs. To come to grips with these possibilities, we need a framework, a perspective, by which we can move within the context of higher education.

The cultural crisis being uncovered by the turbulence, confusion and uncertainty of these times is at its root a religious crisis. The inadequacies of those institutional arrangements against which complaints are being made and protests mounted on campus, are the result of many factors. It is not possible to enumerate and discuss these at this juncture. But in all of the abundant literature on the subject there is a sense of loss as to which direction to take. Many voices offer many solutions. Getting hold of the situation seems impossible. There is a feeling that "everything nailed down is coming loose." Dr. E. J. Shoben, Jr. puts his finger on what lies behind this situation when he says, "Currently, the nation is subject to a panoply of forces that challenge that ancient pattern of dominant values. . . . (There exists) strong suggestion of a sharp decline in the potency of traditional values to guide and animate American life." In this, the institutions of higher education share a like atmosphere and situation with all of society. The crisis is not peculiar to higher education: it exists as a cultural phenomenon.

In the midst of such a reality, we are required to confront the most fundamental of issues. The masks and myths no longer do: the unreality, what protestors call "phoniness," of our systems and institutions have been exposed. Everything is "up for grabs."

One type of response to this understanding of what's happening to us, is the possibility of moving to grasp at straws, seek the simplistic resolution, actually opt out because we cannot bear the tensions of ambiguity. Yet to say with Rollo May that myths are breaking down, does not have to end in a "cop out." It can, and does, call us to face that fact and to await, and work toward, the birth of myths and symbols adequate to our life in this grave new world.

And this is where the religious factor comes to light. It must be quite clear that what we are concerned with here is not primarily the religious factor in campus life as expressed in the formalized, institutionalized expressions of religion. True, the religious institutions of our land are as much caught up in crises as the others. And thankfully, some of the most awake and courageous of those working to reform the churches and synagogues are present on the campus.

When we speak of the religious factor we are referring to the hunger and quest for meaning that emerges within human beings when they bump up against reality. . . . when they become aware that the systems by which order and freedom are held in balance, and in which balance human beings live, are not final in their shape or authority. . . . when they realize that if there is to be change, they must initiate and manage it. It is when this movement toward the world takes hold of a person, that that person enters into the depth and breadth of religion, for it is at that point that the person risks himself in shaping his own world. This is what religion is all about, the process by which things hold together and through which a man 'stands upright.' This self-awareness is both the ultimate challenge to being human and offers the ultimate promise of wholeness. It is, if you will, the movement of faith: it is faithfulness. It is both scary and joyful, threatening and fulfilling. It is the meeting between the self and the world that ties one with everyman, and in the process leads to a continuous process of becoming.

I am not at all convinced—in fact I highly doubt—that those concerned with the cultural crisis as it emerges in the campus setting would find meaning in this analysis of the situation. I do feel that those who are working for creative change on campus—faculty, students, administrators, staff and maintenance people—are aware that they are dealing with root issues. They are conscious that they are confronted with "principalities and powers," not just recalcitrant defenders of outmoded systems.

In the midst of the types of issues and situations confronting communities of higher education, the moralisms, obscurantisms and ghettoisms of institutionalized religion are seen for what they are: bleeders of hope, blinders to truth, bastions against reality. There may well be an arrogance toward religious expressions unbecoming among those claiming to follow the path of Milton as he talked of truth-seeking: "come whence it may, cost what it will." Their own religion, their own idolatry, may blind them as much as religion of the professed religionists imprisons them.

But as we go behind the forms of religion we are grasped with the religious issues confronting every man, and the oneness of all men in seeking a world-view adequate to the measure of all men. The question is not whether a person will be religious: the question is, what religion is adequate? What symbols, what myths, will enable men to deal with this world, will lead them to the heights of their potential and to the depths of their power? A world is struggling to be born. Human beings are reaching out and through things as they are, to make them roomy for growth.

PATTERNS FOR PARTICIPATION

'Caught,' as is every other human being in this cultural shift, and assigned the task of coordinating religious affairs, what then is the role of coordinator? In a very real sense, and understanding religion as we have interpreted it, the coordinator is called to be more of an initiator than one who facilitates all that presently goes by the name of religion on campus. At present, the coordinator is in a relatively powerless position. He is located bureaucratically within a section of the university traditionally considered peripheral to the academy's 'real' task. His role is seen to be that of keeping things calm in what is known as a conflictual area. He is hung with the albatross of moralism and obscurantism. As initiator he is called to move procedurally and substantively—procedurally, to be a change agent; substantively, to participate in and encourage the dialogue about the religious dimensions of the cultural crisis.

A word is in order about the pattern of participation as a change agent and articulator of the religious issues within higher education. This viewpoint assumes what might be called commitments or values, things for which one is willing to pay a price. The prime need of the educational community is for moral courage, that style of life that stands for, and calls out of others, such a joyfulness in one's own self that one cannot rest until all men find such room in which to live until they, too, know self-acceptance and release from the fears and despair that emerge as defensiveness and respond to change as threatening. Moral courage rests on self-confidence and consequent trust in others. It is catching: it touches a yearning in every man. It is hopeful: it has a vision of restoration, and breeds strength in others.

The coordinator is no better or worse than any other member of the campus community in terms of moral strength and insight. Yet, because of his education and experiences, and because of the position he occupies, he holds a unique responsibility for articulating the value issues inherent in the crises on campus. He finds ready allies in students and faculty and administrators sensitive to the pain arising from the present modes of university operation. He knows a kinship with those desirous of initiating change. He sees the stakes, not in terms of his position within a bureaucracy, not in terms of religion being honored, not even in terms of the necessary continuance of his university. He sees the stakes in terms of his own integrity, and finds that integrity directly related to the possibility of giving every man a chance to stand upright. Thus, his concern to become a change agent is understandable. That is the religious service he can provide. It calls for training and skill. It doesn't emerge automatically from good intentions. It is essential if the values of human dignity and worth are to be incarnated in systems that nurture and educate human beings.

But even more significant is the fact that understanding of how this happens and can be helped to happen is available through the resources of the behavioural sciences. Those resources will provide methods, not answers. This yearning and work for change to reshape social systems more humanely is not new. This is the story of every recorded revolution. When the pain has become too much, explosions follow. Reforms sometimes work. The signs of the times point toward changes that could result in revolutions of violence rather than revolutions of hope. The new idea awaiting full application not only to higher education, but to all of our spheres of activity by which human needs are met, is the resources that can raise up agents of change.

Working in such a way, understanding one's role in such a way, will free up the coordinator to be real as a person and necessary to the educational enterprise. His commitment to human values will make him functional. His need for an identity will be matched as he confronts the need of his institution. His religion, conceptually and existentially, will be coordinate with the reality of these revolutionary times.

Maybe if he wakes up, he will wake others. Hopefully, he will be able to join and serve those now awakened, as all work to reshape and reorder the forms and systems now revealing their inadequacy. We have often thought of the Coordinator as a bridge, drawing together those of great diversity into a common functioning. Perhaps we don't need to change this model of bridge builder, but rather change its substance: a bridge builder between those who would keep things as they are and those who would change them. The common value undergirding both sides of the riverbank to which the coordinator can appeal, is commitment to the value of the human person. . . . an awakening of higher education to its function as an innovative agent in society.

BIBLIOGRAPHY

The sources for much of the conceptual material in this chapter is found in the following documents. The key to the bibliography lies in the basic thesis of this chapter, namely, that creating and living into models for the role of coordinator is dependent on seeing this function within the context of the religious, educational and cultural revolutions of these days. The very nature of this task of creating models for participation in these revolutions means that much of this material is available in articles, mimeographed material and some unpublished papers. Adequate reflection rests on continuous investigation through involvement. Occasional and informal references keep one awake to, and in touch with, the fast moving, spontaneous actions of demand and response taking place everywhere. Permanent publications offer long-range perspective; involvement is invited by the briefer, more pointed, and contemporaneous resource.

History, Structure, System

1. Bennett, Edwin de F. *Religion Center: Symbol of Reality*—an address to the Association of Ministers of Greater Houston, 6 Apr. 64—mimeographed.
2. Robinson, Allyn B., *And Crown Thy Good*—National Conference of Christians and Jews, New York, 1955—paper.
3. Tremmel, William C., *A Different Drum: A Manual on Interreligious Campus Affairs*—National Conference of Christians and Jews, New York, 1964—paper.
4. Walter, Erich A., *Religion and the State University*—Univ. of Michigan Press, Ann Arbor, 1958.

The Educational Crisis

5. Allport, Gordon W., *The Person in Psychology: Selected Essays*—Beacon Press, Boston, 1968; esp. Part II, "Personal Conditions for Growth."
   8. Behavioural Sciences, Religion and Mental Health
   9. Values and Our Youth
   10. Crises in Normal Personality Development
6. Bennett, Edwin de F., *Innovation, or Invocation?* Religious Programming by State Universities: The University Owned Religion Center, a paper given at APGA Convention, 8 Apr. 68, Detroit, Mich.—unpublished.
7. Katz, Joseph and Assoc., *No Time for Youth:* growth and constraint in college students—Jossey-Bass, San Francisco, 1968.
8. Muscatine, Charles, chr. *Education at Berkeley,* report of the select committee on education—University of California Press, Berkeley, 1966—paper.

9. Novak, Michael, "The Realists and the Radicals," *Christianity and Crisis,* 3 Mar. 69, 29:3, pp. 34–36.
10. Sanford, Nevitt, *Where Colleges Fail*: a study of the student as person—Jossey-Bass, San Francisco, 1967.
11. Shoben, Edward J. Jr., "Toward Remedies for Restlessness: Issues in Student Unrest," *Liberal Education,* Vol. 56, May 68, pp. 221–230.
12. Smith, Huston, "LIKE IT IS: The University Today," *The Key Reporter,* 34:2, Winter 1968–69, pp. 2–4.

The Religious Crisis

13. Berger, Peter L., *The Precarious Vision,* a sociologist looks at social fictions and Christian faith—Doubleday, New York, 1961.
14. Brown, Robert Mc A., *America: No Promise without Agony*—Keynote Address, 24th National Conference on Higher Education, American Association for Higher Education, Chicago, 2 Mar. 69—mimeograph.
15. Coulson, William R., *The Problem of Community*—Delivered in connection with a presentation, 29 Apr. 68, to an extension course on the Future of Religious Belief at the University of California at San Diego—mimeographed.
16. Coulson, William R., *To a Friend*—an interview at United States International University, Nov. 68—mimeographed.
17. *Daedalus,* "Religion in America," 96:1, Winter 1967.
18. Novak, Michael, "Hypocrisies Unmasked," *Christianity and Crisis,* 12 May 69, 29:8, pp. 125–127.
19. Pelz, Werner and Lotte, *God Is No More,* Victor Gollanoz, London, 1963.
20. "Playboy Interview: William Sloane Coffin—Candid Conversation," *Playboy,* 15:8, Aug. 68, pp. 45–54, 114, 134–140.

The Cultural Crisis

21. Bennett, Edwin de F., *Students, Business, and Revolution*—a paper delivered at the Southwestern Bell Telephone Company Socioeconomic Seminar, 8 Oct. 69—mimeographed.
22. Bloy, Myron B. Jr., *The Crisis of Cultural Change,* a Christian viewpoint—Seabury, New York, 1965.
23. Cox, Harvey, *The Secular City,* a celebration of its liberties and an invitation to its disciplines—MacMillan, New York 1965—paper.
24. Gibb, Jack R., *Dynamics of Leadership*—22nd National Conference on Higher Education, American Association for Higher Education, Chicago, Mar. 67—mimeographed.
25. Leonard, George B. "How to Have a Bloodless Riot," *Look,* 10 June 69, 33:12, pp. 24–28.
26. Leonard, George B., "Beyond Campus Chaos: A Bold Plan for Peace," *Look,* 10 June 69, 33:12, pp. 73–82.

27. May, Rollo, *Reality Beyond Rationalism,* the function of myth in psychological health—24th National Conference on Higher Education, American Association for Higher Education, 3 Mar. 69—mimeographed.
28 "Re-Thinking Ethics," *Student World* 67:3:225, Third Quarter 1964–especially, Dumas, Andre, "The Quest of Man," pp. 248–259.
Wren-Lewis, John, "Science, Technology, and the Dilemma of Ethics," pp. 260–272.
"Called to Be Human," pp. 287–294.
29. Taylor, John F. A., *The Masks of Society,* an inquiry into the covenants of civilization—Appleton-Century-Crofts, New York, 1966.

President of the Association for the Coordination of University Religious Affairs in its tenth anniversary year, George W. Jones serves in the student affairs division at Ball State University as director of religious programs. He represents ACURA in the Council of Student Personnel Associations.

The Co-Curriculum in Religion

George W. Jones

1969 may well be used by historians as the year to mark a watershed in the self-perception of American higher education. The contrast between the meetings of educators during that year and previous years was striking. Absent was much of the heady optimism that had been fed by pyramiding budgets, a crescendo of demands for research and consultation, and lines of would-be collegians waiting outside the doors of admission offices. Instead, doubt was being expressed as to whether or not education should ever have expected to fulfill the promises implicit in being hailed as the "new religion" from which all blessings desired by Americans could flow.

Student protests over higher education's irrelevance and compromise had mounted. Institutional self-studies failed to demonstrate the competence of colleges generally to reach professed goals. Legislatures and philanthropists were questioning by deed as well as by word the utility of much of what higher education had done or was proposing to do. As a result, educators were talking openly to each other about the limitations of their institutions' competence, higher education's lack of omniscience about society's or even its own problems, and the truth of accusations that colleges and universities do engage in self-serving efforts.

A tendency to seek the counsel and assistance of other institutions in meeting the pressing needs of the day could be noted. The American Association for Higher Education, at its annual meeting spoke to its constituency through its resolutions committee in chastened terms:

> . . . *higher education, more influential, more pervasive, more success-*

> *ful than it has ever been as part of America's promise is also experiencing part of America's agony. . . .*
>
> *Part of the agony of American Higher Education grows out of grave conflict over the aims and purposes of higher education, based on misconceptions outside the institutions and confusion within them. . . . Since no institution can be all things to all men, each higher institution must order its priorities.*
>
> *Furthermore, it must inform its many publics of its limitations as well as its scope. Some characteristics are essential to its existence. For example, a college or university emphasizes reason and the rational approach to establishing priorities and to resolving disagreements. . . . It should also—more than ever before—significantly involve all portions of the collegiate community in the re-examination process.*

In line with this stance, the program committee of the Association invited a theologian to keynote the annual conference and recognized the co-sponsorship of the National Campus Ministry Association of a part of the program.

Sociologists employ the concept of differentiation in describing the phenomenon which was becoming visible in American higher education in 1969. An institution limits the scope of its efforts in order to pursue at greater depth and competence its primary purpose. The corollary of differentiation is interdependence. Cooperation with other institutions of the society is needed in those matters which lie beyond the adopted area of primary concentration.

Evidence of differentiation and interdependence in American higher education today is seen in the many structures being developed by colleges and universities for relating to other institutions. Officers whose functions are primarily liaison or coordination with the programs of other institutions are multiplying. Each to some degree meet a need of the university to integrate, on its own terms, the input from or the output to other institutions with its total educational process. Because of the longstanding interest of the churches in higher education, one of the early officers of this liaison or coordinative type in the public universities was in the area of religion.

Dependence on other institutions for the furtherance of the religious commitment of students and faculty took a definite nationwide form with the development of the collegiate YM-YWCA's after the Civil War. The beginnings were marked by the formation of voluntary student religious groups on widely scattered campuses "for the specific purpose of cultivating their member's religious life and for the extension of religion among their colleagues and fellow students."[1] By relating to each other these voluntary associations developed into the collegiate YMCA's and YWCA's. Professional Y secretaries first appeared in 1886 when former Y officers were asked to stay on after graduation at Yale and Toronto to supervise the Y building and assist student officers with their programs. Universities in some cases soon were contributing the salary of these Y secretaries. With the development of church-related and synagogue-related campus ministries in the twentieth century, some universities began to look to the Y secretaries as their employees who, in addition to what else they were doing, could coordinate the university's interests with these other religious efforts.

In the 1930's, a number of the Y secretaries dropped their relationship to a Y organization as such and began to devote their time exclusively to being the university's officer for relating to the ministries sponsored by churches and synagogues. Typically they worked with a student inter-faith council composed of representatives of student religious organizations and sometimes also served as heads of the staff of clergy assigned to their campuses. They thus assumed responsibility for on-campus co-curricular programming in the religious area and were called upon to assist in the evaluation of the programs of the religious groups. The Association for the Coordination of University Religious Affairs (ACURA) was organized in 1959 as a means of bringing together university staff persons with religious coordination responsibility for the purposes of professional stimulation and liaison on a regional and national basis with other religious and student personnel associations.

Typically religious affairs officers have found their home in the university in the student personnel division. Historically Y secretaries, with their concern for the human and liberal aspects of education, had pioneered in the development of many of the programs which came to be known as student personnel services. William S. Guthrie, former Dean of Student Services at Ohio State University, listed 16 student personnel services the concept and practices of which "can be traced in some part at least, to earlier campus religious work agencies of 20 years ago." When the Dean of Men's office was established at Ohio State University in 1927, the YMCA secretary was employed to be the first incumbent and brought "along from the Y office . . . the housing bureau, foreign student work, part-time jobs, and personnel counseling services."[2] In the student personnel philosophy the convictions about the wholeness of education inherited from the liberal arts tradition were reinforced by mounting evidence from the emerging social sciences about the nature of learning. "To a large extent, this new emphasis (after 1918) on religion was related to the growing interest in guidance and counseling. The assertion that on psychological grounds higher education must concern itself with the 'whole' person led inevitably to the argument, that, on this ground alone, the religious life of the student should not be slighted."[3]

Today on some 60 university campuses, religious coordinators are the means of interrelating their university's concern for the total education of their students with the resources of personnel, programs, and facilities provided by religious agencies. In a 1967 study these persons reported that their efforts are focused on four primary functions. Counseling occupies nearly one-fourth of their time with co-curricular programming holding a similar time priority. They also reported that coordinating and communicating each required an additional twenty per cent of their time. These efforts included such activities as working with religious institutions and university agencies, as well as public speaking engagements, research and publicity.[4]

Nearly 75 percent of the four-year public colleges and universities in the United States in 1968, in response to a survey by the writer, indicated that some officer of the institution had been assigned or had assumed some responsibility for religious affairs on their campus. Most frequently this was the dean of students or one of his associates. On the majority of the campuses this was a part-time responsibility, mainly liaison or coordination with student religious organization officers and members and with campus ministers, written into a larger job portfolio.

A RATIONALE FOR RELIGIOUS PROGRAMMING.

Whenever a university takes seriously the need to deal with religious matters in its total educational mission, it must also recognize its limitations in the area of religion and therefore its interdependence with other agencies of society. The churches, the synagogues, and certain humanistic and social service associations also have legitimate concerns and responsibilities in this area.

Recent Supreme Court decisions, in establishing principles for determining the constitutionality of certain religious exercises in the public schools, made distinctions which provide helpful guidelines for higher education as well. Justice Clark in writing the majority opinion in the Abingdon School District vs. Schempp Case of 1963, differentiated between the practice of religion, in that case devotional Bible reading, and the study of religions. Fostering the practice of a religion was held to be a function of an ecclesiastical institution and therefore was held to be unconstitutional if state-sponsored. The study of religion however, was clearly seen to be an obligation of an educational institution.

> . . . *It might well be said that one's education is not complete without a study of comparative religion or the history of religion and its relationship to the advancement of civilization. It certainly may be said that the Bible is worthy of study for its literary and historic qualities. Nothing we have said here indicates that such study of the Bible or of religion, when presented objectively as part of a secular program of education, may not be effected consistent with the First Amendment. (374 U.S. 203, 225)*[5]

The university's concern for religion, in line with its educational purposes, would be to further the understanding of the several religions—their systems of thought; their rites and ceremonies; their codes of behavior; their histories; their impact on individuals, societies, and cultures; and their relevance to contemporary issues. If the college is in the liberal tradition, it will further be concerned that students utilize their understandings in answering the basic questions forced on them by life experiences—questions of identity, purpose, meaning, vocation, and social relationship.

On the other hand a religious group may have as one of its unique purposes the securing of personal commitments to its faith, nurturing persons in that faith, and aiding members in expressing that faith in their daily lives. In furthering these concerns, a religious group may provide opportunities for any or all of the following functions: worship, study, service, evangelism, pastoral care. If it is an ethical religion, as the religions of the West are, there may also be study and strategy sessions in which the group criticizes and makes plans to reform itself and the larger society along the lines of the ethical vision of the group.

How can these differences in function of an educational institution and a religious group be expressed so that they complement rather than infringe upon each other? The matter of personal religious commitment may be used as an illustration. Obviously this is a concern which is primary for many religious groups, but the university also has some concern because of its commitment to knowledge about all phenomena and to the total growth of persons under its tutelage. A distinction may be made in the nature and degree of responsibility of each institution. The religious body has responsibility for calling individuals to a particular religious commitment and for nurturing that commitment. The university is responsible for investigating and teaching about the meaning and effect of particular commitments on individuals, societies, and in history, the arts, and other disciplines. Eliciting and developing the phenomenon is the function of the religious group. Understanding the phenomenon is the function of the educational institution.

Since the processes of experiencing and understanding are intimately related in the development of an individual, cooperation between the two institutions is needed if each is to be effective even in its unique contribution. The task of the university's religious program officer is to effect this cooperation, to integrate the input of resources of the religious institutions with the provision of the university for the total education of the student. In turn the religious program officer may function as a channel for an outflow of information and skills which may be utilized by the religious institutions. The arena in which he does this particularly is through personal relationships with and in the group life of students. Thus he works to complement the classroom experiences the students may be having with religious phenomena.

Religious coordination officers have articulated principles whereby they may carry out their educational mandates while at the same time fully recognizing the full religious pluralism of their campuses. By following these principles in their work they have been able to secure the respect and cooperation of religious groups of all stripes on many kinds of campuses:

1. A part of the constitutional right of each student is access to the resources necessary for the practice of his particular faith.

2. The various religious bodies rather than the university as such are responsible for providing these resources.
3. The university works impartially with all religious groups as they seek to provide these resources.
4. The religious groups, rather than the university, determine whether they will work separately, cooperatively, or unitedly with each other.
5. The university's only basis for accepting or rejecting resources offered by religious groups is on grounds of compatibility with the educational goals and orderly processes of the university.
6. No person or group is required to participate in some program or organizational arrangement which causes him to feel that he is violating a principle of his faith.
7. Students have as much right to organize for religious purposes as for any other purpose.
8. Curricular or co-curricular programs officially sponsored by the university should be conducted because of their educational value rather than because they promote a particular sect or religion.[6]

STRATEGIES FOR RELIGIOUS AFFAIRS PROGRAMMING

Once a university has clarified its own purposes in dealing with religious matters and defined its own role in transmission of the religious aspects of cultures; it is in a position to determine the arrangements or structures by which it may best do this. A variety of possibilities may be available.

A single religious group, or some ecumenical or interfaith coalition, may initiate a particular program with the university's tacit assent or cooperation. This has been the predominate pattern in the past. Architecturally this pattern has taken visible form as religious groups have built, at the periphery of the campus, buildings in which to house their programs.

Again a religious group or groups may originate an idea and come to a university officer or committee for sanction or support. The university might accept or reject the program on the basis of its value to its total educational offerings and its availability to all students. Religious Emphasis Weeks planned by the religious groups but with university sanction are an example of this approach to programming. Building-wise this arrangement is illustrated in the incorporation of religious facilities provided by religious groups in the campus plan of the university in order to insure maximum accessibility and integration.

Still another approach is one in which both the university and religious groups exercise joint initiative in planning and executing a project. The university participates because of the educational value of the enterprise whereas the motivation of the religious groups may be the propagation of their own positions. For example, the University of Hawaii a few years ago invited Billy Graham, the Christian evangelist, to speak on the campus under university auspices. The usual public call to Christian commitment was not included as this would have involved official university sponsorship of a call to a particular religious commitment. However, from the standpoint of the Graham Team and the local sponsoring committee, this was part of the Greater Honolulu Crusade for Christ. From the University's point of view it was part of the annual religious emphasis week which that year included spokesmen for the Buddhist, Muslim, and Jewish faiths.

This third approach is illustrated architecturally in the newly completed Grosberg Religion Center at Wayne State University. An integral part of the University's new union building, the religion center is the result of nearly 15 years of cooperative planning between the University through its Office of Religious Affairs and the religious groups serving the University. A Religion Center Board was formed by the religious groups to represent them in negotiations with the University. One of the religious affairs staff members served the Board as executive-secretary. All funds needed for the building were raised by the Board or its member groups. The University received the funds from the Board as a gift and contracted for construction of the building. In return the Religious Board received a long-term lease for use of the building and entered into contract with the University for maintenance of the center. The University located its Office of Religious Affairs in the building to provide general supervision and management. Each religious group has, through this arrangement, secured the facilities it needs for its own programs and for possible joint or ecumenical programs in a building located at the heart of the campus. The University on the other hand, has made arrangements whereby its students may have readily available to them the necessary resources for the exercising of their faith as a part of their total educational development.

Other approaches to dealing with religion in the university would emphasize the initiative of the university with the possible cooperation or assent of the religious groups. In this arrangement the university assumes responsibility for planning programs which have as their goal aiding students in the understanding of their faith or other faiths in order that they might better answer basic life questions or confirm personal commitments. Eastern Michigan University, for example, provides a Religious Affairs Center which is headquarters for extensive cultural and social service programs of student and university-staff origin. Religious groups provide facilities for their own unique programs in their own near-campus buildings. The University's Coordinator of Religious Affairs also works in a liaison relationship with these ministers and groups.

Even though, for purposes of examination, these approaches have been presented as distinct, in actual practice on a college campus each may be employed during a year depending on the purposes of the project and nature and amount of resources available from the religious groups and from the university. Thus, programs which become an official part of a university's co-curricular programming may originate from several sources: (1) a director of religious programs, an educational officer provided for this purpose; (2) a religious or interfaith council functioning as an official part of the student life of the university;[7] (3) some other campus agency, such as a residence hall or an inter-fraternity council; (4) a joint committee or board composed of student and/or representatives from the university, and from the religious groups with possible representation from clergy, students, and alumni; (5) an ecumenical group composed entirely of persons from the religious groups; or (6) a single religious group. Numerous examples of programs on college campuses which become an officially sponsored part of the university's educational offerings could be cited.

The degree of involvement of the campus religious office will vary, depending on the origin of the program, from full responsibility for initiating the idea, planning the program, and securing financing, facilities and personnel to merely facilitating a program initiated and planned by others by lending advice and moral support. On the other hand a religious group's contribution may vary from full provision to mere cooperation in promotion.

On the contemporary American college campus, given the variants discussed above, a flexible strategy to religious programming is in order. The amount of initiative and input of resources from the college and from the religious groups will vary depending on the nature of the particular concern, the resources available, the structures which may be utilized, and the initiative of the persons involved. Basic to any strategy is a shared understanding of the limitations of both the college and of the religious groups in dealing with religion in co-curricular programming, a consensus on basic principles of cooperation, and personnel in both the university and the religious groups who have the ability and willingness to communicate with and command the respect of the other. Given these conditions, in recent years programs have been promulgated on many campuses which have been helpful to students in gaining a critical understanding of their cultural and religious heritage and in determining their own responses to the issues of belief, value, and commitment confronting them in their daily living.

EXAMPLES OF PROGRAMS

Programs about religion as a part of co-curricular educational offerings may have a part in any of several educational goals—(1) the transmission of the religious aspects of the cultural heritage, (2) criticism of the culture or an analysis of current problems from a vantage point of religious positions, and (3) the development of new cultural forms and structures to convey religious meaning and ethical values. The interest of students in curricular programs dealing with religion has been called a "quiet revolution" by Robert

Michaelson, Chairman of the Department of Religious Studies at the University of California, Santa Barbara.

> *For whatever reason, the present student generation is definitely interested in the study of religion. This includes both the "kooks" and the conformers. I am not saying that this student generation is more or less* religious *than a previous one or that a revival of religion is taking place. But there is a remarkable amount of interest in the study of religion. This interest springs to no small degree from personal probing and searching. To some extent it is non- or even anti-institutional in nature. . . .*
>
> *The nature of this interest ranges from the dilettante to the deeply serious, but the mood of the present generation appears to be more serious than casual. . . . Such a mood expresses itself religiously in a radical asking of ultimate questions, in a disgust with institutions and the complacent patterns of the adult world, and in a profession of attachment to the basic ethical position of the historic religious traditions. . . . Here is a desire to relate to something authentic in the tradition coupled with a feeling of disgust or betrayal with regard to the institutions of religion. . . .*
>
> *In their present mood students tend to shy away from a cut-and-dried, catechetical, or trivial approach to the study of religion. They are attracted to the existential, to a "no holds barred" kind of probing. . . . Curriculum devisors and professors are confronted today by a keen challenge to be both relevant and substantial. . . . There is a temptation to concentrate on the contemporary to the exclusion of the historical, on the surface while overlooking the deeper movements of the stream, to capitalize upon current student interests while shying away from the deeper probings that are conducive to the achievement of perspective. What is needed is a combination of sensitivity to the live issues of the present and a rigorous scholarship which sees these issues in their context and which may learn from the fact that human beings have confronted a variety of issues—some similar to and some quite different from the live ones of the present—in a variety of contexts. It is an awesome and exciting responsibility which demands the best that is in us.*[8]

The challenge upheld for "curriculum devisors" holds equally for co-curriculum devisors. Many extra-classroom religious programs have been purveyors of "cut-and-dried" answers from which all uncertainty had been removed; have been offered in a "catechetical" manner which implied, if not stated, that the only possible response was uncritical submission; or have dealt only with trivial matters, of concern primarily to an older generation interested in maintaining things as they remember them to have been. As a result many of the approaches to programming used in the past have lost effectiveness. Among these are reliance on programs which attract students through socials, mass rallies, speaker-type programs, and strictly sectarian programs.

Co-curricular programs which seem to be meeting with student response today have several hallmarks. Opportunity for high level involvement is one such mark. Students welcome opportunities to become actively involved in developing the implications of ideas, in making applications to themselves, and in efforts to alleviate problems or to meet critical needs. This involvement may be at the ideational level as in a discussion, or it may be at the level of action as in a service project or by participation in the life of a group or through relationships with another. Priority interest in both instances focuses most frequently on campus and societal problems affecting students rather than on more philosophical matters. Those programs which permit confrontation with the live alternatives in contemporary issues as they are expressed by honestly committed persons enjoy high student participation. Currently popular programs often utilize a multi-media approach. Oftentimes they may feed into some type of action project.

Specifically, debates have special appeal; likewise lectures in which the scholar presents his case against an absentee opponent. A film series, concert series, or a dramatic presentation are effective in raising issues, presenting alternatives or in illustrating creative efforts which struggle for ground on which to stand. Service projects complement consideration of personal and social needs. The observation of many working with university religious programs is that students today are more moved by appeals to human values than by religious slogans. These approaches to programming permit students to build relationships, to see connections, to unite thought and feeling in action, to see the abstract and ideal incarnated in the possible and the real, and to erase the distinction between the campus and the "real world."

The 1968 survey by the writer showed that the lecture series is the most frequently sponsored program dealing with religion at the public institutions (36 percent). The corollary fact is the popularity of many theologians and ministers with student audiences.

The University of Michigan through its Religious Affairs Office, which has a professional staff of four, during the 1968–69 academic year sponsored 19 speakers. Topics ranged from "Buddhism," "Drugs and Religious Experience," "Love and Sex," "Jews and Christians in Roman Egypt," to "Is the Christian Church Relevant or Important in the World Revolution?," "The University in American Society: An End of Ideology?," "Between Tyranny and Chaos: Are We Moving toward a Tyranny of the Right or a Chaos of the Left?," "Is There a Christian-Marxist Dialogue?," and "Christianity and Communism: Coexistence or Conflict?" Some of these speakers were sponsored entirely by the University; others were invited by one or several religious groups and co-sponsored by the Office of Religious Affairs. The lecture series is complemented by a series of book reviews by local professors and campus ministers, a film series, and an arts festival. All seek to deal in some manner and on differing levels of sophistication with theological and ethical issues. Funds from the university, from endowment funds, and from the religious groups go into the program budget for the year.

Another type program which seeks to provide a forum for evaluating various viewpoints on controversial issues and moving participants toward commitment and action is the study seminar or—to use terminology made popular at the Cleveland meeting of the University Christian Movement in December 1967—"the depth education group." The method utilizes a number of modes of presentation and seeks to combine study with action.

An example is a course on "White Racism" which was developed originally by the Wesley Foundation at the University of Kansas and widely copied after its presentation at a national seminar on institutional racism sponsored by the United States National Student Association in November, 1968, at Notre Dame University. At Ball State University, with campus-wide publicity and utilization of popular professors from a number of departments, over 200 students and faculty paid an enrollment fee of $2.00 and attended sessions extending over four weeks.

Since many students need other than verbal means to investigate, test, and affirm their basic values and commitments, action-type programs on the campus and in the community are widely employed in universities' religious co-curricula.[9] These programs encompass many areas, but the most popular seem to be those which involve the tutoring of disadvantaged children. Although sponsored by many kinds of campus groups, they frequently emanate from campus religious groups as the Luv Unlimited program of the Christian Churches' ministry at the University of Cincinnati, or MOVE, the community service branch of the United Campus Christian Ministry at North Carolina College at Durham, or from campus religious affairs centers and councils as Phillips Brooks House at Harvard, Cornell United Religious Work, the chaplain's office at Brown and at Smith, the Starkweather Religious Center at Eastern Michigan University, and Stiles Hall at the University of California at Berkeley.

Through a relationship with a college student, a culturally disadvantaged child may find that "security is someone who cares." The interest directed toward him may evoke within him wider interests. Social reciprocity, a new social model, a more positive self concept, heightened motivation may in turn energize his learning.

University students, too, learn through their voluntary service experiences. Having worked with several thousand Eastern Michigan students over a seven-year period, Charles Minneman, Director of the Eastern Michigan University Office of Religious Affairs asserted:

> *They (university students) may learn of cultural separation and its consequences. They may learn from first-hand experience some of the problems of America's cities. They learn about children and their growth and development. A tutorial subject may come into sharpened focus; a tutor is tutored indirectly by a tutee. Students learn about learning. They may learn the dynamics of pre-profession as they move toward identification of their vocation.*[10]

Ten aspects of a volunteer social service program were identified by representatives attending a regional invitational conference in February 1968 hosted by the Cornell-Ithaca Volunteers in Training and Service, (CIVITAS), the student-directed program at Cornell University and Ithaca College. A *general philosophy* identifies the needs to be met, establishes the goals, limits the scope, and provides standards for evaluation of the program. *Recruitment* is the aspect of the program which attracts students and others to volunteer the time and talents for the service of others. *Publicity* is essential not only to keep the volunteers informed but also the several publics within both the college and the community. *Orientation* is designed to instruct the volunteers in the program's philosophy and goals, their work situations, and skills needed for their specific projects. *In-service training* keeps the volunteers briefed about developments within their projects and the entire program if it is multi-faceted. *Transportation* of the volunteers to their places of service is generally conceded to be the most expensive and the most vexing part of student volunteer programs. Assistance by the university, a foundation, or a civic group is often necessary for continuation of the program. *Extension volunteering* enables students to continue service projects during vacation periods or in other communities or provides a way for non-students to work in the program. *Continuity* of leadership and projects is essential to continued community support and cooperation. A full-time paid coordinator on the campus has enabled some colleges to smooth out problems plaguing a program's continuity and other aspects. *Evaluation* is needed to determine the degree of success or failure of the program in meeting goals and to indicate adjustments which should be made. *Social action* designated efforts beyond the projects themselves to alleviate causes of social and individual need rather than continuing to deal only with effects. Apparently only a few of the programs reporting at the Cornell meeting had moved far in this direction.[11]

Liaison with activist student groups on some campuses has been provided by the religious staff. Mr. John Dart, religion reporter for the *Los Angeles Times,* reporting on West Coast campus ministries wrote recently,

> *The campus ministry, once dedicated to preserving the student for the church, is now trying to help preserve the university.*
>
> *It may not always seem that way.*

Many ministers on larger California campuses, often in ecumenical teams of two to four clergymen, either tend to side with militant students on demands for change or are at least sympathetic to their goals.

Some clergymen oppose get-tough legislation for campuses and other outside pressures, believing that programs can and should be worked out within the educational communities.

But even the most radical clergymen decline to give unqualified support to student activists, partly because they wish to remain available as an acceptable channel for communication between administration and militants.

Neither do they condone extreme solutions to campus problems or the use of violence. Ministers on three recently turbulent campuses are quick to add that violence, in their opinion, has come from the ranks of both students and police.

Like many liberals, the Rev. John Hadsell said he and other members of a Protestant team ministry at UC Berkeley were 'torn between the legitimate demands of the strikers and their intransigence' during the recent student strike for an ethnic studies department.[12]

The International Ministry in Cambridge is a project of religious groups including Jews as well as Roman Catholics and Protestants aimed at increasing intercultural understanding and cooperation in the area's universities and churches. To further these ends, three projects—dialogue groups for foreign students led by interns from area seminaries, training sessions for volunteers from churches to work with foreign persons, and Project Foreign Talent to discover foreign persons who could be used to enrich university course offerings—had been developed by 1967.

An effort to incorporate ministers into the life of residence hall complexes is seen at Pennsylvania State University under the leadership of the Office of Religious Affairs. A planned strategy was needed if the campus ministers were to be able to relate to the 13,000 students living in campus residences. The resultant "Residence Hall Ministry" is a program of volunteer work staffed entirely by local clergy, interested lay persons, and religious affairs interns from various theological institutions. The motives for beginning this ministry in 1960 were both educational and practical. The resources of pastoral counselling and religious activities needed to be made more available and at a more meaningful level for students as a part of their total educational opportunities. Expansion of the residence halls system had necessitated decentralization of many student affairs activities.

Under the direction of the Coordinator of Religious Affairs, office space is available in each of the seven residence hall complexes for the volunteer religious workers. Some religious affairs associates, as the campus clergy and lay volunteers are called in this role, spend as much as 20 hours per week in the halls, others as little as two hours per week. However, informal staff-student contacts in the dining halls and at social gatherings are said to be the most profitable approach to the program. Assignments are made without regard to denominational affiliation since the staff represents the Religious Affairs Office rather than their own religious group in this relationship. Much of the coordinator's activity in the program is devoted to orienting new staff to the University's policies and procedures in the Residence Hall Ministry.

Since its beginning in 1960, the emphasis of Residence Hall Ministry activity has changed from personal and pastoral counseling to program activities of a broad nature. Once the students survived the "collar shock" of 1960, they began to relate freely to ministry staff regardless of either's denominational affiliation. Inter-faith marriage panels, comparative religious traditions, and book and movie discussions were starting points from which in-depth relationships developed between ministry staff and residence hall students.

Mr. Clifford Nelson, Coordinator of Religious Affairs, reports that evaluation of the program is accomplished in several ways.

> *Activities and their attendance give us an indication, however superficial, of the desirability of these programs from the student's viewpoint. The desire on the part of our residence hall student governments to incorporate these staff members into their structure as advisors to educational-cultural committees was a completely unsolicited indication of student acceptance. Indications to date are that the program is educationally and legally sound and desirable from all viewpoints.*[13]

University religious affairs coordinators have demonstrated on campuses widely spread geographically and of diverse types and sizes that they can be a means whereby the resources of personnel and programs of the religious groups may be integrated into the co-curriculum of the university. The university thereby can be not only a forum for ideas but also a place where significant search and affirmation of values and meaning can take place. The opportunity and obligation for developing such structures rests largely with higher education now. Keith Spalding, President of Franklin and Marshall College stated recently,

> *The focus of interest on religion, along with the search for the great and ultimate truths, has shifted from the public community life of our society—and indeed, in many cases, from the organized churches—to the academy.*[14]

If this search is to be more than theoretical, then provision must be made for the co-curriculum as well. By recognizing not only their limitations in this area as they have in the past but also by assuming their responsibility by forging channels of interdependence, universities can provide a new generation of students an opportunity to learn to come to grips with the vital issues of their day in light of the diversity of values they meet in public life. Perhaps in the absence of a cultural religious establishment, they can learn better than an older generation how to find that necessary consensus on specific moral issues essential to "domestic tranquility," "the general welfare," and the other benefits of public life. At least directors of religious affairs are committed to the task as they seek to effect frameworks whereby students may become actively involved in the transmission, sifting, reformation, and renewal of their culture.

NOTES
THE CO-CURRICULUM IN RELIGION

1. Thornton W. Merriam, "Religious Programs," *Encyclopedia of Educational Research,* ed. Walter S. Monroe (New York: The MacMillan Co., 1947) p. 321.
2. William S. Guthrie, "Changes during the Last Half Century in Student Personnel Services," *Religious Education,* LIV (March 1959), p. 96.
3. John S. Brubacher and Willis Rudy, *Higher Education in Transition* (New York: Harper & Bros., 1958) p. 331.
4. John Paul Eddy, "A Comparison of the Characteristics and Activities of Religious Personnel Employed in Selected Four-Year State Colleges and Universities in the United States" (Ph.D. dissertation, Southern Illinois University, 1968) p. 66.
5. For a fuller consideration of legal issues, see Paul G. Kauper, *Religion and the Constitution* (Baton Rouge: Louisiana State University Press, 1964) and American Association of School Administrators, *Religion in the Public Schools* (Washington, D.C.: The Association, 1964).
6. Some of these principles are discussed in greater detail in the ACURA-sponsored manual on interreligious campus programming, W. C. Tremmel, *A Different Drum* (New York: National Conference of Christians and Jews, 1964).
7. Forty-five percent of the four-year public colleges and universities responding to the writer's 1968 survey indicated that an interfaith council with responsibility for campus-wide religious programming was functioning on their campus. Thirty percent reported that an officer of the university was designated to work with the council.
8. Robert Michaelsen, "The Study of Religion: A Quiet Revolution in American Universities," *Religious Studies in Public Universities,* ed. Milton D. McLean (Carbondale: Central Publications, Southern Illinois University, 1967), pp. 9, 13–14.

9. Twenty-two percent of the university officers responding to the 1968 religious coordination survey by the writer indicated that they had some responsibility for a campus service project.
10. Charles Minneman, "Innovations in Religious Programming by State Universities: Student Volunteer Service Programs," *Detroit Convention Abstracts* (Washington, D.C.: American Personnel and Guidance Association, 1968), p. 132.
11. The Evaluation Committee, *Issues and Recommendations of a Regional Conference for College Social Service Organizations* (Ithaca, New York: CIVITAS, 1968) pp. IVB, 1–5.
12. *Los Angeles Times,* April 1, 1969, p. 1.
13. Clifford Nelson, "Innovations in Religious Programming by State Universities: Residence Hall Ministries," *Detroit Convention Abstracts* (Washington, D.C.: American Personnel and Guidance Association, 1968). p. 133.
14. *The Muncie Star,* May 18, 1969, Sec. B, p. 10.

Located in the Helen Eakin Eisenhower Chapel on the University Park campus of the Pennsylvania State University, Richard E. Wentz serves as educational director in the Office of Religious Affairs and as assistant professor of religious studies.

The Sanctions of Celebration

Richard E. Wentz

Since both the ideal of destiny under God and the way of democracy were based upon a dynamic or experimental conception of human life under God, the primarily important thing is not where the society and the government now are in the process of the great experiment, but the sureness of the people's sense of direction—the firmness of their belief in the essential rightness of the general tendency or movement.[1]

it's a great life, go get the things that you're after
hold out for good times and laughter
this is your chance so go for today
it's a great life, why don't you reach out and take it
jump for the top and you'll make it
stick with your dreams and you'll find your way[2]

The first quotation is a statement of fundamental orientation. It serves as the sanction for a sense of hope—full involvement in human destiny. The second selection represents a stance. It is a rocking incantation of the breakthrough of hope. Whatever joy is present in it is feigned. There is no sense of involvement in anything greater than one's dreams and laughter, no quality of dependence on sanctions for existence. The postures represented in both citations are ingredient in the culture of America and its microcosm—the university. The former orientation is less fashionable than the latter—especially among intellectuals and the educational elite. The latter posture is much more attractive because of the allure and youthfulness of its devotees.

Modish or not, I am convinced of the truthfulness and necessity of the first posture. But I have an affinity for the candor of the second. There have been those in past and present history who have mouthed as platitudes the articles of the first quotation without comprehending its depth and the charge to its followers. Those who chant the second creed are aware of this superficiality. They permit their bodies, their minds, and their words to range freely and without inhibition in rhythmic rejection of the first posture. But in spite of all the "soul" that is released, the second stance is not genuine "celebration" of life. If the first posture is a stolid awareness of the sanctioning of life—lingering today as a kind of sanction without celebration, the second is a celebration without sanction. What I want to propose is that the latter is therefore no celebration at all, just as the former is no longer a living sanction.

Celebration is not a contrived act or program. It springs forth out of the drama of life. Celebration is not the individual doing of one's "own thing." It is not a privatized promotion of sensory and psychic phenomena. It is a natural response to a destiny that is for one because it is at the same time for others. The great gap between the two quotations at the head of the Chapter suggests a crisis that some might term a liturgical crisis. Man is a liturgical creature. He must be able to 'take part' in acts of celebration. He must have vehicles that provide for self-enlargement. He must be able to be engaged fully in an action that is a channel for the irruption of the unexpected. Setting aside for the moment the more ecclesiological manifestation of such power, we can point to illustrations in the national heritage. Independence Day parades, Memorial Day ceremonies, Thanksgiving festivities—all were at one time bearers of a liturgical power for Americans. Now they bear only a peripheral and superficial significance—especially among the educational elite and alienated youth. How has it come about that we are a culture without the ability to celebrate? On college and university campuses the only thing left to celebrate is the victories of a football team. But many of us are too sophisticated in our latter-day scholasticism to be caught participating in such a liturgy as that. The university today is an arid and prosaic place. The only ripples on the placid surface are caused by those who clench their fists and gnash their teeth out of a deep and gnawing dissatisfaction which they do not fully comprehend.

THE PROVISION OF SANCTIONS

The preceding paragraph presents a view of life that requires further exposition. I should like to clarify what I have been saying by the use of the term "appositional." Funk & Wagnalls provides two definitions. Grammatically, apposition is "the placing of one substantive beside another to add to or explain the first." Grammar deals with structure, arrangement, and interrelationships. So, according to this first definition, apposition indicates that the fabric of language permits one independent, self-subsisting individual to add to or explain another. Biologically, apposition is "growth or increase by juxtaposition, as of tissue." Together the definitions form a total concept, which deals with two important aspects of existence: First, they offer a way of understanding, of knowing, of communicating that is drawn from relationship. Secondly, they provide for a means of *nurture* derived from relationship.

I would argue that life is appositional in character and is not existential in the sense of the individual's absolute decision and control over his character and existence. Life is not the defiant 'Camus-ian' resolve to remain human in the face of threats and plagues to the contrary. In life we find ourselves constantly standing in relationship to something that explains us and contributes to our growth—sometimes to our advantage, at other times to our detriment. We do not explain ourselves or add to our growth by simply taking thought or action. There may be numerous relationships that provide a curtailed form of apposition. Family, friends, professional life (among others) may offer such potential. But a full relationship of apposition calls for a milieu that is abundantly larger, and greater than the tangibility of existence itself and its furnishings.

The truly appositional is what Kees Bolle is talking about in his discussion of myth, when he writes of the "deadening contrasts" that exist in life. Life is full of opposites—possibilities and impossibilities, cruelties and joys, yeas and nays, "proven" truths and "unproven" truths. We are only free to live when the opposites are joined to make room for life.[3] "In this sense," continues Bolle, "but only in this sense, is what Malinowski said true, that myth is 'not an idle rhapsody, not an aimless outpouring of vain imaginings, but a hard-working, extremely important cultural force.' It is true in the sense that myth gives a form to the freedom which makes man *man*. But this form is not 'a system,' although no system, economic, societal, cultural or otherwise, could function without such form."[4] The appositional is the milieu of meaning that makes it possible for man to live in freedom. It feeds man's rational and systematic propensities as well as his need for celebration. When the appositional does not offer us this freedom, we become the slaves of our own systems and programs as they exist in "deadening contrast" to each other.

Another way of stating it—in terms related to our earlier description of the impasse of celebration in modern life—is to say that true apposition is the provision of sanctions for living. Sanctions dare never be purely a matter of legalistic prescription or contractual agreement. A society that tries to function in that manner will experience breakdown. There are signs that this is precisely what is happening today. When a people are devoid of an appositional milieu that offers a fundamental sanction for living, then nothing remains but the "deadening contrasts" of law-and-order and doctrinaire freedom. Nothing remains but the legalistic opposites—one man's "law" vis-a-vis another's. "The age of science, the age of power, the nuclear age, the age of world wars and dictatorships, the age of anxiety and frustration—this age of unfulfilled promises and dire threats—constrains us, willy-nilly, to reconsider. . . . to ask with a new seriousness whether the true and the good as envisaged by individualism are not to us a source of lies and evil that may become the undoing of the gains of civilized life in the West."[5]

True apposition provides the sanctions for living. That is, we are given confirmation for our universe and our selves in relation to other selves. We are given a structure of organic relationships that serve as a foundation for thoughts and actions. The structures are organic as distinguished from the contrived opposites (Bolle) that exist among the other structures of human life. "Every human community is both organism and artifact. It is an organism insofar as it is integrated by loyalties, forms of cohesion and hierarchies of authority which have grown unconsciously with a minimum of conscious contrivance. . . . The community and its authorities are artifacts insofar as the form of cohesion and the integration of the community have been consciously contrived."[6]

THREE TYPES OF SANCTIONS

True apposition must provide three types of sanctions: sanctions for movement and change, sanctions for participation, sanctions for celebration. These three sanctions are provided insofar as the criteria of meaning, freedom, and hope (respectively) are present. The absence of these three criteria marks the failure of whatever appositional power is present in existence. The point is that the provision of the criteria of meaning, freedom, and hope is only possible when the appositional milieu is greater than that to which it exists in apposite relationship—*than we are.* If it is possible for us to exhaust the power of the appositional, it can no longer offer us meaning, freedom, and hope. If the power of the appositional is exhausted, it means that we have become greater than it is; consequently, it no longer tells us anything about ourselves. If the power of the appositional is exhausted, it means that it has been reduced to the point where its ingredients are purely contrived, with no organic dimensions (in the sense of the quotation from Niebuhr above).

If the power of the appositional is exhausted, it no longer carries meaning to life and to us because it now consists of concepts and symbols which can be questioned by something of superior power—by us. If the power of the appositional is exhausted, then it no longer affords freedom because it has become one more of the "opposites" that Bolle spoke of in our earlier reference. That is, it has become just one more rational possibility—capable of being curtailed, refuted, vanquished. If the power of the appositional is exhausted, then it no longer offers hope because hope is an attitude of expectant openness toward the future. Hope is the quality of awareness of a destiny that offers *possibility* to the individual and to the human race. True apposition is able to sacrifice itself, to offer itself to the end of providing meaning, freedom, and hope without exhausting its power. True apposition is an inexhaustible matrix of concepts and symbols bearing personal and historical power.

What Robert Bellah calls "civil religion" and Sidney E. Mead the "Religion of the Republic" or "The Nation With the Soul of a Church" points to an example of such true appositionalism in the history of our nation, particularly in the 19th Century. Since the Second World War the gradual loss of appositional power derived from the "civil religion" has been acute. In that microcosm of the culture—the university—the consequent loss of sanctions has been traumatic. Meaning, freedom, and hope are absent, and accordingly, their absence forces many people, especially students, to attempt to contrive the sanctions.

What has been experienced is much akin to what Walter Prescott Webb tells us happened when man first encountered the Great Plains. Webb refers to the experience of Coronado's Army in the sixteenth century (as related by Castineda): "Many fellows were lost at this time who went out hunting and did not get back to the army for two or three days, wandering about the country as if they were crazy, in one direction or another, not knowing how to get back where they started from . . ."[7] Webb also quotes a comment by John Noble, the painter: "You look on, on, on, out into space, out almost beyond time itself. You see nothing but the rise and swell of land and grass, and then more grass—the monotonous, endless prairie! A stranger traveling on the prairie would get his hopes up, expecting to see something different on making the next rise. To him the disappointment and monotony were terrible. 'He's got loneliness,' we would say of such a man."[8] What is suggested is the vertiginous discovery that one's frame of reference is no longer valid. Normal expectations are no longer satisfied. In such a situation we can only pretend that this is not so and seek some means of support and sustenance in whatever the situation has to offer. We must contrive. We must find sanctions for celebration, and finding none, we end up in a hysterical dervish of drugs, drinks, and desecration. True apposition cannot be composed of contrived elements.

When the criterion of *meaning* is present in life, we are provided with sanctions for *responding to the changes* occurring in society. If there is meaning to existence other than what we fashion by rebellion, defiance, or even constructive effort, then we gain a sense of movement and change to which we can respond without having the world collapse if we choose improperly. Meaning gives us a sense of perspective for the continuing changes of existence. John F. Kennedy's final State of the Union message gave this truth rhetorical expression:

> *We are not lulled by the momentary calm of the sea or the somewhat clearer skies above. We know the turbulence that lies*

> *below, and the storms that are beyond the horizon this year. But now the winds of change appear to be blowing more strongly than ever, in the world of communism as well as our own. For 175 years we have sailed with those winds at our back, and with the tides of human freedom in our favor. We steer our ship with hope, as Thomas Jefferson said, 'leaving fear astern.' Today we still welcome these winds of change, and we have every reason to believe that our tide is running strong.*

What is being portrayed is a concept of life in process of realization, never consummately realized according to some model (Utopia or Armageddon), never fully embodied at any one time. William Wolf clarifies this thought further as he explores the meaning of the idea that "all men are created equal": "For Jefferson the phrase was a geometrical *axiom* needing no proof, but resting on the basis of a 'self-evident truth.' For Lincoln in his maturer years the phrase was a *proposition* that was in continual process of being demonstrated."[9] After all, meaning must be indulged by memory in order to be lasting and dependable. For the amnesiac, the present has no resources other than his ability to learn how to find sustenance and kindly-disposed humans. Memory takes place in movement—linking the present to signposts from the past. It is an organic process. Therefore, when meaning is present, life is prepared for change and abides in movement.

When the criterion of *freedom* is present in life, we are provided with sanctions for *participation* in the movement we have just discussed. Man is more than the descriptions he provides of himself. He is more than the proscribed and reductionist notions in which some methodologies and disciplines in a university seek to confine him. As Bolle pointed out, man is more than the "deadening contrasts" and "opposites" he observes. He exists fully when there is "room for life," when he is not dependent on one of those "deadening contrasts." Dependencies of this type curtail freedom. Man can *participate* in the movement of change because it has become an experience of *freedom's* dramatic realization. This is what Peter Schrag described as he editorialized about Martin Luther King, Jr.:

> *in fashioning from native materials—the revival, the Constitution, the resilience of the Southern Negro—a new vision not only for blacks but for all Americans, he was simultaneously more radical and intrinsic than his critics. He was ready to use power—did use power in political action and economic boycotts—but he also believed that any relation of subservience corrupts the oppressor even as it demeans the oppressed and that therefore the* real revolution can come only through the liberation of the American spirit. (emphasis mine.)[10]

Real revolution, in that sense, is the discovery of the ability to participate in the realization of a freedom in process. Participation comes from knowing that liberation is greater than the "deadening contrasts" that may go by the name of freedom. Participation comes from knowing that the realization of freedom is not dependent entirely on our definitions of it, or our mobilization for it. We are free from the onus—free to *participate* rather than to prove ourselves.

When the criterion of *hope* is present in life, we are provided with sanctions for *celebration*. Something liturgical can "turn us on" in joy or sorrow if it is a vehicle that expresses something of the hope that is interrelated with meaning and freedom. Bolle writes: "It was not only because of the greatness of the event that the burial of President Kennedy was not 'just a ceremony.' Rather, it was true liturgy because its meaning obviously did not depend on the accurate rehearsal of each participant in each detail. No one could have regulated the mourning by so many on that day. Conflicting and piecemeal theories become irrelevant; spontaneously, people subjected themselves to an order which appeared to govern both life and death."[11]

Celebration is more than mere joy over animal appetites. It is more than delight in flowers and sunshine, more than Rod McKuen's rhapsody for the love of a pussycat. Celebration is hopeful participation in a drama that links the past, the present, and the future. It draws into its action the dimensions of nature, of history, of existential events. Love, sexuality, birth, injury, ecstasy, hurt, abuse, pain, error, insult, denial, death—all are involved in the action. What goes on today under the heading of celebration is often mere ceremony. It is done by those who now dabble in externals because they have lost touch with the appositional reality that catches one up in recitation, chant, and dramatic enactment. Those are the people who play at churchiness, patriotistics, and moralisms. But there are others for whom true celebration has also been replaced by ceremony. They are the young—the children of those just mentioned who consciously and unconsciously, are in anguish over the absence of appositional power. They are defiantly and anxiously trying to contrive that power. But, as we have seen, it is a power that cannot be contrived. Their celebrations without sanctions become lopsided, half-true ceremonies, or chants of torment.

EVANGELICAL PROTESTANTISM AS A BEARER OF SANCTIONS

At one point in our nation's history something called Evangelical Protestantism was the bearer of the appositional power required to provide the sanctions of meaning, freedom, and hope. Let it be understood immediately that this essay is no jeremiad calling for a return to any kind of Protestant cultural hegemony. As Sidney E. Mead, Ralph G. Gabriel, and (to some extent) Robert Bellah have pointed out, the nineteenth century experienced an intermingling of two religious forces. One was denominational Protestantism, by which we mean a cluster of elements shared by churches and the benevolent associations and reform societies used by Protestant Christians to affect the moral climate of society. That cluster included the rhetoric of a kind of orthodoxy, an interest in experiential religion, perfectionism, and revivalistic practices. The other force was the religion of the democratic society and nation, which had roots in both the rationalism of the Enlightenment and Christian ideas of Providence and Commonwealth. These two religious forces mingled and operated under the rubric of an Evangelical Protestant consciousness. The commingling afforded a mainstream within which a diversity of forms and interpretations existed. A clear example of this diversity can be seen in the shared friendship and agenda of Dwight L. Moody and Henry Drummond. Moody was the coarse, homespun, pragmatic revivalist for whom orthodox propositions and new intellectual currents formed no conflict. Drummond was the educated Scot whose concern for the discoveries of Darwin and Spencer was an occasion for an evangelical program of reconciliation between Christian truth and the new thought, and he conducted his program as a sophisticated plea for experiential religion.

Ralph Henry Gabriel saw the ingredients from the two religious forces running parallel and interrelating in the consciousness of the American culture. There was the fundamental moral law in the democratic faith, relating to the laws of Protestant versions of the Kingdom and divine sovereignty. There was the restraint of evil in individuals and government fundamental to democratic constitutionalism, relating to parallel doctrines in the Calvinist tradition of Protestantism. There was the democratic conception of free individuals learning to obey the moral law and finding release from too much political authority, relating to evangelical ideas of the freedom for the regenerated man from the terrors of the Old Testament code. And the philosophy of human progress found in the democratic faith related to the millenial hopes of Protestant Christianity.[12] To this we should add a doctrine of Providence in Protestantism that related to the conception of destiny inherent in the democratic faith. The nineteenth century use of the doctrine of Providence requires more careful development by historians of thought. For it was a fluid concept not at all confined to the stereotypical notions of mechanistic determinism associated with it. To the prevailing consciousness Providence was a movement of purpose and hope in which the nation and its people participated. Paul Tillich has written what has by now become an abused truth. We risk further abuse by citing it:

> *Religion as ultimate concern is the meaning—giving substance of culture, and culture is the totality of forms in which the basic concern of religion expresses itself. In abbreviation: religion is the substance of culture, culture is the form of religion.*[13]

Sidney Mead builds on Tillich's definition to point out that "If a culture is the tangible form of a religion, in the United States that religion was Protestantism."[14] We shall call it Evangelical Protestantism to distinguish it as a kind of ideological consciousness rather than as denominational or theological Protestantism per se; also to place in relief those characteristics acquired during the 19th century (cited earlier in this section).

SANCTIONS IN HIGHER EDUCATION

Evangelical Protestantism provided an intellectual frame of reference, a rhetoric, and a liturgy for America. And what must be brought to light for our purposes here is that higher education shared in those provisions. The appositional sanctions of meaning, freedom, and hope were present in the life of virtually every college and university in America. They assumed several operational contours, which we shall list as holism, missionary impulse, and climate of morality. The three are obviously interrelated, but sufficiently distinctive to call attention to them.

First, higher education reflected a holistic milieu. This might be variously described as world view or unifying principle. Philosophers and theologians thought of it as dependence on an ultimate principle of being and reality that gives everything its place in the one scheme-of-the-whole. Social scientists and empirical philosophers in our own day, impressed with their own measure of Bolle's "deadening contrasts," have been telling us a holistic view of being is no longer possible. The "deadening contrasts" of a technological and pluralistic society have no time for a scheme-of-the-whole. Instead they tell us that multiplicity of experience and thought without overview or underlying interrelationship is the only stance for modern man. They regard a holistic view of man as an outmoded enterprise. The nineteenth century did not think so. Knowledge was of a whole and whatever one studied and learned had to be resolved and related to the scheme-of-the-whole.

As an example of this holism, we need but single out those courses of study in the curriculum known as mental and moral philosophy (sometimes the word 'science' is used in place of philosophy). These were often taught by the president of the faculty to the senior class. The assumption was that students who had learned many things during their careers had one final task to accomplish: they had to be given a frame of reference for dealing with life and putting their learning to the proper use. It was also assumed that they possessed the rudimentary predilection for goodness; it had only to be uncovered, called to their attention. Skills for proper understanding and development of that propensity had to be sharpened.

A survey of the texts that were used for these courses of study would form an interesting history. They were written and revised by clergyman-educators like Noah Porter of Yale. For a long while they reflected the natural theology of men like Paley and Butler. They used the philosophical tools of Scottish Common Sense Realism and later of Kantian idealism. Whatever was used, basic Christian motifs and principles held sway. Another factor in the development of this unifying approach to education was the time-honored "faculty" psychology, which prevailed through most of the nineteenth century even though experimental psychology had begun in the latter half of the century. Many will be surprised to learn that the "faculty" psychology did not refer to the techniques used by the faculty to deal with students. "Faculty" psychology assumed that the human mind was possessed of various faculties of thought and conceptualizing—each of which was developed by a different kind of study. Parenthetically, we should consider whether we gave up that assumption too soon, having concluded that the findings of the newer psychologies demanded an absolute rejection of the"faculty" psychology. It should be easy to see that an educational philosophy dominated by the study of mental and moral science as we have described it communicated a unified world view. And a point to bear in mind is that this kind of study, along with courses like "Evidences of Christianity," took place in the land-grant colleges and state universities as well as in the classical colleges of American Protestantism.

The use of scientific methods, no less than classical studies, was thought to impart knowledge of the Creator whose providential spirit participated in the ongoing destiny of America. Which brings us to a second contour in higher education. It possessed a missionary impulse. There was present a zeal for realizing the hopes for mankind that Providence had offered to that strange breed of man—the American. The impulse pressed education to reach all Americans with its 'christianizing' influence so that America could then fulfill her mission in the society of nations. "This whole process of training and experience of the race in its upward movement from barbarism toward the destiny of the 'sons of God,' may properly be called its education," said Dr. George W. Atherton in 1898. Atherton was president of The Pennsylvania State College, which was finally acquiring institutional stability after almost forty years of existence. "This law of progress," continued Atherton, "is not only declared by revelation, but is written in the constitution of the race; the man who says man is retrograding has misread history, providence, and his own nature." As American youth study, said Atherton, they will discover that their understanding of political institutions will show them "that the fundamental idea of republican institutions is the same as the fundamental principle of Christianity. . . . Is it too much to say that all these evidences of God's providential care point to the fact that He has duties for this nation in the future?"[15] Naive? Perhaps from our vantage point (whatever that may be). But it was an expression of the way in which Evangelical Protestantism had diverted the attention of its millennial hope to the needs of the nation. One could supply similar references (to Atherton's) from the mouths and pens of clergymen and laymen in the world of politics and education. They constitute a pervasive force in the nation from early in the nineteenth century on down to the first impress of disillusionment after the '14–'18 war. People and institutions were caught up in the missionary impulse quite as much as they understood that the "Creating Spirit of the Universe" was a principle for the scheme-of-the-whole in knowledge and action.

The third of the contours of Evangelical Protestantism that I shall emphasize is the climate of morality. I have purposely used the phrase "climate of morality." It seems rather obvious that this is precisely what does not exist today. We should not assume that the "rites of adolescence" which earlier took place in higher education are identical to the moral chaos of our times. For in the 19th century they were precisely that—rites of adolescence, for which the collegiate system had made no provision (our culture still has no provision for such rites). They were neither overt rejections of the moral tone of the culture nor symptomatic of chaos. Dsicussions of morality today reflect the chaos in that they are representative of Bolle's "deadening contrasts" with no room for life. So-called "situation ethics" tries to decide on which of the "contrasts" is the proper option in a given situation. The representatives of "ethics of principle" assume they are applying the demand of an abstract principle to a given situation. Both methods are precisely that—methods. They represent morality as a matter of contrivance rather than as response to an organic climate.

I emphasize the need for a *climate* of morality because it is precisely in our current dilemma that we live with the oppressive character of our own machinations. There is little but our animal nature that enables us to respond to life-situations with spontaneity. I would grant that it has been at least a partial good for us to have re-discovered that man has hungers and drives like other animals. That discovery, however, may be quite sufficient for the animals; it is hardly sufficient for man. Yet we seem to have entered a period in history when man has only two facilities on which he can rely: his animal instincts and his ability to master a technological use of reason—a use that can become his tool for whatever he may desire. But man is more than a calculating animal and needs to be able to take responsible actions without calculating them. Calculation is for crisis—individual, societal, and political. But even that kind of calculation-for-decision must take place in some frame of reference. We must have meaning, freedom, and hope that are not entirely dependent on mere ideas. Our equipment for decision-making must be able to respond to something that transcends us and our time, yet gives itself to us. It is neither possible nor desirable for me as an individual to make the necessary calculation of ideas, concepts, and options before every action. My response must, in most cases, be spontaneous. What Eliade says of the poet applies here to some extent:

> *the past does not exist for the true poet; the poet discovers the world as if he were present at the world's origin, as if he were contemporary with the first day of Creation. One might say that every great poet refashions the world, for he attempts to look at it as if time and history did not exist.*

What Eliade's description of the poet points to is the uniqueness of man we have just been talking about. It is the mysterious character of man to be able to rise above the calculating contrasts.

It should be evident that the climate of morality I have claimed is essential comes about only when true apposition exists. The nineteenth century Evangelical Protestant ethos was the transmitter of such a climate. That statement will naturally conjure up all the objections that have by now become a blatant bore. We are aware of the fact that the climate of which we speak produced a host of moralistic and rigoristic notions about human behavior. Pejorative use of the adjectives puritanical and Victorian has become commonplace. But all this pejoration gets us nowhere and it is somehow unseemly for us to indulge in it—we who have hardly come up with any more suitable mode of behavior. The climate of morality of the last century may have issued in attitudes and actions suitable for their time. That possibility we have no way of measuring except to say: these were the principles that guided them, and these are the events of history in which these principles were articulated. What is equally clear is the fact that the climate of morality issued forth in many more diverse forms than we are prone to realize. The climate was comprehensive. One could point to the accents on faithfulness and courage—trite and banal to us, but affirmative values to our forefathers of benighted yore. They accented manliness and strength of character as "Christian virtues" even more than they expressed negative concern for drunkenness and improper sexual intimacy. This was especially true in the colleges and universities of the land. The following quotation could be duplicated from the archival files of virtually every college president, chaplain, or faculty member of the 19th century. The author is a historian and philosopher, writing about one, who at the turn of the century had served as a professor, a dean of the School of Language and Literature, and Chaplain at what was then The Pennsylvania State College:

> *Greater than all else, he was a prophet of the larger view of things. He believed in the essential reasonableness of the Christian life, as a life of service; and his devotion and faithfulness in little as well as great duties, developed a character which bespoke immortality. Letters, written, as it were, at the very brink of the grave have the spiritual vigor and potency of the more abundant life, the life everlasting.*[16]

The work of the YMCA and the Student Christian Movement is representative of a clear call to the educated man to convert to the manhood of Christ. It was a call to physical and moral grandeur, a call to the equality and responsibility thrust upon the individual in a Republic in the throes of progressive acceleration. The clarity of the call became manifest from the seventies on, but its beginnings are traceable to the student societies of colleges early in the century. When the land-grant college and state university movement began gathering momentum, those student societies and Christian Associations became a regular and dynamic feature of the institutional life. Their existence everywhere in institutions of higher education was a direct reflection of the climate of morality provided by the Evangelical Protestant milieu. In this heritage prayer and virtue became not sanctimonious and joyless exercises, but virile characteristics. So dynamic and successful was the moral force that John R. Mott could write in 1915:

> *The present situation is immeasurably more urgent than that of other days because of the recent unparalleled triumphs of Christianity. It is a remarkable fact that the most extensive victories of Christian missions have been those of the recent past.* [17]

Contrary to current popular opinion, the moral climate of Evangelical Protestantism gave stimulus to many important movements for reform and service to mankind. The rhetoric of the actions and speech of the entire 19th century is a reflection of that moral climate. And rhetoric must not be dismissed as "mere rhetoric." For it is true of rhetoric what Robert Bellah points out in reference to ritual: "we know enough about the function of ceremonial and ritual in various societies to make us suspicious of dismissing something as unimportant because it is 'only a ritual.' What people say on solemn occasions need not be taken at face value, but it is often indicative of deep-seated values and commitments that are not made explicit in the course of every-day life."[18]

The moral climate had its detrimental effects, of course. In the sphere of personal ethics, certain patterns became rigid and stultified. In part it was because colleges in a frontier society had to be concerned with the deteriorating effects of living in coarse and isolated surroundings. They had to provide accommodations for their students, and with such accommodations went the problems of maintenance and order among a grading of ages much lower than that of today. The "collegiate way" of *in loco parentis* was born. And if the fact of housing and guardianship was not sufficient cause for austere regulation of behavior, there were other causes. There was the fear of those who saw the nation growing and expanding at so brisk a pace that there had to be concern for its education in the civilizing virtues (which in that point of history were readily identifiable with something called Christianity). Then, too, we must remember that the churches had accepted the mission of establishing their Christianity in the moral fibre of the nation after they had been disestablished as churches after the Revolution. They had been remarkably successful in a campaign which was encouraged by men like Benjamin Franklin and Thomas Jefferson.

Colleges and universities were responsive to the moral climate. They represented it in its diversity. On the one hand, they were concerned that education be "the process by which a man becomes *what he is;* by which his physical, intellectual, and moral powers are rounded out into a complete and symmetrical manhood."[19] On the other hand, they assumed that this symmetry required body and mind to have the same care and development. Pure and disciplined thoughts, attitudes, and behavior belonged together. They believed that every impression made on the mind continued to exert influence throughout eternity. According to their holistic philosophical outlook, everything in the physical and moral world operated to general laws of interrelationship. Therefore, even reason could only function properly if it remained untainted by the crudeness of those "sins" whereby man dulls his senses and makes his body unfit to exalt and support the work of the mind. To many representatives of this milieu, science itself was a servant of the whole of man. That is to say, scientific progress stood in relation to moral and religious advance as "does the engine upon the railroad to human freight."[20]

TOWARD A RECOVERY OF APPOSITIONAL POWER

We have been trying to establish the presence of a climate of morality in contrast to a situation of contrived ethics. This climate was one of the contours that operated in the culture of America's past. We have called that culture Evangelical Protestantism, and we have described the holism and the missionary impulse that shared life with the climate of morality. We have said that Evangelical Protestantism was the form of appositional power that provided the sanctions of meaning, freedom, and hope—sanctions that energize for change, participation, and celebration. Somewhere around the turn of the twentieth century the appositional power of Evangelical Protestantism began to decline. It was the beginning of a slow breakdown, which is almost complete at present. As a consequence, we are left with a need for meaning, freedom, and hope—with nothing but our own "deadening contrasts" of definition and contrivance to provide them. We have a need to know how to respond to change, to be able to experience a sense of free and spontaneous participation, to be able to celebrate; but there are no sanctions to activate us. The youth of our culture are trying to pull this all off without sanctions.

So let us ask what happened to account for the loss of sanctions? And how can we regain them? We could spend time arguing that the increased urbanization and the overwhelming character of technological advance have pushed aside the concern for the nurture and articulation of the sanctions. Having to build and re-build cities, find food and work, remove garbage—this is an oppressive clime that leaves little time for reflection. Inundated by the demands of technology and often convinced of its panacean nobility, we gradually lost the memory of our sanctions. In addition, the increasing reliance on government and the growth of large corporate entities of labor and capital resources began to remove the need for those life-giving sanctions that motivate the beliefs of the individual and "the people." Consequently, we have been living within the sway of a very dangerous and deceptive illusion—that an informed populace can turn the state and private corporate capital in the direction of problem-solving.[21] There is profound truth in all of these factors as an explanation for the loss of sanctions.

However, we shall leave the analysis of those factors for the moment to the sociologists and political scientists. Instead, we return to the style of the historian of religion.

> *The end of the religious age. . . . is an impossible concept. The religious principle cannot come to an end. For the question of the ultimate meaning of life cannot be silenced as long as men are men. Religion cannot come to an end, and a particular religion will be lasting to the degree in which it negates itself as a religion. Thus Christianity will be a bearer of the religious answer as long as it breaks through its own particularity.*
>
> *The way to achieve this is not to relinquish one's religious tradition for the sake of a universal concept which would be nothing but a concept. The way is to penetrate into the depth of one's own religion, in devotion, thought and action. In the depth of every living religion there is a point at which the religion itself loses its importance, and that to which it points breaks through its particularity, elevating it to spiritual freedom and with it to a vision of the spiritual presence in other expressions of the ultimate meaning of man's existence.*[22]

We suggest that the appositional power of Evangelical Protestantism as the bearer of sanctions has accomplished just what Tillich outlines. The religious character has been lost because that to which it pointed has broken through its particularity; it has been elevated to freedom for larger service. In this sense it has been universalized, which I take it is what Tillich means when he speaks of "the spiritual presence in other expressions of the ultimate meaning of man's existence." Now, I would argue that this has been the continuing experience of religion in America. The difference is that, at this particular moment, the elevation and universalizing has reached the point where the language is no longer recognizable. The languge of religion is no longer understandable on this new level of universality. This is partially due to the fact that we have forgotten the significance of Tillich's prior assertion: the breakthrough of particularity is not achieved by relinquishing one's "religious tradition *for the sake of* a universal concept which would be *nothing but a concept* (my earlier point about "contrivance"). The way is to penetrate into the depth of one's own religion, in devotion, thought and action."

In other words, the sanctions for life's meaning and celebration are not really gone. They are present in our culture. They have been universalized and are seemingly dormant, ready for larger service. They await the attention of higher education because they have broken through the particularity of religious tradition and must now be dealt with by that sphere of the culture charged with "preparation for life." Higher education, meanwhile, still persists in a stance and method appropriate to a previous age when religious tradition informed the heart of culture, leaving education to reflect that tradition while going about its task of furnishing the tools for a technological age. Higher education today is under a religious mandate. It must release appositional power for the continuance and well-being of mankind. It can no longer be content with analysis, technique, and scholarly acumen.

Going about this new task, higher education will be tempted by its most recent mode of academic proficiency. It will be tempted to analyze concepts and to try to build and contrive a philosophy. It must reject that temptation and turn to the difficult task of understanding knowledge-and-experience, taken together. A penetration of depths must occur, not a vivisection or fragmentation of the whole into parts. Penetration for understanding deals in "devotion, thought and action." Higher education must learn how to perform such penetration with integrity. In so doing higher education will help to uncover the interrelatedness of truth. It will recover the appositional character of life appropriate to our day. We will have organic sanctions by which we may celebrate life without the vengeful clashing of contrasts, or the bitterness of those defiant and superficial celebrations which are the style of searching youth today.

None of this relieves theology and the churches of a profound task of their own. Theology here refers to the intellectual clarification and interpretation of the continuing tradition of the liturgical community. Theology and liturgy have always taken place within the general history of mankind. At their best they have stood in prophetic distance from that general history, learning from it, using it, and voicing judgment on it. Theology and liturgy have partaken of the material of general history and also made their contributions to it. The churches as celebrating communities must continue their operations in that manner. They will accomplish their assignments best by penetrating into the depth of their own continuing tradition in devotion, thought and action.

This means that such penetration will be taking place on two levels. On the one level higher education will penetrate the religious power of the *culture* to permit a creative appositional relationship to offer itself once again. On the second level theology and the churches will encounter the religious power of their living tradition in order to break through the particularity and lift new contributions of judgment and freedom onto the more universal levels of the culture. In this manner the appositional needs of man will be recovered and renewed. Both the culture and the communities of faith will regain their own sanctions for celebration. And they will have gained them not by *contriving* "relevance," but by discovering it. Meaning, freedom, and hope will again alter the sanctions for movement and change, for participation, and for celebration. Those are the marks of true relevance.

NOTES
THE SANCTIONS OF CELEBRATION

1. Sidney E. Mead, "Abraham Lincoln's 'Last, Best Hope of Earth'" *The Lively Experiment* (New York: Harper and Row, 1963), p. 84.
2. O'Hara and McReynolds, "It's a Great Life" (Topez Music Corp., 1967). Sung by "The Fifth Dimension."
3. Kees W. Bolle, *The Freedom of Man in Myth* (Nashville: Vanderbilt University Press, 1968), pp. 48–50.
4. Bolle, *op. cit.,* p. 50.
5. Joseph Haroutunian, *God With Us, A Theology of Transpersonal Life* (Phila.: Westminster Press, 1965), p. 16.
6. Reinhold Niebuhr, *The Self and the Dramas of History* (New York: Charles Scribner's Sons, 1955), p. 163.
7. Walter Prescott Webb, *The Great Plains* (New York: Grosset & Dunlap, 1931), p. 105.
8. Webb, *op. cit.,* p. 488.
9. William J. Wolf, *The Religion of Abraham Lincoln* (New York: The Seabury Press, 1963), p. 171
10. Peter Schrag, *Saturday Review of Literature,* April 20, 1968, p. 28.
11. Bolle, *op. cit.,* p. 85.
12. Ralph Henry Gabriel, *The Course of American Democratic Thought* (New York: Ronald Press Co., 1940, 1956), p. 28.
13. Paul Tillich, *Theology of Culture,* Robert C. Kimball, ed. (New York: Oxford University Press, 1959), p. 42.
14. Sidney E. Mead, *The Lively Experiment,* p. 134.
15. George W. Atherton, "Public Education under a Republican System of Government" *Pennsylvania School Journal,* 47 (August, 1898) pp. 79–82.
16. Erwin W. Runkle, ed., *Sermons and Addresses* of Benjamin Gill (State College, Pa., 1913), p. 14.
17. Quoted in Edwin S. Gaustad, *Religious Issues in American History* (New York: Harper and Row, 1968), p. 218.
18. Donald R. Cutler, Ed. *The Religious Situation: 1968* (Boston: Beacon Press, 1968), p. 333.
19. George W. Atherton, "The Place of Industrial Training in the System of Higher Education," Inaugural Address, 1883, p. 1. Penn State Collection.
20. Evan Pugh, "Address to the Cumberland County Agricultural Society" (Carlisle, Pa., October, 1860), p. 4, 5. Pugh was the first president of what was to become the Pennsylvania State College. He was one of those rare products of German university education— a Ph.D. from Göttingen in 1856.

21. See Jacques Ellul *The Political Illusion* (New York: Alfred A. Knopf, 1967)
22. Paul Tillich, *Christianity and the Encounter of the World Religions* (New York: Columbia University Press, 1963), p. 97.

Charles Wellborn is associate professor of religion and university chaplain at the Florida State University. TWENTIETH CENTURY PILGRIMAGE: Walter Lippmann and the Public Philosophy is Wellborn's most recent publication (Louisiana State University Press, 1969)

Moral Exercise in the Intellectual Community

Charles Wellborn

From, of all places, Tascosa, Texas, comes a pungent summary comment on the contemporary world. The *Tascosa Pioneer* editorially observes: "Truly this is a world which has no regard for the established order of things, but knocks them sky west and crooked, and lo, the upstart hath the land and its fatness."

Nowhere is the sky more acutely tilted or the upstart more raucous than on the contemporary college campus. At least, it seems that way to many of us who live in the midst of today's academic uproar. No doubt each student generation in turn has been a puzzle to its predecessors, but such long-range historical reflection is little comfort to today's elders, struggling to stay in communication with young people who have been counseled by some of their own number never to trust anyone over thirty years of age.

For a considerable portion—the majority, perhaps—of today's generation the values, standards, and traditions of the past are suspect by definition, rejected largely because they are hangovers from yesterday—which may literally mean twenty-four hours ago. Little is sacred, and the ideal is a pattern of moral action as fresh as the situation of the moment. The words of Paul Goodman, originally addressed to campus chaplains, have a much broader implication: "Admittedly, for the majority of young people today, the Western tradition is quite dead . . . Chaplains neither can revive it, nor in my opinion, do they have *anything* to teach. But they can provide centers, and be centers, for confusion."[1]

"Centers for confusion?" This is one astute observer's estimate of the most creative thing which can be done by someone who wants to act positively on today's campus. Others may feel that more creative contributions are possible, but this prescription does seem to supply a valid clue to the understanding of our time. A look at the newspaper front page or at a television news report seems to support the pertinence of the observation. Moreover, most college and university administrators would have no difficulty in agreeing with Goodman's emphasis on confusion as a campus keynote. Unrest, dissension, violence—these are major ingredients in the cultural mix of twentieth-century Academe. One function of that mix, most observers agree, is a moral revolution, a destructive shake-up of traditional mores and ancestral values.

Max Lerner reminds us that the term "revolution" can be employed in at least two senses. In one sense it refers to the transfer of power from one class to another by means of some type of direct action violence. In the second sense it denotes a highly accelerated rate of change, so rapid that the result is an almost constant phenomenon of breakthrough. Each breakthrough projects a new level from which further change takes place. In this sense, we are experiencing all sorts of revolutions: technological, cybernetic, communications, civil rights. In such a context, Lerner notes, it would be surprising if we were not also having a morals revolution.[2]

If there is a genuine and observable happening which can accurately be labeled a moral revolution, and if (as I would argue) this revolution is of fundamental importance to the young adults who are concentrated in great numbers on the university campus, then certain questions are implied. If the task of the university is the task of education, what is its educative role within the context of the moral revolution? If we grant that the American university can no longer legitimately conceive of itself as *in loco parentis,* does it then follow that the university has neither role nor responsibility in the lives of students outside the classroom? The university, having discarded the model of pseudo-parent, must discover another model. To discover such a model in the area of problems indicated by the title of this chapter is a particularly perplexing and challenging one. Is there a defensible involvement by the university structure in the moral and religious life of students?

Obviously, the existence of a university-supported and sanctioned position—a Coordinator of Religious Affairs—implies some concept of such involvement, however unformed and inchoate the concept may be. The initial rationale for such a position rests on the recognition that religious organizations and activities do exist on any campus and that such organizations and activities do elicit the support and interest of a sizable number of students. Furthermore, the empirical religious pluralism of any campus—a steadily increasing pattern of complexity—seems to require that some concrete protection be given to each individual student's freedom to express himself religiously (or anti-religiously). Legally, we have come to realize that the full implementation of religious liberty within a healthy, functioning pluralistic society requires not simply a policy of official neutrality on the part of the state and its agencies, but also the permission for, and sometimes even the requiring that, special provisions be made for religion. These provisions may be necessary to neutralize the otherwise restrictive effects of the expanding activities of the state, along with other societal or community structures.[3]

Relevant here is the recognition that many—perhaps most—universities actually function today, particulary for the undergraduate student, as contexts of living with their own distinctive ethos and life-style. Perennial town-gown conflict is neither accidental nor erratic; it is endemic, since the two communities constitute distinct organisms. Students do not ordinarily live in *both* the university and the surrounding city. Rather, their life centers in the university, out of which they periodically emerge to visit the city. Religiously, this means that the mere fact that there are churches available to students in the city does not sufficiently guarantee actual pluralism and maximized religious opportunity for the intellectual community; therefore, additional provisions become necessary.

It is partly against this background that an increasing number of universities have recognized the need for a Coordinator of Religious Affairs, or an equivalent officer with various titles, as an essential part of the student personnel staff. At the minimum, this officer's responsibilities include what the most commonly used title implies—coordination and facilitation of organized student religious activities and organizations. It must be clear that, at least in theory, the Coordinator does not represent a futile attempt to reinforce an anachronistic parental model for the university. The Coordinator's job is not to "sell" religion, or any sectarian version of it, nor to impose traditional standards of moral behavior; rather, he is the guardian and promoter, in both positive and negative ways, of the student's right to maximum religious freedom. The efforts of a coordinator to encourage and assist Muslim or Hindu students on a particular campus to form their own student religious organization may represent part of his positive function. On the other hand, his interpretation of university policy in such a way as to protect the privacy of the individual student from unwarranted invasion in the name of evangelism or religious proselytizing may represent a negative function.

But these activities of the Coordinator as *coordinator* can represent, even at best, a kind of sterile and "bare-bones" approach to the phenomenon of religion on campus. Coordination easily degenerates into paper-shuffling, calendar-keeping, and space-assigning. Recognition of this judgment is reflected in the widespread dissatisfaction of many university Coordinators with their titles. No alternative title for the office has yet achieved any consensus, but at scattered institutions the equivalent official is known as Dean of Religious Affairs, Dean of the Chapel, Director of Religious Affairs, or, even, in some few cases, by the historically suspect title of University Chaplain.

Clearly, much of the title problem is semantic, but the uneasiness about titles reflects a deeper issue: should not the Coordinator actually do much more on campus than coordinate? In actuality, as the John Paul Eddy study of religious coordination indicates,[4] Coordinators are involved, normally and routinely, in a wide variety of functions which extend far beyond coordination. These may include program planning, the promotion of religious dialogue on campus, the organization and supervision of student service work projects, and, not least of all, religious or moral counseling. Such a multiplicity of functions, added to the lack of clear job description, leaves many Coordinators frustrated.

In one of Thomas Hardy's novels there is a character who, whenever he drinks too much, suffers from a curious affliction called "the multiplying eye." Coordinators have a similar complaint. They are uncertain "about their true ends in work and life; they have become cross-eyed from trying to keep in view a treacherous dazzle of purposes. It is enough to make anyone's eye multiply."[5] And each task has its special demands and unique problems. Even if one narrows his focus specifically to the counseling task undertaken by many Coordinators, he does little to simplify the analysis.

To function on the contemporary university campus as an effective religious and moral counselor is a challenging job, full of pitfalls and exceedingly narrow lines to be walked with great caution. To recognize the difficulties of the task, however, does not invalidate it. The Coordinator who sees his job as more than bureaucratic maneuvering will inevitably be drawn, to a degree largely dependent on his zest for the task, into the arena of moral exercise in the academic community. As he moves into this phase of his professional responsibility, his role may well define itself in a number of diverse ways.

THE COORDINATOR AS CAMPUS CONSCIENCE

The traditional college or university chaplain,[6] acknowledged with some embarrassment by religious coordinators as a kind of primordial and not quite respectable ancestor, had as a principal function the pastoral task, including the leadership of worship services and preaching. His role was made viable by the fact that the academic community to which he ministered was not genuinely pluralistic. The university faithfully reflected, in most cases, the white, Anglo-Saxon, Protestant, middle-class society dominant in the country as a whole. As a preacher, the chaplain had both the continuing opportunity and the accepted responsibility to exercise some level of prophetic thrust. In terms of his own understanding of the moral and ethical demands of his particular religious faith, he operated as a campus conscience.

Today's Coordinator, placed within an almost totally different academic context, obviously cannot and ought not to call university policies or structures to judgment with a resounding "Thus saith the Lord." Should he do so, he may be answered with justification by a question made relevant by a pluralistic culture, "which Lord?" Yet the need for steady and consistent voices of conscience within Academe is as vital today as ever; perhaps they are even more drastically needed. The prophetic role of the Coordinator in the moral arena cannot emanate specifically from a sectarian religious stance. But it can be maintained that there is ample room for meaningful and prophetic action within the broad context of the Western moral tradition, drawing strongly as it does on both Christianity and Judaism, as well as on secular humanistic sources. All strands of the tradition emphasize the moral responsibility of men in terms of the central value of persons. They stress the recognition that man is not finally the manipulator of his own values but that he is accountable in some way to patterns of moral action outside himself. They emphasize the significance of such virtues as honesty, integrity, fairness, and justice.[7]

True, the Coordinator's role as campus conscience cannot be equated with that of the denominational clergyman or campus minister, who speaks out of his own faith tradition without the necessary limitations placed on one who functions within a public structure in a religious pluralism. But I reject the contention that there is no role for the Coordinator in this regard. The Coordinator possesses, despite his limitations, a unique stance from which to exercise moral leverage within the university; indeed, his impact may well be strengthened by the consideration that he does not speak out of sectarian bias but out of the empirical moral concern of the community. Granted, his approach must be distinctive. Where those outside the university's structure are prepared to give possible positive, even detailed, answers to the ethical dilemmas arising in academic life, it may well be that the Coordinator's most effective function is simply to raise the embarrassing questions so often swept under the rug in the name of pragmatic efficiency—to uncover possible injustice and lack of integrity wherever it may exist.

One example may be given. Recently I sat, as I regularly do, with the Cabinet of the Vice-President for Student Affairs in the university where I work. The subject under discussion dealt with certain policies affecting personnel employed in the university's housing system. The policies were discussed in terms of cost involved, effect on employee recruitment, worker efficiency, expected results, and similar concerns. I conceived my responsibility as that of asking questions about certain relatively hidden racial discrimination factors in the policies. I questioned, for instance, why dormitory switchboard operators on some shifts were required to wear maids' uniforms while those on other shifts were not. I pointed out that the facts were that all operators on the shifts required to wear uniforms were blacks, while almost all of those on the other shifts were whites. Whether or not discrimination was intended, the visible results of the policy appeared discriminatory. Black students on the campus had already called this to my attention. They had also appraised me of the fact that two different manuals of job practice were being used in housing employment—one for student assistants (mostly white), the other for full-time employees (almost entirely blacks.) The differences between the two manuals were relatively minor but striking, and they seemed to me to constitute a legitimate grievance point for black employees. It was my task in this context to raise questions of moral concern.

One of the other university administrators responded initially to my questions with some resentment. "Inevitably" he said, "you seem to cause trouble!" Yet, later, he pointed with some pride to the changes made in the policies and in the manuals, reflecting the recognition of moral and ethical, as well as pragmatic, concerns.

Though this incident involved minor matters, it is typical. Possibly, the Coordinator may find some assurance that he is doing his job well if he is occasionally labeled a troublemaker. Who else, on most university campuses, has the specifically defined responsibility to question discriminatory policies and procedures? Or to quiz administrators about the degree of fairness to students involved in registration procedures, housing deposits, food plans, bookstore policies, campus security operations, overly-large classes, unreasonable examination schedules, etc.? The list is almost endless.

It may be argued that the raising of such issues is the responsibility of every member of the university community. While this contention is true in theory, the fact remains that what is everyone's general business but no one's specific concern rarely gets accomplished. The recent appearance of the university official known as an "ombudsman" on many campuses is one recognition of this fact. The ombudsman reacts to specific student or faculty complaints of injustice. The Coordinator can and often does function as a kind of ombudsman, but he may go far beyond specific cases to question and analyze broad, general policies and procedures, attitudes and relationships, from the moral or ethical standpoint. How well he can accomplish this task—even the way in which he goes about it—will, of course, vary. The kind of institution, the organizational position of the Coordinator in the over-all university structure, the strength of the tradition supporting his office, the willingness of university officials to listen to him, the personality of the individual Coordinator—all of these factors influence the character of his ethical thrust in this regard. Such men as William Sloane Coffin at Yale or Beverly Asbury at Vanderbilt have distinctive and highly visible styles as campus consciences. Other men in other situations function more unobtrusively though with at least equal effectiveness.

Differences of style and structure must not be allowed to obscure the need for this function, however varied the approaches to the task may be. Neither should the Coordinator (by whatever name he is identified) be unduly intimidated because he is not prepared to propose concrete plans of action for solving campus situations of stress and moral tension. There is a legitimate division of labor on campus, and the responsibility of the Coordinator is primarily to challenge the injustice and inequity, the depersonalization and inhumanity so often present in the academic community. Others in the university are better qualified and directly charged with the positive devising and implementation of more satisfactory policies and procedures. The Coordinator can often make his most effective contribution as a "boat-rocker," a question-raiser, a somewhat abrasive and troublesome critic of the status quo.

In this connection it can be noted in passing that perhaps the most frequent charge made against religious affairs officials on university campuses is that they are simply irrelevant to the major concerns of the academic community. Almost paradoxically, a major task of the Coordinator may well be to challenge the "irrelevance" of Academe. Irrelevant to what? To life in its fullness—a fullness which includes dimensions of moral, religious, and human significance often sadly overlooked in the intellectual process. In a recent open forum discussion of curriculum and teaching problems on the Florida State University campus, by far the loudest student applause was given to a young man who asked from the floor the blunt question, "Can anyone here tell us what most of this crap we are required to study has to do with flesh and blood living?"

Thomas Leatherwood quotes William Sloane Coffin as commenting on the familiar academic pattern of years spent in shedding light on something which appears, finally, not worth illuminating. There is abundant and apparent need, he argues, for a prophetic voice *within* the university, one which will speak forcefully about "the university's reluctance to 'humanize' its own structures and to turn outside in more creative forms of service to society."[8] The intellectual community requires a constant calling to account in terms of both its internal structures and its external concerns.

Our discussion to this point has dealt largely with the Coordinator's possible role as a critic of structures and policies, working within the moral arena of the university as a whole. Even more significant can be his involvement as a moral counselor, dealing with individual students (and faculty members). To understand this facet of the task, we now look briefly at the context in which the Coordinator must function as a moral and religious counselor.

THE CAMPUS AS A MORAL COMMUNITY

More than one observer of the contemporary campus has been forced, sometimes reluctantly, to the conclusion that the moral dimensions of academic life, considerably neglected in recent days, are now the area of prime need and concern. So, Philip H. Phenix writes, "Within the past three or four years there has occurred one of those changes in the American scene that radically alters the entire climate of common presuppositions and expectations. While in previous periods the central issues might be characterized as ideological, technical, political, and the like, I think the most apt term for what is new in the present atmosphere is moral concern."[9]

Phenix goes on to explain that he is definitely not referring to the type of "moralistic" concern so typical of much nineteenth and early twentieth century higher education. Rather he contends that "questions of conscience have now moved into the foreground of the American cultural scene. The immediate stimulus is, of course, Vietnam, but Vietnam only symbolizes the conflicts of conscience in a wide range of social and personal issues, including those of race, poverty, sex, drugs, and politics, both national and international."[10] The strain and frustration involved in facing these issues, so central in the lives of most American students today, emphasize the conclusion that material and technological approaches are inadequate, supplying at best only the raw information beyond which personal decision making must take place. For students such problems are not academic, in the sense of detached theoretical analysis; rather they are existential. Their lives and futures are authentically at stake in the struggles arising out of these issues. In addition, many of us who have worked with students for years would argue that this is, by and large, the most idealistic, "compassion-oriented" generation of students we have ever known. It is no wonder that the universities should have become cauldrons of ferment. Underneath the frequent aberrations and not infrequent inanities of contemporary student unrest lies, I am convinced, a powerful undercurrent of profound moral concern. "What the morally concerned students are asking is nothing less than a thorough moral reconstruction of education itself. Most of them would not couch their protest and their aspiration in those terms. They would rather use a term like 'relevant,' meaning an education that will enable them to transform a world that their consciences bid them reject in its present form."[11]

The world outside the campus normally tends to regard the campus as a kind of tangential society, largely divorced from the practical concerns of mainstream life. The "ivory tower" concept is still typical of much external thinking about the university. Student foibles have, at least in past days, usually been regarded as part of a transient passage over Fool's Hill, a kind of necessary disease from which, once recovered, the young person stands to gain valuable immunity from future infection. After Commencement "real life" begins, and the erstwhile student can then devote his energies to the serious task of existence, accepting with a minimum of complaint the preformed patterns of success and status.

Whether this view ever had any support in reality or not, it is a fanciful delusion today. For one thing, exposure to college or university experience of some type has become the experience of the majority. And we have come to understand more clearly that "Commencement" is a gross misnomer. Life does not begin after one's senior year in college. Indeed the most important and "real" segment of one's total existence often turns out to be the campus years.

Max Lerner reminds us that America has never developed a code-making or code-keeping class as have most other countries. There is no clearly defined American aristocracy to set standards in taste, fashion, or morality. As long ago as the Colonial period, de Tocqueville noted this significant difference between Europe and America. But, if there is no code-making class, how does a country develop its codes? In the early American experience the church stepped in, operating in cooperation with a small-town agrarian community structure to shape and enforce standards and codes. But this did not last long. What happened was that the middle classes moved into central importance, fashioning codes directly relevant to middle class life in a flexible society.[12]

But neither life nor history ever stands still. If the middle-class, operating with an emphasis on severely-modified Puritanism in an acquisitive, expanding society, once shaped the mores and the standards, that too is changing. A good case can be made, I think, for the contention that tomorrow's codes are being most dramatically and forcefully shaped on today's campuses. Obviously, the college or university constitutes a sub-culture in our society, but it is also a vanguard culture. What happens on the campus eventually percolates down to the rest of society. However frightening the prospect may appear to an older generation, the contemporary college student is forming standards which will apply not only to himself but eventually to the larger culture of which he is a part. University students constitute the code-making (and code-destroying) class in modern American society.

William Hamilton is another observer who has traced out this phenomenon. Hamilton recognizes the important fact that significant codes or moral standards are never developed autonomously or privately. They arise out of the interaction of life within community. "More interesting than the death of the moral absolute and less understood is the more subtle death of the institutions in American culture that men have ordinarily trusted in communicating values from one generation to another. The death of the absolute may not be particulary sad, but the death of the family and the death of the church are among the most sophisticated and subtle and bewildering and offense-giving moral facts of our time."[13] Hamilton contends that the family and the church are "sick communities," that is, they no longer have the capacity to deliver moral values from one generation to the next. As a result, men are morally ill. They seek a healing or therapeutic community within which to discover their identities and anchor their values. But this community must offer a special kind of ethos not ordinarily characteristic of social organisms. Albert Camus argued that the necessary moral category of our time is *rebellion*. Only when an individual learns largely by trial and error, the creative art of rebellious freedom is he prepared to launch himself on the quest for meaning and integrity. From this perspective, the morally therapeutic society is that one which can best tolerate, even encourage, rebellion while, at the same time, opening up the possibility of creativity in that rebellion by offering the resources of a supportive, accepting, challenging community. The moral climate so desperately required by today's student is one which inculcates "a selective, careful, moderate, yet profound rebellion against the sick communities. When we spy health, we will delight in it, and when we spy sickness or mediocrity or disease, we will say as decisive and clear an absolute 'no' as we can. We will combine rebellion against the sick communities that introduce demons into our systems with the struggle for new communities, on the principle that we cannot heal ourselves and that only community can heal."[14]

Hamilton's guess—and his guess reflects his hope—is that the university can become the place where the creative combination of rebellion and search for the therapeutic community can go on. He believes that there are signs that this process is occurring. The troublesome rebellion of students on campus can be interpreted, on the one hand, as a rejection of the prepackaged, non-existential absolutes handed down by entrenched traditional moralistic structures, but also, on the other, as an indictment of the frequent attempt of the academic community to "cop out" on moral issues and involvement. The rebellion is offensive to those who want to keep education clean, neat, and conventional, and it is also offensive to the academist who does not want moral values intruding themselves between his mastery of his subject material and his students. "But the conception of the university as a moral community or, if you like, a place where young men and women are searching for somebody else who has their secret, or for somebody who's got the same set of clues so that the clues can be tested and examined—this is becoming more and more the real meaning of the university."[15]

Whether ot not one agrees with Hamilton's total thesis, his understanding of the dynamic at work on the university campus seems to me to make sense. And it relates immediately and vitally to the problem of what a religious affairs person ought to be doing in the academic community. The implication of Hamilton's argument is that, to the horror of the academicians, the real life of the community is increasingly not academic at all, at least not in any conventional sense. What is happening at the university is the "search for comrades" or for community, "the looking out for those who have your secret." One wonders if this is not, today, a more viable explanation of that worrisome university phenomenon, the "popular" teacher, than the standard charge that he is either a cheap entertainer or else that he offers a "crip" course. Perhaps students flock to the teacher who seems to them to care about people as persons and education as a confrontation with life.

Many college administrators are concerned today because so many students do not seem to be as interested in curriculum and degrees as they once were. The common response by people outside the university to student unrest is to demand that the trouble-makers settle down to their studies and "do what you're supposed to do in college—get an education!" But what if students are more interested in the good life than they are in facts and speculations? What if they seek as models, not the detached, amoral, "objective" image which so many academics attempt to project in the classroom, but men and women involved in the moral dimensions of life and both sympathetic to and empathetic with the moral search? The problem is, as we all know, that it is widely accepted that the better educational institution a university is, the less it is interested in providing models for the good life.

And so students take matters into their own hands. They search for different levels of experience in which the quest for comrades can go on. And this search can open up all kinds of possibilities, both constructive and destructive. The search leads to campus riots and picket lines. It results in "free" universities and in dorm discussions which, more often than adults realize, turn from routine "bull sessions" into depth encounters; it directs young men and women to LSD and marijuana; to arrest and jail; to Peace Corps and ghetto projects; and, most frequently perhaps, to bed.

Whether the student in this search is finally helped or hindered by the university depends on many factors. If the academic pattern is, as it often turns out to be, one in which literature is presented as pure form, economics as computer analysis, philosophy as a language game, and political science as quantitative summaries of voting behavior, the student is not likely to be helped very much. If the university's student affairs people are still striving to operate *in loco parentis,* thereby effectively cutting meaningful lines of communication with students, there is little help available from this quarter.

Just as certainly, if the university has pushed the panic button, totally discarding the parental model, but has found no new model to put in its place, resources for help will be sadly lacking. The pendulum swing from pseudo-parent to non-concerned, non-involved bureaucrat leaves the university even more sterile than before. Whatever can be done on campus to experiment with new models of student-faculty and student-administrator relationships must be given top priority. To abolish the possibilities for faculty and administration identification with students in their needs and struggles, using the excuse that we can no longer prescribe rigid standards for them, is to surrender to the absurdity of the pendulum swing with instant over-reaction. To eliminate those avenues by which the student may discover concern and care for him on the part of the mature images in his community is to cripple drastically his search for identity and growth.

THE COORDINATOR AS MORAL RESOURCE

It is certainly not the contention of this article that the hiring by the university of a Coordinator of Religious Affairs is a solution to the whole problem of providing possibilities for therapeutic community on university campuses. Indeed it must be recognized that increasingly the center of life for the student is with his peers in the living unit, whether that be a dormitory or an off-campus apartment (as it more and more frequently is). This, as the saying goes, is where the action is. Too often in the classroom the modern university strives to educate people to live in a world they have no intention of living in. With their peers they seek to learn to live in the world they have accepted, not the one they have already rejected.

What this seems to mean is that the university's part in the moral and ethical phase of student life must necessarily be non-directive, voluntaristic, and supportive. Parietal rules on curfew, liquor, sex, etc., are largely ineffective anywhere and almost totally unenforceable in off-campus apartments. Neat moral bundles of authoritarian standards are existentially rejected by students before the packages are ever opened.

In this context I would suggest that the most appropriate model for the university's relationship to students is one which is already in existence: the "counselor-client model." Instead of relating to students *in loco parentis,* or as detached and personally uninvolved academic figures, or as objects of hostile confrontation, student personnel workers should seek to apply the counselor-client model to their total relationship with students. The religious affairs officer is in a particularly favorable position to develop and pattern out this kind of model, though it is clearly recognized that he is only one of many university officials with whom students should relate in this manner.

Obviously this type of model is already functioning in university counseling centers, though sometimes the professionals in these centers are hampered by an unwillingness to become overly involved in moral and value problems or a reluctance to identify with the reality of student struggles in this area. But the task of the Coordinator of religious affairs as a moral resource is not to compete with other counseling services on campus. Instead, it is to supplement and help render more effective these services in the lives of students.

Within the structure of a counselor-client model the counselor obviously offers himself as a resource for the client, but there is no compulsion upon the client either to seek help or to accept it. The Coordinator of Religious Affairs, as a religious counselor, fits this pattern. He is provided by the university as a resource, and it is essential for students to recognize that he is available. In fact, the more available he or his staff can be, the more likely students are to use their services.[16] He must also be accepted as non-disciplinarian and non-authoritarian, having absolutely no connection with either university disciplinary processes or rules-making procedures. As an available, voluntaristic resource, able to enter into unstructured, open-ended conversations with students, the Coordinator may operate in the moral arena in a number of rather distinctive ways.

First, he can function as one who speaks the language of those students (there still are and, I am convinced, will continue to be many of them) who approach their moral problems and struggles within a religious value-context. In my own work at Florida State University I find myself talking to a fairly steady flow of students who are seeking "someone who knows what I'm talking about when I refer to things like sin and salvation." In many cases, these students have tried other campus counseling resources with disappointing results. This does not necessarily reflect upon the competence of other counselors. What it does mean is that many students are repelled by the counselor who either does not understand them in the religiously-oriented terms in which they themselves perceive their problems, or who does not take seriously the student's problems expressed in those terms, or who seeks to translate the student's struggles into non-religious concepts. This is not to deny the effectiveness of any particular counseling approach used in an appropriate situation. But there are students whose background and personal commitments require them to deal with their problems in a manner commensurate with their world-view. They need someone who is willing and prepared to relate to them on their own terms *but* who is also competent enough as a counselor to recognize the emerging outline of problems which can be more effectively dealt with by other counselors with different perspectives and training. Individuals wrestling with problems of guilt, for instance, may well see their difficulty as primarily theological; that is, they perceive themselves as guilty over against God and in need of divine forgiveness. The religiously-oriented counselor is often better fitted to deal with such a problem within the student's own context. It is also worth noting that a number of students are conditioned to a greater willingness to enter into a meaningful counseling relationship with a person identified by them as a "religious" figure than with a university employee perceived by them as a professional counselor who is simply doing his job.

Second, the Coordinator can provide a moral resource as an accepting and supporting individual who is willing to deal with students as unique individuals and on a non-judgmental basis. Of course, this is what any good counselor seeks to do. Yet my own experience is that it is often especially helpful to students to find acceptance and support from a religiously-identified counselor. It has been interesting to those of us in the Office of the University Chaplain at Florida State University to note the high percentage of students characterizing themselves as "non-religious" who come to us for this type of relationship. Whatever the psychological dynamics of this situation may be, many of the "non-religious" students who seek counseling help from the religious counselor respond in meaningful ways. Perhaps, at this point, if nowhere else, the Coordinator does function in a "pastoral" role. It has been our experience, on the other hand, that most students who are identified with campus religious organizations and local churches do not come to our office for help. Instead, they seek out their own campus minister or pastor. To us, as more neutral figures identified not with established or organized religion, but with the university, come the unaffiliated, the disaffected, the searchers.

It is my own conviction that a Coordinator of Religious Affairs should be openly and definitely student-oriented. Ideally, he should be the kind of person to whom students may come with confidence that his basic stance is sympathetic to them and identified with their concerns. To the extent that this image is concretized and accepted, the Coordinator will discover increased avenues of communication and counseling with students.

Third, the Coordinator can act as a moral resource by serving as an effective and knowledgeable referral person. In problem-situations dealing with specific religious commitment and belief, the Coordinator knows the availability, competence, and concerns of campus ministers, local church officials, and faculty advisors to specific religious groups. When a student seeks specific help best given by one of these persons, the Coordinator can facilitate contact and conference between student and counselor. The Coordinator must cultivate sensitivity to a student's background and needs so as to be able to refer him properly. He will also discover that his interest in proper referral, skillfully manifested, is interpreted by the student as a positive act of concern and personal interest.

THE CONTENT OF MORAL COUNSELING

What are the specific aims of the Coordinator as he offers himself as a resource for moral counseling? This is perhaps the most difficult area to pin down. Clearly, in his organizational responsibilities the Coordinator is not justified in favoring one campus religious group over another or in proselytizing for any sect. Just as certainly, however, he is not justified in attempting to "sell a bill of goods" in the counseling situation. To many people this seems to render his task impossible. Either, they argue, the religious counselor will impose his own views on the students or their encounter will be so generalized as to become vapid and unproductive.

But is the task of the religious counselor actually more complex or difficult than that of any other counselor? The aim of any effective counselor is to assist the counselee in understanding himself and his problem and to provide the kind of resources—personal, relational, and informational—which will assist in a responsible handling or resolution of the problem. Within the context problems, often only vaguely identified by the student as "religious" or "moral," the counselor may assist in bringing the perspective of moral responsibility and the central value of persons to bear. He may supply information about religious views, Biblical or other moral teachings, as well as sharing the experiences of other persons who have faced similar problems. Most importantly, perhaps, he can demonstrate his concern and acceptance by listening, by assisting the student to articulate his own feelings, by encouraging him to uncover the full dimensions and complexities of his problem. He may remind the student that, experientially and empirically, he does not live in a solitary world, and others have a legitimate stake in any decision which is made. He can demonstrate in concrete ways that the university—the most immediate community in which the student lives and moves and has his being—is neither as faceless nor as impersonally unconcerned as it so often appears.

The essential point to remember is that the Coordinator functions most adequately and appropriately as a *client-centered* counselor. His concern is consistent with his job description: he is not interested in prescribing either moral or religious patterns of belief and behavior upon his counselees. He is attempting to "open up" the problem, to assist the student in understanding where his anxieties or uncertainties have their focus, to remind the student of complexities or issues which have been overlooked, and to provide either informationally or by referral, relevant additional resources directly related to the student and his problem.

At Florida State University, over a period of several years, we have seen students in considerable numbers respond positively to this kind of approach. The University Chaplain and his staff have also been able to function effectively, within the boundaries of this model, in frequent dorm discussions (floor and hall groups, for example), in fraternities and sororities, and with other natural groupings of students. Almost invariably, such group sessions provide opportunities for additional individual student contact. Since we see students and their problems as our "business," the more business we have, the better.

The field of endeavor in which religious affairs student personnel workers are engaged is still largely uncharted, at least in the context of the state university campus. Mistakes have been made and will continue to be made, as Coordinators attempt to work out an understanding of their own role within the boundaries of their two worlds: the domain of human religious commitments and the pluralistic multiversity of today's educational scene. But, if we are to take seriously the concepts that the college years are not merely preparational, but central in life experience, and that the vocation of the student as a student is total and not segmented, then the university must find its model for involvement in every dimension of student life. The concept of the Coordinator as not only a facilitator of religious activities and dialogue on campus, but as a moral counselor, provides new opportunities for the university to function in terms which help to make sense, from the student perspective, of the modern higher educational process.

The words of John R. Mott spoken several decades ago, seem to many of us to be more realistic today than ever before: "If I had my life to live over again, I would place myself alongside a great university, for in the university are the greatest needs and the greatest opportunities in the world."[17]

NOTES
MORAL EXERCISE IN THE INTELLECTUAL COMMUNITY

1. Paul Goodman, "Introduction: Chaplains and Students," in Albert H. Friedlander (ed.), *Never Trust a God Over 30* (New York, 1967), XII.

2. Max Lerner, "Morals and the College Campus," in Charles Wellborn (ed.), *Challenge to Morality* (Tallahassee, Florida, 1966), p. 22.
3. See the significant article by Wilbur G. Katz and Harold P. Southerland, "Religious Pluralism and the Supreme Court," *Daedalus,* Winter, 1967, pp. 180–92.
4. See John Paul Eddy, *Comparison of the Characteristics and Activities of Religious Personnel Employed in Selected Four-Year State Colleges and Universities in the United States.* Research Studies Series from Associated Educational Services Corporation, New York, 1969.
5. Irving Howe, "Beleaguered Professors," in *The Troubled Campus* (edited by the Editors of *The Atlantic*), Boston, 1965, p. 53.
6. The reference here is to the college or university official, so common in an earlier period of American educational history, not to the denominational campus chaplains who are still visible parts of the normal campus scene.
7. For detailed elaboration of this general theme, see Walter Lippmann, *The Public Philosophy* (Boston, 1955), esp. pp. 72–138. See also Robert N. Bellah, "Civil Religion in America," *Daedalus,* Winter, 1967, pp. 1–21.
8. Thomas O. Leatherwood, "Prophets in Academe," *Humanity,* December, 1968, p. 4.
9. Philip H. Phenix, "The Moral Imperative in Contemporary American Education," paper prepared for *Perspectives in Education* (Columbia University), Winter, 1969, p. 1.
10. *Ibid.*
11. *Ibid.*
12. Lerner, "Morals and the College Campus," p. 26.
13. William Hamilton, "The University and Our Moral Situation," in Wellborn (ed.), *Challenge to Morality,* p. 67.
14. *Ibid.*, p. 70.
15. *Ibid.*, p. 71.
16. This is a major argument for the type of experimental residence hall religious counseling programs which are under way at such institutions as Pennsylvania State University and Florida Staate University.
17. Quoted in Charles F. Kemp, "Counseling the College Student," in George L. Earnshaw (ed.), *The Campus Ministry* (Valley Forge, Pa., 1964), p. 225.

Luther H. Harshbarger heads the department of religious studies at the Pennsylvania State University and served for seven years on the Danforth Foundation's Commission on the Study of the Campus Ministry. His observations are informed by close association with the director of the Danforth Study, the late Kenneth Underwood, and over twenty years as sometimes campus minister, chaplain and coordinator of religious affairs, and now professor and department head.

The Search for Church-University Relational Models

Luther H. Harshbarger

For 2,000 years, education and religion have been inextricably related, heroically and tragically. This must always be so if the task of transmitting, inculcating and criticizing their cultures is to continue, for education and religion deal with the questions which are at the very center of human society and culture.

Both education and religion are in deep trouble today. Perhaps they always have been. Historically, education has always represented a great concern and a special problem. Higher education, especially, has proved both a bane and a blessing to religious institutions and society. The new pattern of social and political stability developing in the Middle Ages was accompanied by intellectual revival. Out of this intellectual revival were born Cathedral and Monastic schools, marking the beginning of Scholasticism as the context for teaching of the Bible and the Qur'an. At the same time, in the Spanish academies at Toledo and Cordova, Arabs, Jews and Christians sat together in the same classroom, listened to the same lectures, learned the same New Metaphysics based on the Neoplatonic version of Aristotle. These scholars were intent upon showing the compatibility of the Qur'an, the Bible, and the Torah and Talmud to the best scientific thought of the day. The University of Paris, arising out of these schools in later Middle Ages, hoped its students would withdraw from general society for a three to seven year period in order to continue their learning. In the 14th century it was the Church that protected twenty thousand to thirty thousand students against secular pressures.

This remarkable conviction on the part of the Church, historically, and now on the part of contemporary society, incidentally, that it must support its own critics, is something we ought not to forget. Neither society nor religious institutions, however, has ever been comfortable with this creature turned critic. Note this remarkable fact: every major heresy since the 14th century has stemmed from intellectuals. Recall also that never in the history of higher education has there been a major educational reform apart from the initiative of students. Today Protestants applaud Martin Luther for posting the 95 Theses on the doors of Wittenberg. But the university authorities then were no more happy with Martin Luther than President Pusey is today with the Students for a Democratic Society. This protection on the part of the Church fomented heresy everywhere, and when the Church attempted to protect itself by requiring a formal adherence to the Apostle's Creed, even as late as the 19th century in Cambridge and Oxford, Jeremy Bentham remarked that the streets of Cambridge were paved with perjury.

The 20th century has seen a series of revolts which add up to something resembling a creed of total rebellion against Western culture. Now youth, world wide and uncoordinated, are outspoken in antagonism to the character of contemporary life and its social settings. They appear to be caught in a web of concepts which have broken with historical continuity and engendered a quest for new patterns of interpretation. Once again in contemporary culture there appears a convergence of forces causing religious institutions and universities to go through a painful and controversial transition. The whole society appears to be floundering, both in terms of the goals it seeks and the means to achieve them.

Universities, the paradigm of the New Technotronic Age, are uncertain of their role. In their uncertainty, they are torn by internal strife, subject to conflicting pressures from all sides, and staggered by the proliferation of knowledge—a knowledge that springs from technology and from the whole rational, logical system that students so contemptuously challenge as irrelevant.

At issue is the reconsideration of the relevance of the whole learning experience in its traditional setting and the reapplication of the knowledge explosion to the demands of contemporary society. Robert Hutchins has remarked that everything that is wrong with the American university has been wrong with it for the last 50 years. The difference is, he notes, that until recently nobody cared; the university was a peripheral institution, but now it has moved from the periphery to the center and become the central factory of the knowledge industry.[1]

As the University has moved to the center, changes are forced in other basic social structures which affect the status of individuals. Religious institutions, once the organizing and directing institutions of their cultures, are now voluntary societies of only peripheral significance. This shift forces a search for the relationship of religious experience to its traditional organizations, and of the religious mythos to traditional historical/theological convictions.

Changing structures within universities and churches are clues to the developments in the culture. On one hand, the university mediates both the new knowledge and reconstructed religious beliefs to the whole culture and its task "is the creation of the future, so far as rational thought, and civilized modes of appreciation can affect the issue."[2] On the other hand, Kenneth Underwood has prophetically pointed out that, "In periods of history when a society is in transition from one way of life, thought and faith to another, its religious leadership is among the first and most serious objects of criticism and rebellion, for religion symbolizes and articulates the society's most basic values and commitments. Confusion and loss of morale in the religious leadership of the society is usually an indication of serious problems, in meaning and purpose, to come in other leadership and institutions."[3]

We are going through a revolution in the consciousness of Western man so profound that it necessarily requires an appraisal of many of our most cherished assumptions and beliefs. Such revolutions are always marked both by phenomenal change in the social structure and culture and by concomitant crises. De Tocqueville accurately describes this situation: "There are no revolutions that do not shake existing belief, enervate authority, and throw doubts over commonly received ideas. Every revolution has more or less the effect of releasing men to their own conduct and of opening before the mind of each one of them an almost limitless perspective. . . . Men are no longer bound together by ideas, but by interests, and it would seem as if human opinions were reduced to a sort of intellectual dust, scattered on every side, unable to collect, unable to cohere."[4] In such periods of profound instability, great demands are placed on the intellect—leaps of imagination and expansions in perspective; a new dedication to reason, an acceptance of the world as it is, and a crying awareness of the world as it ought to be. In such periods of revolutionary transition there are always discrepancies between the older forms of knowledge and faith, and the emerging socio-technical forms of social and cultural life. Such is the period we are living through.

Many are convinced that education and religion are in disarray and chaos to a far deeper extent than we have yet to comprehend. To what extent the contemporary revolutionary ambience is morally serious or just rebelling conformism, it is too early to say. It does seem clear, however, that many people have become deeply disillusioned about themselves, their idols, national hopes, and technocratic civilization. Universities, churches, and even seminaries, are filled with persons living in a void of half-gods or none, experiencing the emptiness of holocaust, anomie, or the trivialization of existence constitutes something like a culture of unbelief.

In general, Western culture seems beset by a peculiar spiritual malaise which is very difficult to analyze. There is a loss of bouyancy and zest about its most characteristic enterprises. Religiously, there's a kind of cultural shock which produces cravings for faith and meaning, but fragmented men seem to be ill equipped to give or to receive such gifts. The culture is marked by increasing alienation, polarization and even open hostility. One of the striking marks is the seemingly sudden erosion of the authority of our educational and religious systems, their leadership and cherished beliefs and canons, which until recent times, had borne the weight of our social hopes. Indeed, many of the cherished ideals of the university community and of the religious traditions now appear as problems rather than as sources of a solution. Both personal and official authority have waned in a manner akin to Turgenev's description of a nihilist as "a man who does not bow down before any authority, and does not take principle on faith, whatever reverence that principle may be enshrined in."[5]

At the very least, the educational and religious systems seem no longer to be coherent enterprises. Their policies consist of just so many arbitrary decisions made in unplanned, almost sub-rational response and adjustment to diverse strains and practical pressures. This contributes to a wave of discontent. The cities are in crisis. Students are in turmoil, and in a "revolutionary" mood which rejects both history and the prevailing social consensus. They are impatient with all traditional modes and goals, and deeply question national goals and the bases of public and private morality, finally focusing an unrelentless criticism on educational and religious institutions.

THE MISSION OF THE UNIVERSITY

In the current situation it is not at all surprising that there are debates and serious questionings about the nature and mission of the university in modern society. Widespread disagreement is apparent in public discussion, in bewilderment, and in the spirited discussions on the nature and style of scholarship going on among academicians. It is dramatically illustrated by the gathering storm of student unrest and revolt. The strident charges of meaninglessness, irrelevance, and even immorality against the university may be excessive, but they can provide categories for our further analysis.

By *meaninglessness* they apparently mean that the piece-meal approach to learning as exemplified in the departmental organization and its specialization is so fragmented that it lacks any character, coherence or central purpose.

There is a certain faceless character about the knowledge enterprise. Norman Mailer amusingly describes this lack of character of universities as he approached the Manned Space Center at Houston. He says that there was no way to determine whether one was confronting an industrial complex, a minimum security prison, a large insurance and finance corporation, or the newest and finest kind of hospital for radiological research. "Or perhaps it was a college campus—one of those miserable, brand new college campuses with buildings white as toothpaste, windows set in aluminum casements, paths drawn by a right angle or a carefully calculated zigzag to breed right angles and a general air of studies in business administration, a college campus in short to replace the one burned in the last revolution of students."[6]

For the first time in the history of the university, there *is no organizing motif* or higher principle structurally written into the entire curricular program. The programs are specialized and departmentalized and thus they appear to reduce the universe to an assemblage of parts, the mind of man to an aggregate of sense perceptions. Even the casual observer may feel the thrust of the poet's comment:

> *. . . upon this gifted age, in its dark hour*
> *Reigns from the sky a meteoric shower*
> *Of facts . . . they lie unquestioned, uncombined,*
> *Wisdom enough to teach us of our ill*
> *Is daily spun, but there exists no loom to weave it into fabric.*[7]

There is a distinction between an aggregate of parts and a vital whole, between a discrete many and a living unity. The result for the institution and the student is a vacuum of purpose because education lacks what Samuel Taylor Coleridge called "the self unraveling clue."[8]

The earliest universities were organized around central motifs in what we would call professional schools which had a specific purpose. Lectures were focused and subject matter inter-connected to train the elite for the churches as in Paris; or to train civil service to run the empire as at Oxford or Cambridge; or clergy, doctors and lawyers to meet the needs of the new church in the new city as at Harvard and Yale. But this observation hardly meets the point. Theology at Paris and other universities in the Middle Ages was the "superior faculty." Russian education also has a unifying ideology and organizing principle for all scholarly activity with explicit purpose. Is this what we need?

To my mind such comparisons are invidious and miss the really significant point: the growth of knowledge in the 20th century has been so enormous and still increases at such acceleration that it cannot be assimilated by the university or the culture. The doctor of the Middle Ages could master all the knowledge there was in breadth and depth in his life time, could brood over it, and then in mellow wisdom, organize it around some principle of selection. But today, every professor knows the rigors required and the perilous speed at which he must work to keep from being swamped by the expanding scholarship and new knowledge in his own narrow field. "There is a curious illusion," Whitehead writes, "that a more complex culture was possible when there was less to know. Surely the only gain was, that it was more possible to remain unconscious of ignorance. It cannot have been a gain to Plato to have read neither Shakespeare, nor Newton, nor Darwin."[9]

But still we can agree that the university does not completely fulfill its mission in the modern world, if it does nothing more than provide a collection of information and intellectual bric-a-brac. There must be a search for a certain unity of the self, a certain method in feeling. For unity and method are qualities of the educated mind and these require what Coleridge called a "*surview* which enables a man to foresee the whole of what he is to convey,"[10] or what amounts to the same thing, the educated mind has a "passion for an ordered intellectual vision of the connection of events."[11]

The charge of *irrelevance* has special force at a particular point where contemporary universities have ignored their environment. This point is the lack of organic connection before and after student years. Furthermore, the Land Grant tradition, which responded dramatically and successfully to the demands of the culture in the late 19th century in food production, for example, has been largely irrelevant to the present cultural revolution. We need to replace this tradition with one more contemporary in its concern for the black community and urban affairs.

Students are rebelling against the restrictive orthodoxies of higher education and have shown real desire for more opportunity to participate in the formulation of academic policies and to relate the gathering storm of social issues to campus concerns. But they have little knowledge or experience at being heard in councils of authority. If this state of affairs continues, the next step in the "student revolution" is likely to bypass entirely the question of restructuring the university in an effort to get out "where the action is." Students already seem to be deserting the campus as a locus for life in an effort to immerse themselves in more natural social communities, and the concept of the campus as a cloister is rapidly disappearing. This is illustrated in the recent SDS participation in the protests and strike against the Long Island Rail Road, with students associating themselves with the middle and the upper classes.

Furthermore, I think it is fair to say that the educational scene in America can be characterized by a tension between two influential views about the mission of higher education among public leaders and academicians which press upon the university in partial and inadequate terms. In cryptic fashion the question can be formulated this way: Is the university a public utility or a community of disinterested scholars?

The first view assumes that the crisis in the cultural order is so enormous that the university should relegate everything else to second place and concentrate upon meeting it directly. To many people in all walks of life this is not at all a novel or disturbing point of view. In some such fashion, many have long believed that colleges and universities are service agencies of society, dedicated to upholding the American way of life, the system of free enterprise, and the values inherent in a "Christian" culture. This point of view draws upon a tradition in American higher education when the college professed character development as its primary interest and expected the student to discover a calling which served society. He not only learned skills, but was expected to be a self-conscious citizen and serve the community.

There is a second prominent view found among scholars and teachers in response or reaction to the first point of view. In this view the university must be free from partisan interest, from any defense of cultural values, moral considerations and it must escape the press of utilitarian applicability. The scholar's first obligation is to his discipline, the pursuit of his craft. His method is one of objective analysis, freed from "unscientific" points of view. The strength of this position stems largely from the scientific-empirical tradition in which men have employed very successful methods in gaining knowledge and controlling the natural and physical world for the analysis of the social world. They have attempted to let the facts speak for themselves. But the very nature of the method causes it to study those aspects of human activity which can be measured, quantified, and embodied in some kind of abstract categories or principles. In its initial stance, this kind of technical reason requires an objectivity which permits no moral judgment as to personal duty or public purpose.

In an era when the operational uses of knowledge seem almost a social necessity it is natural that there should be a reinterpretation of the tensions and significance of these two traditions in learning in an attempt to respond constructively to world events and national need.[12]

The indifference to its environment, on the one hand, and the apparent willingness to serve as bastions of special interest, on the other, has opened the university to the charge of *immorality*. Universities in the eyes of an articulate minority have been captured by the military-industrial-political-complex—"the establishment"—government, industry, even agriculture. There was a land grant act to serve a changing milieu, why not an "urban affairs act?" Why the plea for detachment now?

The 55th Annual Meeting of the American Association of University Professors, concerned about institutional autonomy, recognized that campus demonstrations are in part "a manifestation of deep and sometimes profoundly moral discontent arising out of social injustice, public policy, and, in some cases, out of inefficiency, irresponsibility, and unresponsiveness within the institutions themselves."[13] Mayor John Lindsay in a recent speech at Yale, asking why many students take radicals seriously said, "Is it the university, which calls itself a special institution, divorced from worldly pursuits, while it engages in real estate speculation and helps plan and evaluate projects for the military in Vietnam?"

The pathos of concern for coherence, relevance and morality of knowledge is expressed poignantly, if naively, in John Fischer's recent proposal for re-forming colleges and universities around "the idea of survival" as "the organizing principle for many fields of scholarly inquiry; which is relevant to the needs of our times; and which would not . . . impose an ideological straightjacket, as both ecclesiastical and Marxist education attempts to do."[14] Here is an idea, he thinks, which would give students "coherence and visible purpose," and equip them to do something about "what is going on in the world." No multiversity this, offering a plethora of unrelated courses, and "no detached, dispassionate scholars" need apply. All courses will seek to answer the question, "what must we do to be saved?" And every professor "will have to demonstrate a commitment to this goal . . . he will be expected to be a moralist; for this generation of students, like no other in my lifetime, is hungering and thirsting after righteousness. What it wants is a moral system it can believe in—and that is what our university will try to provide. In every class it will preach *the primordial ethic of survival.*" (emphasis mine). "Saving knowledge" is no longer the slogan of the eschatological imagination to be sought by the religious enthusiast only and scorned by the modern educated organizational man. We must learn how knowledge saves and can be saved!

Fischer is not the first one to make this suggestion. Eugen Rosenstock-Huessy, in 1937, demanded of the university for the sake of humanity that, "it should learn to think in a different way, in the sense that scholarship and science should be pursued in communication with the neighbor and as such become an act of pastoral care *(Seelsorge)* for the neighbor and the community."[15] Whether the university is a proper agency of salvation in any of the senses of that word is another question. Higher education certainly is a noble enterprise, but is there any salvation in it? It does underline the important point, however, that any successful reform of higher education will have to be radical, founded on a single idea capable of knitting together all the strands of study, giving them coherence and visible purpose.

Yet this comment should give us pause, for a definition of the primary vocation of the academic community has not come easily in Western history. There has been a pattern of development which demands consideration. Although this is not the place to write that history, we can make some observations rather quickly by historical illustration.

Today, we are surprised and shocked that students reject the proud achievement of universities and we abhor their resort to protest and violence as instruments of change. Looking back we should rather be impressed by the violence of struggles through which the university came to understand its proper purpose and prize its independence. Special relationships between town and gown have developed over a period of 500 years, culminating in the just previous generations of special privilege for the university community and its students as a kind of third order, where students were protected against civil procedures and social and community responsibilities. Members of the university were given a special license, a detachment from town, crown and mitre, a functional independence that, hopefully, would allow it to find its own way towards its true aims and fulfillment.

This functional independence has been and is derived from the fact that a culture cannot exist without a reasonable process. The distinctive vocation of the educational community is to raise critical, constructive issues—for the whole State and the whole Church—on an *intellectual* level. The essential function of the university is critical reflection, evaluation and foresight, not, first of all, action. Feverish dilettantism and desire for radical action leads to premature activity, and such action without thought may impoverish a culture as seriously as grosser forms of hesitation, conservatism or gradualism.

The present quest for a "surview" is multi-dimensional, yet there is something tragic in the rejection of any body of systematic, hard, discursive knowledge as inhumane. Many students do not trust the coherence of experience and they reject the reflective, verbal and intellectual traditions of learning. There is a certain pathos in the sentimentality of their search for values amid the clutter of curricula, in their belief that knowledge is somehow a system to be intuited. The present student generation is a NOW generation, expressing a sense of alarm, concern and compassion, and wanting to perform immediately the action that is definitive. They want immediacy of experience and are impatient with gradualism and the older generation when it asks for reflection. The slogans are community, co-control, relevance, legitimacy, with no part of the past. They want only the future and it is difficult for the university to remake the age according to a vision of spontaneity, love and an immediate end to all injustices.

I am fully aware that such a statement can easily be misunderstood. There is now, however, almost tragic irony in President Pusey's first address to Harvard freshmen. It will be, he said, "a tragic lack, and unwise wisdom, if your generation feels no compelling urge to mold the world over after its own heart's desire." Yet, "the heart's desire" and relevance cannot necessarily be equated with contemporaneity. The student concern for morality of knowledge is laudable, but knowledge does not begin with morals, rather with facts and theories. Otherwise, a university simply becomes another community of pious secularism. A university must be first of all an intellectual community *before* it is a moral community. As Jacob Burckhardt once put it, truth is something to be apprehended intellectually and to be lived morally.

This age, any age, demands more than a sense of urgency and something more than frenetic casting about for new schemes, new courses, patterns of governance, etc. It requires an exacting task of reflection as a real base from which to launch a radical attack on society. The crises of our time provide opportunity for rethinking on theoretical and intellectual dimensions. Developing the art of careful reflection provides the means of search for new forms of community and relevant forms of action which are truly revolutionary. "The true revolutionary is a very patient man, and one who rarely acts at the spur of present impulse; for he looks so far ahead into a future of his own, guides himself so by this future, that his actions acquire a deliberate consistency unattainable by most of us who live in a present that is not wholly our own."[16] Scholarship does not mean a state of repose, inaction or the putting off of all activity until later; it is not separate from pioneering, it is not an inert state. Scholarship does mean the recognition that in periods of upheaval some enterprises can be launched only in a limited way and successes remain centripetal and indecisive. More attention needs to be paid, I believe, to the moderate youth culture and the learning of the techniques of responsibility, change and renewal within established social structures. Systematic, intelligent discussion is required to develop human beings with the power to discriminate, to think not in axioms, but in terms of social achievement. Students have a right to expect the university to be free from extremist pressures if the faculty, in turn, have a right to be heard. They have a right to expect that members of the faculty be serious and faithful to the craft of learning and to the demand that the university community life be vivid in its proper passion and peculiar reverence for knowledge. The university cannot be a captive of any other enterprise, however worthy, and still be itself. Its special freedom in a culture is justified only in so far as it is disinterested, that is, freedom in pursuit of its own purposes, not being used by others for their purposes. Whitehead says it well. "Fools act on imagination without knowledge; pedants act on knowledge without imagination. The task of a university is to weld together imagination and experience."[17]

A further observation can be made very quickly again by way of historical illustration. Learning at its best is always related to its social milieu. The great scholars from Plato, the Prophets, and the Sages, were profoundly concerned with the basic social issues and had a deep sense of vocational obligation towards their own times. To be sure, this was often on different levels than political or business or industrial concerns, for example. But it has been historically true that the scholars have been the ones that have seen the problems of their culture long before any one else had begun to worry about them. Writing about the 17th century as the age of genius, Alfred North Whitehead makes the interesting comment that the impetus and direction for that development was given by the experimental method and by its attitude to "irreducible and stubborn facts." He illustrates this with reference to Francis Bacon's *Natural History*. Bacon apparently believed that science begins with an understanding of the mechanical arts and, therefore, the factory as the locus of invention provides the way for the laboratory to become the locus of research and the home of science. The study of the crafts, therefore, becomes an important clue to the knowledge of nature. There grew up in that century an interest in technical knowledge, which grew out of the late medieval interest in technology as the way for man to control and reshape the powers and materials of nature.[18] With Luther, Bacon exalts the values of experience and the dignities of labor. "Men must know," he wrote, "that in this theatre of man's life it is reserved only for God and the angels to be lookers on."[19]

This apparently is the beginning of the cultural belief in knowledge as power to transform the world and has important application in American history in the Morrill Land Grant Act of 1862. With the post-Civil War, the industrial revolution arrived in America and the rise of state and land grant universities redesigned the aims of higher education consonant with the needs of the new industrial society, and related the university closely to the American culture milieu and ethos. The impact of these ideas and techniques changed and continues to change the whole culture. As Clark Kerr says "the ideopolis is now the center of the city and the university is increasingly the center of attempts by an entire people to know what is happening to them."

In this expanding age university leaders are being asked to use their special knowledge and skills experimentally and flexibly for the sake of the community.

To say that a university must be related to its social and cultural milieu, however, is a different thing than saying that it should be judged by reference to its utility to the community. The town is often interested in the university only as a market, and church and state very often only support it as an organ to express their own wills. All three, state, church, and industry, tend to ignore the essential life of the university and evaluate it as a tool-making industry. This is a special temptation in the contemporary world where specialized knowledge and advanced education have become more and more useful operationally. Of course the university may be an instrument of social policy, but it still must remain, at the same time, the natural critic of social policy and file its own evaluations thereof.

Studies in universities should be pursued in response to the demands of the present age. And they can lose nothing, in fact, can only gain, academically by the deepening of this sense of responsibility. From the history of education we can learn that it is just those ideas and yearnings of a particular milieu that furnish the relevant issues for research and study. In fact, many issues become ripe for solution and new areas are opened up for research simply because they are relevant to the destiny of a given age. The university must not only live with its history and its concerns for the future, but must also live intensively in the present.

In the university, hopefully, the adventure of action meets the adventure of thought.

RELIGION AND THE LEARNING ENTERPRISE

From the beginning we have stressed the important point that educational institutions and religious institutions and their professionals represent the vanguard in periods of radical transition. Their changing structures and ideologies are clues to the profound developments in a culture. Periods of crises in consciousness and their events have a paradigmatic quality which forces re-orientation of thought and experience and seem to impose their own categories of interpretation and significance. Each age seems to have its gestalt and generates its own unique kind of knowledge in order to express its spirit and destiny.

In such periods of disquietude, universities mediate the newer knowledge and changing beliefs and cannot confine themselves to pure abstract learning unrelated to cultural change. They are rather communities striving for a relevant understanding of the vastness, complexity and meaning of the cultural process.

Religion and its institutions provide models which symbolize and articulate the basic values and commitments of a culture and represent a standpoint, or a way of looking at human existence, offering images for interpreting the elemental facts of life. Religion is at the vanguard of cultural criticism because such criticism usually implies rejection of the vortex of meaning depending upon any holy ultimate or transcendence. The contemporary crisis in religious commitment and consciousness appear as contradictions between traditional modes of religious faith, thought and behavior and the emergence of socio-technological forms of cultural life. Therefore, American society faces the acute problem of finding religious and general symbols which will adequately express the spiritual and moral problems and the occasions which grip the nation and its primary institutions.

The discussion of the mission of the university thrusts us naturally and inevitably into the question of the appropriate role of religion in the learning enterprise. The soteriological and cognitive converge in the university because education at all levels is increasingly the cultural paradigm of this age and the university increasingly is that place in society where the knowledge explosion occurs, is evaluated, and persons prepared for responsible policy decisions for the whole society.

The fundamental question is whether we have the kind of knowledge and ability to apprehend the nature of change at its very depth and not just on the surface.

I do not have the answer to that question, but I think it is significant that in our search for church and university relational models and the characteristics of a profession that we have now recently completed a model of research which attempts to probe the very depths of the structures of learning and religious communities.

The appearance, in late Fall 1969, of the late Kenneth Underwood's *The Church, the University, and Social Policy* as the report of the Danforth Study of the Campus Ministry, will mark the conclusion of what must be the most substantial and intensive study of religious commitments and actions of American religious institutions and leadership ever undertaken.[20] While the study focusses on a single profession, it goes far beyond the usual confines of such research. It will be useful for our purposes to describe the study at some length and then explore its ramifications for church-university relations and the character of the religious professions.

Underwood saw three forces converging to produce the occasion for critical reflection and decision: first of all, clerical and lay ministries within the structures of the institutional church; secondly, the leaders of higher education who are involved in the knowledge revolution; and third, public figures who formulate policies in the major organizations and professions of American society. The leaders of these three forces are involved at every point in the study.

Underwood's undertaking was the consequence of no small vision. His was a labyrinthian and serendipitous mind, searching all depths and reaching out for all pertinent connections. It is important to understand the unique character of his venture. The study represents a method of collective inquiry and research, using both the insights of theological reflection and social sciences, although being careful not to reduce religious categories to other forms of causation and experience. It focused upon the ministry, the church, and higher education. The self conceptions of the people being studied were taken seriously, and they themselves participated in the process of research and reflection; and the people and the institutions under study visibly changed in the process. The goal was nothing less than to effect the ministry, the university, and social policy in such a way that the professions are re-formed and the institutional structures reshaped.

Later in this chapter we may explore further the methods and major organizing ideas of the Danforth Study, but for now a comprehension of the ethos is more important than a precise understanding of the methodology. Underwood called the study social policy research or prophetic inquiry. For him, this was a process combining ethical inquiry and judgment with all the relevant modes of technical knowledge. There is a kind of socio-technical knowledge and learning, he felt, being created in the university in its involvement with the problems and processes of contemporary society which necessitates the understanding of the relationship of science, technology, social ethics, and institutional policies. This socio-technical knowledge creates new forms of social organization and reshapes forms of human culture in accordance with an imaginative vision of the good life and the general welfare. Socio-technical knowledge is neither an art or a science, but is a third kind of knowing which assumes a participant attitude, where the investigator actually influences the subject or object of his study by his questions and his questions, in turn, are shaped by the answers he receives. So there is a continual cycle of inquiry and feedback where before there had been only one-way flow. This circuit seeks a comprehensive vision or organic unity rather than a detailed description of a particular reality.

Underwood, using this "new discipline" resolutely refused to isolate the study of a part of a profession from its wider context—the churches, the modes of ministry, the ideologies, the universities, their structures of learning and teaching, students and their aspirations and anxieties, and the (relationship to) American culture. This process brought an end then to the old dichotomies of culture and technology, art and commerce, or sacred and profane. The methods of inquiry and the criteria are in flux all the time, but they do require honesty in reporting, rigor in the pursuit of truth, fairness toward the autonomy of disciplines. This is not a simple linear development. One must keep all of these modes simultaneously under intensive scrutiny. There is complexity and richness to the reality described and envisioned in the variety of disciplines and perspectives brought by the participants to the inquiry, and the effort is to get a comprehensive vision, a sense of the need for establishing new ways of relating many factors and forces heretofore separate, and an importance of social policies as a focus for restructuring and redefining the purposes and methods of achievement. The result, Underwood hoped, would be that public leaders, laymen and clerics, and academicians would be able to think carefully about what ought to be the course of events for religious and academic institutions at the points where ethical concerns impinge upon one another.[21] For Underwood, the concept of the profession was central, and the professional is one who has the artistry and skill to apply a body of clearly understood cognitive content to the general welfare, and the power to integrate religious belief, technical theory and data, and the varied modes of his profession and apply them to concrete problems. The profession expresses itself in four historic modes—priest, pastor, prophet, and king, as parts of a unified action. The professional is related critically and positively to a very broad context: the churches, their views of the ministry and ideologies; the universities and the structures of learning, teaching and research, students and their aspirations and anxieties; and American culture, its basic trends and the policies and values of professional, technical and popular sub-cultures. None of the four modes of the profession can be separated from each other or from this wider context without grave distortion of the profession.

In the history of religious institutions the order and priority of these particular offices have shifted, signifying changes in religious consciousness, both of the professional and the community. They constantly need new elaboration and reconstruction. What is at stake here is the function of wholeness, a comprehensive vision of new ways to relate factors, forces, and courses of events where religious, academic, ethical and technical concerns impinge upon one another. Unfortunately, in most situations men have been unable to work out a cognitive model of this comprehensive and integrative function. Rather, these modes of ministry have been broken up into specialized subfunctions and trivialized forms of service. So there is counseling without a point of view, evangelism without justice, prophetic utterance without analysis, teaching without intellectual curiosity or passion and administration or governance without community vision.

That the changing character of religious consciousness and the shifting of professional roles and relationships of the academy and the church require new elaboration and construction is plainly evident in American history. Religion has never been divorced from higher education, public or private, although it has been a relationship oscillating between the center and periphery of the culture. De Tocqueville's comment that in the United States religion has "mingled with all the habits of the nation" is clearly evident in American higher education until the early 20th century.

To be sure, the American religious heritage and therefore the religious heritage of American higher education has never been the subject of unambiguous interpretation. Schleiermacher once remarked that every interpretation must begin with misinterpretations and we are dealing here with a field replete in misinterpretations based upon simple linear developments. Yet our students today could certainly profit from the reminder that the puritan roots of our culture constitute a highly developed intellectual system, an organized synthesis of concepts still implicitly operating in American culture.

The interest of the puritan fathers in orthodox doctrine and ritual, by no means excluded a concern for the advancement of learning. Their intellectual life revealed both breadth and depth of learning, including not only theology, but a great interest in the classics and the emerging sciences. Following Augustine, they believed that while a saint must first believe in order to know, after he has come to believe he must endeavor to know as much as possible. As Whitehead notes, the puritans of the 17th and 18th century "were the most intensely imaginative people . . ., racked with the intensity of spiritual truth intellectually imagined. The puritan faculties of those centuries must have been imaginative indeed, and they produced great men whose names have gone round the world."[22]

On the other hand, William Berkeley, the Governor of Virginia in the 17th century, could say, "Thank God there are no free schools or printing, for learning has brought disobedience and heresy into the world, and printing has divulged them. God keep us from both." Since the disintegration of the Puritan synthesis and especially in the 19th century, with the second Great Awakening, religious experience developed in a period which had no intellectual or theological shape. In the post Civil War period the Church turned from reasoning to affectionate kinship support at the very time when the United States was becoming the world leader in genetics, for example, and a fatal split between faith and intelligence was introduced. The religious American became an intellectually disinherited individual and the minister became a messenger who had forgotten his message. Fundamentalism, rationalism, pietism and moralism became the main categories of religion.

The theme of salvation through knowledge was a basis for the founding of colleges to be molders of character with a total religious concern for the morals and characters of students which was reflected in the curriculum and campus life generally. This total ministry required no specificity of professional function such as chaplains or professors of religion. The faculty were primarily concerned "to transmit the learning of the past" in order to develop persons of strong character called to serve God and one's fellow men. The educated mind in this tradition was expected to be the bearer and critic of his culture. In all of his associations, it was hoped, he would be self-conscious of the community, and through the patterns and the crises of his daily life aware of the depths and heights of human desire and suffering. The campus climate of opinion, the curricular leadership of the faculty, the president, all were thought to minister to the student.

The radical cultural shifts which began in the late 19th century are illustrated by a quaint and somewhat humorous anecdote. In 1894, T. C. Mendenhall refused the presidency of Ohio State University because "although he was a church goer and a choir singer, yet he was not a church member and would not pray in public." Shortly thereafter when Professor Adams of Johns Hopkins was invited to take the presidency he asked a similar question: "Is the president necessarily the chaplain of the university or can religious functions which are important be discharged by ministerial members of the faculty?"[23]

The post Civil War period brought major changes in academic life, changes which were concurrent with the rise of state universities and the redesigning of the aims of higher education, consonant with the needs of a new industrial society. The Morrill Land Grant Act of 1862 proved to be a momentous and revolutionary decision in the history of higher education, which related closely the university to the American cultural milieu and ethos. The religious impulse was equally strong in these colleges because state legislatures reflected the religious attitudes of the communities, and the faculties and administration were products of church related colleges. Teachers were still expected to be politically sound, theologically orthodox, and to be concerned about the discipline and the moral and religious needs of students. Nonetheless an historic shift was imminent, brought about by the necessary redirections of the aims of higher education. This historic shift is symbolized by Henry Commager's comment that in 1840 the president of every important university was a clergyman, whereas in 1940, there was not a clergyman president of a single leading institution.

While religious concerns both in scholarship and practice appear in the 20th century to be altogether marginal to the mainstream of higher education, that does not mean that such a minimal role has been or is insignificant. Compatible religious and educational goals have developed not only in spite of but under the aegis of religious pluralism. Since no particular form of religion is normative for the entire society, differences have tended to be submerged into a common generalized conviction which always has about it a vaguely patriotic character. Despite sectarian differences there is a common good which de-emphasizes peculiar items of belief. Moreover, this conviction is not confined to the religious institution. The belief that the "religious life" is not confined to ecclesiastical bodies has characterized religion's role in the public domain throughout American history. This can be seen in several dimensions. One, there is a public domain to which all men belong and in which they act. Americans are simultaneously Jews or Christians; local, state, national, world citizens; students, professors, administrators. They function in a variety of cultural contacts in which they are inextricably involved. To each of these areas and simultaneously they bring their own history and commitments. Two, there is a religious sub-stratum in American national life which is expressed in the myth, symbols, ceremonies, and rituals common to all Americans and expressed in proclamations, political addresses, and the celebration of holidays. Three, religious organizations have spawned throughout American history, voluntary associations to fight against some social evil or for some cause be it slavery, liquor, war, Sunday observance, anti-Vietnam. Indeed the voluntary character of the denomination as an organization of purposeful activity has placed great emphasis on this kind of pragmatic achievement. In these dimensions, at least, there is impressive evidence that religious influence has been pervasive in American political and cultural life.

It is this tradition which has been influential on campuses since the latter part of the 19th century, and was no less operative in state colleges and universities. So President Calder of the Pennsylvania State College could hold a revival meeting on the campus and report that "all the students were converted." There followed courses in religion and character building, appointment of chaplains, the founding of voluntary associations, especially the student YMCA, for all forms of religious discussion and practice, social amelioration, and protest, and most of the activities characteristic of student political groups and student personnel offices characteristic of today's campus.

The dilemma of a Mendenhall and Adams has been resolved in the 20th century. The "total ministry" of colleges and universities long since has given way to the proliferation of functions and the development of specializations. So the modern university is rather a collection of diverse and discrete disciplines where technological considerations tend to dominate. It is a "city of the intellect" or "knowledge factory" usually characterized by sharp divisions among those who would "gladly learn and gladly teach," those who run research laboratories, those who determine educational policy, and a corporation with an administration to govern the city.

The concern for the religion, morals and character of the student has been assigned to offices of student personnel which sometimes have a division of religious affairs manned by professionals in religion with such varied titles as Chaplain, Dean of the Chapel, Coordinator of Religious Affairs, Religious Counselor, YMCA-YWCA Secretary, or Campus Minister. The very variety of titles attests to the fact that the "total ministry" has been institutionalized as separate specializations or professionalizations. In the sixties there are approximately three thousand such persons employed full-time either by churches, colleges or universities and who belong to a variety of professional associations such as the National Association of College and University Chaplains, the Association of Coordinators of University Religious Affairs, the United Ministries of Higher Education, Hillel Directors Associations, Newman Apostolates, the National Campus Ministry Association, and so on, and who work in denominational centers or foundations, Christian Associations, Hillel Foundations, Newman Clubs, university and college chapels and student personnel offices.[24]

A radical shift has taken place also in the curriculum and the scholarly enterprise in religion. In the 19th century the President and faculty offered courses in Evidences of Christianity, Moral Science, English Bible, Classical Language, etc. so that the teaching of religion has always been characteristic of American colleges and universities. The teaching of religion generally was seen as an extension of the church onto the campus and its teaching was for moral and evangelistic purposes. The content of the tradition and phenomena of religion are the functions of religious traditions. The corpus of religious knowledge organized itself around faith traditions and represented the legitimate means of study. Hence, the members of the faculty would represent the dominant religious traditions. Nowadays this is commonly known in professional circles as the "zoo" theory and this mode has been characteristic of church colleges, schools and seminaries although very little of this type of teaching exists any longer. Further development took place in the 1920's and 1930's with the development of Bible Chairs, Schools of Religion and following that in the 30's and 40's the establishment of some departments of religion, in private and state universities.

There is an intellectual revolution taking place in the modern university which seems to mark a major shift on the part of students away from religious practice and organization to the study of religion. I doubt that there is a causative relationship but it seems to be a fact that as religious practice declines in the culture, the popularity of the study of religion increases. The clear signs of change in the climate of opinion is most dramatically exemplified in the changing attitudes concerning the study of religion in public or tax supported universities. It is not necessary to go into detail in this limited space since its development is well documented in a number of publications.[25]

The late 1950's and 1960's mark a significant turning point in this development. At least forty state universities or colleges offer full-blown academic programs in religion, and 90% of the public universities and colleges offer at least some courses in religion. In addition, increasing numbers of both public and private universities are revamping their programs in religious studies. There is also a dramatic shift in point of view. Since the majority of institutions of higher education go well beyond the point where the scholarly study of religion is still debatable, discussion centers around educational policy, the general shape of the curriculum. The questions of objectivity and legality no longer impose any major problem.

The initial problem of religious studies in the university today is not that of adding a few more courses in non-Western religions in order to overcome Western religious parochialism, but that of an adequate definition of the field—its subject matter, methodologies, and epistemologies. What are religious commitments, experiences, world views, and how are they studied? What are the processes and forces which are influential in the formation of religious systems?

The prevailing point of view now holds that the phenomena of religion or religions as a system represent proper objects of study according to the generally accepted canons of the academic community. The central object of study is the *homo-religiosus,* his commitments, experiences, world-views. How are they to be studied? What are the processes or forces that are most influential in the formation of beliefs, character and behavior? Typologies of faith and patterns of religious commitment are subjects of comparative studies in Western and non-Western societies so that the major options of belief concerning man's being and value are studied on a world-wide basis. These studies are conducted in terms of the internal integrity of each option and do not make a particular theistic faith a standard against which all other commitments are to be measured. Patterns of religious thought and action will usually be looked at both internally as seen by the participants, and externally by those who view it from other perspectives. There is continual research for more discriminating criteria for identifying religious world views from non-religious ones.

Beyond that, while there may be debate on the finer points, there is a general agreement that religious studies have the following characteristics:

First, Religion is a discipline in the sense that it has an identifiable subject matter and the various fields or sub-disciplines comprise Religious Studies. Religion is *sui generis* not subject to reductionism or to be described in any other form. But at the same time, it is pervasive in all aspects of culture and, therefore, is a legitimate object of study on the part of any discipline where it is germane.

Second, the methods used are phenomenological, historical, literary, analytical, interpretive, and comparative. That is, they are "objective" in the same sense that any other detached and critical study of a subject is objective.

Here scholars are quite ready to use phenomenological and empirical studies. They are interested in ecumenical approaches in the fullest sense of that term to the study of religious experience in a variety of cultures and traditions. They recognize that the realignment of religious understanding cuts across Western religious traditions, conservative and liberal groups, in complex ways. So they search for new alignments of religious forces in a global way. And they seek an imaginative balance of the major historical and contemporary modes. In any case, the disciplines of Religious Studies are by their very nature related to the existential, and the social, to the present and the past. And the study of religion in this way involves both contemporary issues and historical developments.

Third, the subject matter areas cannot be taught in isolation from relationships with the broader contexts of the many ways of knowing in the university. And, therefore, relationships with other departments are eagerly sought. While religious studies are usually seen as legitimate subject matter for the Humanities and the Social Sciences, they also deal with the questions of the nature of total culture. Many of the themes which have been long neglected in academic specializations such as the classic questions raised in Weber, Troeltsch, and Durkheim about the relationship of personal world views to the processes in modernization, are coming again to the fore not only in departments of religious studies, but in the many cognate fields as well. The general faculties of universities, in contrast to decades ago, develop a growing respect for the disciplines of Sociology and Psychology of Religion. In addition, intellectual religious historical studies are no longer regarded as anachronistic throw-backs to another era. Programs of research, graduate studies, and continuing education in religion are seen as legitimate university enterprises.

These general comments point also to still unresolved problems. The term, religious studies, already indicated drastic changes in the shape of the curriculum and, therefore, in requirements for personnel. In these departments the question of commitment to or ordination in particular religious traditions do not arise. Appointments are made by similar canons to any other department. The only types of persons who are excluded are religionists with highly developed sectarian and specialized expressions of beliefs who have given up any serious critique of religious expressions.

The subject matter is more likely to be ordered in terms of area studies, for example, than in the traditional trivium of Biblical Studies, History and Theology. One is more likely to talk about Near Eastern studies as the context for Biblical Studies. Historical and comparative studies of religious phenomena and their institutions in the culture from which they are derived or where they exist, East or West, are more likely than any emphasis on Church History.

This change in program means that new fields evolve and many fields expand. This points to the dilemma with reference to personnel. It is still a fact that most people teaching in these universities have been trained in seminaries and divinity schools with predominantly Jewish or Christian orientation. Furthermore, this training is heavily concentrated in the traditional fields of Bible, Theology, Church History, and fellowship support is heavily concentrated also in these areas. This means that there are acute shortages in areas like Sociology of Religion, Comparative Ethics, the History of Religions, East and West, Area Studies and Comparative Studies of many kinds.

This rapid development and expansion of Religious Studies in universities is a remarkable event in the history of American education and scarcely could have been anticipated. Religious traditions, layman and cleric, on or off campus, have considerable stake in the nature and quality of this development for many reasons.

This has been a movement largely beyond the influence of ecclesiastical institutions and sparked to a great extent by the interests of the present student generation in the study of religious phenomena. This does not necessarily mean that this student generation is any more religious, and I doubt that there is much profit in probing their motivations for such study. Their remarkable interest, I would suspect, springs to no small degree from personal probing and searching for self identity in this chaotic world. To a large extent the interest is anti-institutional in nature. Whatever their reasons, it is clear that it is becoming academically respectable to take a serious scholarly interest in religion and this interest has developed to such an extent that one can almost say that the present mood is even one of excitement. In any case, their mood challenges curriculum organizers and professors to be relevant and substantial, imaginative and solid.

As the Underwood study implies, we may be reaching in our society the point where the only process by which belief is formed and acted upon for most people is that of genuine inquiry in a college or university setting, and in the testing of it in relation to policies and institutions most influencing their lives. Certainly, the study of religion alters the circumstances in which belief is expressed and commitments lived. Study of religion can lead to both commitment and noncommitment, but in any case, to more informed choices. It is the temptation of every young person and every party to his education to push for premature closure of his options for commitments and style of life. In the study of religion, he can explore with his teachers and peers the great diversifications and patterns of faith available to him.

There is this difficulty in that all beliefs may be placed on the same level and we could be developing a generation of people who stand on the periphery of every religion by profession as well as by conviction. Certainly any intelligent and informed choice could lead to profound conviction and commitment to beliefs and causes intelligently chosen. In any case, this is an important problem, especially since the study of religion is more likely to take place also in secondary schools as well as colleges. Should this happen, then almost certainly it will transform our knowledge of the relationships of belief and action and this has tremendous consequences for parish-sponsored religious education. Problems of coordinating the formal academic study of religion with social action efforts and reinterpretation of traditional dogmas in relation to the processes of secularization and political change, will very likely dominate the next two decades of this relationship.

THE SHAPE OF A PROFESSION

The dramatic shifts in professional roles and the changing character of the study of religion symbolize a revolution in religious consciousness in a socio-technical age. It must, therefore, be a matter of considerable concern to higher education and religious traditions and organizations. We have already said that each cultural period seems to generate its own unique kind of knowledge to express its spirit. The style and structure of the socio-technical age breeds its own peculiar gestalt or ethos which informs the content of all professional thought and work. There is a certain givenness about it. This is expressed by Norman Mailer, again describing the situation at the Manned Space Center in Houston. He says that it was slowly seeping in on journalists in Houston "that they were becoming obsolete. Events were developing a style and structure which made them almost impossible to write about. A process was taking place which was too complex to be reported and so processes began to produce the news for reports. This was taking place everywhere and it represented the *signature of the century.*"[26]

This "signature of the century," willy nilly, shapes the professions. The journalist's sense of obsolescence is a *malaise* common to professions in American society including Chaplains, Coordinators, Campus Ministers of Confessional Groups and, to some extent, professors. Erik Erickson calls it role diffusion or confusion. Given American colleges' and universities' commitment to spectator sports, one would have thought that the football coach would be immune from this academic malaise. Yet a recent issue of *Sports Illustrated* had an article entitled "The Desperate Coach." The headlines of the article in bold face type asked, is the coach "the remaining stronghold of the archaic family structure," or is he as one described himself "the last chance for the preservation of dignity on the campus? . . . The coaches, bewildered, angry and disillusioned, no longer certain of their mission, or in some cases, of their relevance—wonder if they can relinquish authority and still win."[27]

The conception of the profession is central to a definition of the crucial significance and status of leadership. It is a concept in flux, but historically the process of defining the profession takes place in universities. Underwood's intuition was correct. If the university is the paradigmatic institution of the socio-technical culture, then the religious professions related to the university are the precursors of the future because they are defined by the very special constituency and particular relationship to this paradigmatic institution. This is done not only with reference to his own self image but also with the community's image of his role. Many of the functions once performed by the religious profession in academia are now performed elsewhere—in counseling, religious studies, community services, for example—along with declining interest in the practice of religion which has collapsed many of the religious structures and organizations of the campus.

One of the dilemmas of the staff person in religious affairs is that he is associated with a division of personnel. Personnel people are caught in the cross fire between scholar and administration, student and administration, and they represent administration. By and large, the prevailing philosophy of personnel people in the last generation has been a philosophy of social control which resulted in manipulation of student's discipline and regulations. In a society where technological considerations tend to dominate the person has "an agglomeration of functions" to use Gabriel Marcel's phrase. These functions need therapeutic agencies to keep them going so you have to have hospitals, counseling services, religious services, etc. Hence the function of the personnel person in this sort of society is something like a mechanic. His office is the garage that keeps the machine running. The society mechanics consist of vice-presidents for student affairs, deans of student affairs, doctors and hospitals, chapels and chaplains, and coordinators of religious affairs. So the technological society has a different image of the professional than he has of himself. Has he any adequate concept of his profession? Jargon abounds—educational reform, humanizing the educational process, listening to speak, speaking to communicate, waiting to respond, acting to be relevant—jargon is elevated almost to the level of a metaphysic. But does he understand his role to be, in Underwood's terms, a decisive bearer and critic of his culture, dealing with the fundamental issues of life, a profession existing in its own right and not by concession, exercising a leadership that impinges upon academic policy?

It may, therefore, be interesting to apply Underwood's modalities of the profession—priest, pastor, prophet, king—to the signature role of the various forms of the religious professions. But first, this parenthetic note. These traditional images are often thought of simply as Christian categories of the ministry. They represent also the major areas of exploration of religious phenomena and consciousness increasingly applicable to the scholarly study of religion. There is increasing understanding of the importance of myth, symbol and liturgy; the changing nature of man and the protean character of his relationships; the intellectual content of religious faith; and the role of the religious community and its relationships to the culture as fundamental categories for research and study. So the modalities are equally applicable to the professional scholar and the general practitioner. In the space left we can only indicate impressionistically some of the possibilities.

1. The vastness and complexity of the socio-technological university is such that few persons are able to understand all the processes that shape their lives. This points to the importance of liturgy and ritual as symbols of the whole society in which they live. The function of the priest is to develop new symbolic forms of community or help to redeem the traditional ones rather than allowing them to be only signs of reaction.

One of the basic weaknesses of the modern university community is its lack of public expression or symbolization of the university as a community, except, perhaps, on the football field. I once reminded our football coach that he was the chief priest of the university. This shook him somewhat, but there is a grain of truth in the charge.

Chapels and Convocations have a role to play here, if once they recognize the persuasive power of ritual, poetic analogy, myth, legend, liturgy and linguistic associations and modes as carriers of the fears and hopes of men of our time. What could be more irrelevant than singing and praying? Yet the age old office of liturgy may be the most rational of acts for our time. As Rosenstock-Huessy once exclaimed, "From the liturgy I have learned to think rightly!"[28] By these simple, seemingly incongruous acts of kneeling in a chapel, stopping by some wayside altar, chanting the choral antiphon, the reading and hearing of the words of the Torah, Law, and Gospel, by the blessing of the loaf and the cup—these are dramatic enough to be happenings if their true dimensions were ever discovered. But it is by these simple acts that men have spoken across the generations to their children and their children's children concerning their own responses to the mystery in which they found themselves and which gave meaning and direction to the whole of life. Perhaps new liturgical forms need to be developed, but it is the function of liturgy to present the concrete embodiment of the culture in which we live, and by participating, persons find themselves a part of this whole and discover through it the meaning of life. Hence, liturgy will be discovered to be more of a necessity in a cybernetic society.

2. How does the *pastor* care for students in a technological society when the objective of the university is no longer the molding of character? And

where there is what Robert J. Lipton calls the "suspicion of counterfeit nurturance" and that is when people find themselves in need of special help and yet resent whatever help is offered because its assistance is equated with weakness or inferiority?[29]

There is a kind of pathos in this fabric of the culture which Jimmy Breslin calls "a series of rages," when deep alienation develops between the professional and those he would associate with. Indeed, many with whom he was formally associated and worked with in social action, civil rights, protest movements and the like have now become more sophisticated about the powers of bureaucracies and professional structures and the resistance to change than the professional himself. Or, he is used by his identity with social revolt. There is a public relations attempt, perhaps, on both sides, a kind of mutual conning, in the attempt to identify religion with social action where the professional tries to borrow for religion some of the attraction revolt has for the student and students in turn exploit his respectability. In their ready availability for blessing of every fad and latest protest movement, campus ministers are often like the priests in the year of trial in 1848, who were "blessing the trees of liberty" planted by the very people who were trying to destroy the social structure.

Yet counseling quite clearly has become one of the major ways campus clergy use to legitimize their presence on the campus. Members of personnel offices and students tend to look upon pastoral care and counseling of the clergy, however, as related only to a limited range of inter-personal, private, moral and religious problems focussed mainly on sex, personal despair and anguish and the sacramental acts such as marriage.

The present state of chronic unrest signals the development of an important situation vis-a-vis faculty/student relationships and may apply to the ministry as well.

The intellectual over 30 is likely to find the present situation replete with ambiguities, finding himself alternately attracted and repelled, impressed and bedazzled, jaded and bemused, by the behavior of young rebels. He will be tempted to respond by disassociating himself from the young and escape into the pursuits of his own specialty. In another period of kaleidoscopic change, E. T. A. Hoffmann wrote, "So I closed my eyes to all the strife and war in the world and retreated into the land of music as the land of faith, in which all our doubts and sorrows sink into a sea of sounds." Whitehead's observation that "the justification for a university is that it preserves the connection between knowledge and the zest of life, by uniting the young and the old in the imaginative consideration of learning,"[30] may be true enough. I think, however, that it is entirely likely that the alienation of status and of the generations is real, initiated for the most part by the student community. We, therefore, may have to give up the sentimentality of factuly/student friendships and relationships oft enjoyed in the past. Members of the university will have to find a new nexus of relationships based on the bond between knowledge and experience in the fulfillment of necessary tasks. Social relationships derived from objective necessities such as the relationship between doctor and patient, teacher and student, are based upon a division of functions. As someone has said, the meaning of reconciliation with God is that one finds a functional place in the movement of history. But it is not the basic purpose of the university to mold character and to promote friendships between students and faculty. That does not mean unconcern for students, but that's another part of the human dimension. The faculty is concerned with the education of their minds, working with them on their studies. As F. D. Maurice put it with reference to his teaching in the schools for the working classes in the 19th century, we "made our teaching a bond of intercourse with the men whom we taught."[31] Teachers are not mere occasions but are indissolubly related to self knowledge and to the developing of self identification.

The practicing professional must come to see that, whatever the issue, counseling best goes on in the context of community organized to conduct full and frank discussions in which varying points of view are brought to bear on the issues using the technical wisdom of varied dipciplines. He will be the one who cares about what is happening to each student in the concrete structure of the university, where he is going in his work and what he is doing with his knowledge.

Then, perhaps, Margaret Mead may be right when she says, "Once the fact of a deep, new, unprecedented, world-wide generation gap is firmly established in the minds of both the young and the old, community can be established again."[32]

Where there has been a dimension of pastoral concern chaplains often learn some very deeply personal things about the impact of education on students. They have discovered that deep alienation exists not only among those of the hippy subcultures, but also among those alienated from the formal guidance of the health services, counseling services, etc. They have been able to heighten the sense of responsibility of groping students for a meaningful education and to influence the how and what of the entire educational process. They have understood and ministered to the *zerissenheit* (torn-to-piecesness) of conscientious members of faculty and dedicated administrators. It will indeed be a tragedy of historic dimension if a profession based on the notion of *Koinonia* cannot find a basis for genuine community in a day when the whole of society hungers for it.

3. Underwood hypothesized, however, that the religious professional had the least experience and knowledge in prophetic inquiry and governance. Prophetic inquiry meant for him the fusion of knowledge into patterns of coherence, meaning and loyalty so that education could occur in wiser preferences, perspectives of faith, and moralities of knowledge. We need not dwell here on the susceptibility of the religious leader to theological fads in the last generation. We have gone through theologies of the death of God, the mature secular man, and now there's a new Germanic theme, the theology of hope. The professional seems tempted always to give the latest and most controver-

sial piece of theological news to studentsand faculty rather than thrust intellectual struggle into a much more subtle and complex context.

If it is true that this generation may be the first to live wholly in accordance with the credo of the socio-technical culture, then religious thought and theology would have to draw its understanding of the coming epoch from the analysis of this new kind of knowledge which is silent on questions of how a man should live and what he should choose. Such knowledge must be informed with religious and ethical concerns. This will mean less dependence on the humanistic disciplines alone, at least in the traditional forms which often attempt to be more technical and scholarly neutral than the sciences. This means, further, a struggle to re-establish standards of intellectual and social responsibility; that close the gap between literary and philosophical technical criticisms and social criticism. There is much pious talk about humanizing the sciences and technologies by the inter-penetration of human values through history, literature, philosophy, art and religion, but these disciplines hold largely ornamental positions in the life of the university and few seriously seem to believe that they have any relationship to objective reality or serve as guides to human conduct. The liberal arts will need to recover the tradition of Matthew Arnold, John Ruskin and R. H. Tawney and believe with Archibald MacLeish that, "Poetry should deal with public issues and the human heart. And the human heart is a social organ, not just a private one."

Alfred North Whitehead, referring to the originality and value of the contribution to the thought of the world of the early fathers of the schools of Alexandra and Antioch says that, "These Christian theologians have the distinction of being the only thinkers who in a fundamental metaphysical doctrine have improved upon Plato."[33] We should concentrate on that tradition, one that was continued and flourished in America in persons like Ames, Edwards, Bushnell and the Niebuhrs in our own time. Underwood, working in that tradition, believed that theological thought was the gateway to responsible participation in the whole university. It is the inter-penetration of the meaning of faith in exploration and experimentation closely related to technical research, operational skills and the development of social policy.

4. For Underwood, the modes of the profession converged in the symbol of the king or governor. Governance and the involvement in social policy decisions were of paramount importance. There was an especially close relationship between prophetic inquiry and governance. Administration can be a prophetic activity if by being a prophet one means the attempt to change and transform culture. The four modalities carried on in the context of a community of shared beliefs would galvanize into action the community to implement and to give shape to a social good.

Almost without exception the religious professions abhor the role of governance and in their mood runs an undercurrent of alienation from structures. They have also created an image of themselves in the community so that the contemporary evaluation and expectation of the clergyman is that he will not have any expertise or understand the dynamics of public planning and policy.

Religious professionals have had little experience in positions of administrative responsibility where social policy goals are set and so they have tended to perpetuate student views of alienation, and very often to regard the legitimate use of power as unworthy, perhaps even evil. They have not seen the importance of informing policy decisions in the university or influencing the agenda of policy makers, developing principles which guide proposed courses of action, and proposing alternative courses. In other words, to do for our time what Kierkegaard was concerned about, namely that of the "reintroduction of Christianity into Christendom." Too often the idol is the word, speaking out on every issue whether one has anything to say or not, a kind of pediatric social prophetism which is the expression of naive convictions evaporating under immature intellectual analysis and evolutionary change.

There are significant battles going on between peoples of all social organizations who fear vast shifts of power in the action of the blacks, students, the young, the intellectuals, the professionals, and who envision pervasive demonic forces at work at the roots of the system, and who have lost confidence that they can influence significantly the governers or governance. The mode of governance means the exercise of power within the structures and loyalties of society rooted in the status, functions and authority of a society's organizations. The responsible ruler senses the issues and conditions that cut across these divisions in order to express the style and spirit of the culture or the age. He attempts to identify where decisions are made and influences for change are exerted. He views power as the free expression of the people who need to develop their talents and their objectives in an efficacious way. Governance is the effort to channel and persuade and to serve viable and just programs. This is what being a bearer and a critic of the culture means: one who accepts responsibility for transmitting, criticizing, transforming, applying the characteristic religious ethos in the face of changing historical situations, in other words, exercising a leadership that impinges upon public and academic policy. Here the professional exercises a mediating role in the interstices and interfaces where he has something of technical competence as well as generalized responsibility.

The professional precursor then is one capable of uniting the priestly, pastoral, prophetic, and governing modes of ministry. This may be an impossible task for any one person. Therefore, the precursor ministry would be an ecumenical team ministry which was supported by adequate structures of governance in the church and clear in its relationship to the university and staffed by men of complementary competences. The precursor I envisage, however dimly, is one who will be able to carry out this integrative function in his own person or in a staff competent in these four modalities. The definition of his profession will allow him deep roots in one of the religious traditions though not necessarily institutionally responsible to any ecclesiastical organization. His definition will symbolize his integrative role within the university and his task will be so defined, and informally will establish relationships with many offices and departments in the university including, but not necessarily limited to student affairs. He will be able to speak for the university's interest in the religious traditions and their values as well as defend the freedom of the dissenters and be in a position to influence the development of policy for the university community. He will see an essential relationship between faith and technology, between theory, doctrine and practical experience. And the ability to integrate religious beliefs, technical theory and data and the modalities of ministry in facing human need is the mark of all great professionals. And when the professional tries to express in symbols and cognitive forms his deepest convictions and knowledge about human problems, there is a necessity to act out that meaning in concrete service.

Obviously, the professional scholar and teacher and the campus minister have much in common. Relationships between these two groups on most campuses are much like Schopenhauer's porcupines who learned how to huddle close enough together for warmth but not too close to prick each other! We know the historical reasons for this development as departments of religious studies sought academic respectability and campus ministers were jealous of the disciples who were to be protected from the corrosions of the faculty and administration. Yet each has much to contribute to the other.

The pluralistic scholarship in religious studies can be an intellectual center where students and faculty examine and change their own commitments and formulate beliefs on the basis of learning about other religions as well as their own, while at the same time they are testing their ethical insights and beliefs in relationships to specific policies of the institutions in which they are located. This experience can, at the same time, create a cycle of learning, the feedback from which would richly infuse the teaching and research of departments. The time is ripe for both to seek out the real feelings and thoughts of participants in situations and if the traditional modes of acting have no relevance or meaning, to abandon them. There are just too many important things to be done in the world to permit outmoded forms of scholarship, accretions of ritual piety and organization which have lost their meaning to impede discernment of the real occasions in the modern world for thought and action. We need to heed Bertrand DeJouvenal's warning that there is a constant dying of possible futures about which two mistakes are common. One is to be unaware of them while they are alive, the other, to be unaware of their death when they have been killed off by lack of discovery.

What the future holds for the religious professional and the religious institution in the life of the university, who can foresee? The religious professional at least can be an artist in the sense defined by Marshall McLuhan, "The artist is the man in any field, science or humanities, who grasps the implications of his actions and of new knowledge in his own time. He is the man of integral awareness."[34] He and his community can participate in all areas of the university's life as instruments where needed, exploring the pertinent connections of theology, social policy and self-perception, ready for new forms, less concerned about life and death alternatives. Professors and chaplains can have a depth of understanding which can continually ask what has happened, why it has happened, and then begin to see what they can do. That at least would be worth a try.

NOTES
THE SEARCH FOR CHURCH-UNIVERSITY RELATIONAL MODELS

1. *The Center Magazine,* Volume Two, No. 3, May, 1969.
2. Alfred North Whitehead, *Modes of Thought,* (New York: The Free Press, 1968), p. 171.
3. Kenneth Underwood, *The Church, The University, and Social Policy,* pp. 5–6. A manuscript to be published by the Wesleyan University in late 1969.
4. *Democracy in America,* II. 1. 7.
5. Ivan S. Turgenev, *Fathers and Sons,* trans. by Constance Garnett, (New York: Modern Library, 1950), p. 24.
6. Norman Mailer, "A Fire on the Moon", *Life Magazine,* August 29, 1969, p. 26.
7. *Collected Sonnets of Edna St. Vincent Millay,* (New York: Washington Square Press, 1959).
8. *The Friend,* I, 14.
9. Alfred North Whitehead, *The Aims of Education,* (New York: New American Library, Mentor Books, 1954), p. 57.
10. *Biographia Literaria,* XVII.
11. Whitehead, op. cit., p. 57.
12. For a sophisticated discussion of the debate now going on within the university see James S. Ackerman, "Two Styles: A Challenge to Higher Education", *Daedelus,* Summer, 1969, pp. 855–869.
13. "The AAUP and Campus Disruption", May 3, 1969.
14. "Survival U: Prospects for a Really Relevant University", *Harpers,* September, 1969, pp. 12–22.
15. Quoted in Kornelis H. Miskotte, *When the Gods are Silent,* trans. by John W. Doberstein, (London: Collins, 1967), p. 338.
16. Crane Brinton, *The Political Ideas of the English Romanticists,* (Ann Arbor: University of Michigan, 1966), pp. 88–89.
17. *The Aims of Education,* op.cit., p. 98.
18. *Science and the Modern World,* (New York: New American Library, Mentor Books, 1958), pp. 42–43.
19. *The Advancement of Learning,* VII, 1.

20. Kenneth Underwood, *The Church, the University, and Social Policy,* (Middletown, Conn.: Wesleyan University Press, 1969), 2 vols. The first volume is the director's report on the process of inquiry, the data, and their policy implications. The second volume contains working and technical papers of scholars, ministers, university and church administrators, and others who participated in this study. In addition, the Commission's report will be published in early Autumn, 1969, under the title *New Wine,* edited by William Kolb, Chairman of the Commission, and Dean of Beloit College. The other members of the Commission were: William Cole, Luther Harshbarger, Edith Lerrigo, Charles McCoy, Robert Rankin, J. Paul Reynolds, Harold H. Viehman, and Robert Watson. There have been a number of "spin-off" studies, including Phillip E. Hammond, *The Campus Clergyman,* (New York: Basic Books, Inc., 1966); Jeffrey Hadden, *The Gathering Storm in the Churches* (Garden City: Doubleday, 1969) already published. Further there is Elden E. Jacobson, *The Berkeley Crisis,* unpublished Ph.D. dissertation, Yale University, 1966. And there are other sociological studies, either still incomplete or to be published in other ways. The dimensions of the Study can be illustrated by the fact that the Danforth Foundation funding amounted to approximately $450,000. The cost factor never ceased to appall Underwood, especially when he realized, and constantly emphasized, that this study was only the beginning of a process and itself was part of that process by which the church and the university could reform ministry to campus and, thereby, point the way to the reformation of all the ministry for the sake of the world. As William Kolb put it in his introduction to *New Wine,* "In Underwood's mind his study was only the first of many studies, and of them it would never be possible to say that they were done, for they would be intimately bound up in a continuing process of research, action, and reflection upon action."
21. For examples of this sort of inquiry, see Marshall McLuhan, *Understanding Media: The Extensions of Man* (New York: McGraw-Hill, 1965); Herbert W. Richardson, *Toward an American Theology* (New York: Harper and Row, 1967), ch. 1; Bernard Meland, *The Realities of Faith* (New York: Oxford University Press, 1962).
22. *The Aims of Education,* op. cit., p. 105.
23. Reported in C. P. Shedd, "Religion in the State University", Hazen Pamphlet No. 16, p. 9.
24. The story of this development has been told many times but see especially Clarence Prouty Shedd, *Two Centuries of Student Christian Movement* (New York: Association Press, 1934); *The Church Follows Its Students* (New Haven: Yale University Press, 1938); Merrimon Cuninggim, *The College Seeks Religion* (New Haven: Yale University Press, 1947); Seymour A. Smith, *The American College Chaplaincy,* (New York: Association Press, 1954).

25. The latest statistical information is available in Milton D. McLean, ed. *Religious Studies in Public Universities* (Carbondale: Southern Illinois University, 1967); Erich A. Walker, ed. *Religion and the State University* (Ann Arbor: The University of Michigan Press, 1958); Robert Michaelsen, *The Study of Religion in American Universities: Ten Case Studies* (New Haven: The Society for Religion in Higher Education, 1965), and *The Scholarly Study of Religion* (New Haven: The Society for Religion in Higher Education, 1964); *The Study of Religion in College and University* (New York: National Council of Churches, 1967); *The Study of Religion in the State University* (New Haven: Society for Religion in Higher Education, 1964). Two books dealing with the character of Religious Studies are Clyde A. Holbrook, *Religion, A Humanistic Field* (Englewood Cliffs: Prentice-Hall, 1963), and Paul Ramsey, ed. *Religion* (Englewood Cliffs: Prentice-Hall, 1964). On the place of the study of Religion in General Education see the *Journal of General Education* (University Park: The Pennsylvania State University, vol. 13, no. 3) October, 1961.
26. *Life Magazine,* op.cit., p. 37.
27. John Underwood, "The Desperate Coach," *Sports Illustrated,* August 25, 1969, pp. 66–76.
28. Eugen Rosenstock-Huessy, *The Christian Future,* op. cit., p. xl.
29. Robert J. Lipton, "Protean Man", *Partisan Review,* Winter 1968, Vol. 35, 1:13–27.
30. *The Aims of Education,* op. cit., p. 97.
31. Raymond Williams, *Culture and Society 1780–1950* (London: Chatto and Windus, Pelican Book, 1963), p. 122.
32. *New York Times,* March 16, 1969.
33. *Adventure of Ideas* (New York: MacMillan, 1933), pp. 214–215.
34. Marshall McLuhan, *Understanding Media* (New York: McGraw-Hill, 1965, p. 65.

Part Three

CHALLENGES AND PROSPECTS

Albert Schaffer is professor of sociology in the College of Arts and Sciences at the University of Alabama. Partner in a well-known husband and wife team of sociologists, both Drs. Albert and Ruth Schaffer focus a heavy concentration of their professional and organizational work in the area of contemporary social problems.

Toward an International Community of Man Under God

Albert Schaffer

America and possibly all nations in the western world confront an anomalous situation. The cumulative processes of technological change and organizational complexity have created the definite prospect of solving one major functional problem for all societies, adapting to the environment through production and distribution of material culture. These nations are on the verge of eliminating poverty, of making each family prosperous. Alfred Marshall's prediction, made almost a hundred years ago, that in terms of occupation, every man will be a gentleman, may be validated.[1]

Enjoyment of this circumstance may be short-lived. The technological developments responsible for affluence have also created the capacity of destroying nations and civilization by nuclear weapons and biological warfare. The technology which "solved" one functional problem of society increased the importance of a related problem, avoiding a nuclear war and the destruction of society. The complexities of adjusting institutions and beliefs to cope with this functional challenge make the outcome problematic. This paper explores some of the factors, especially religion, theologians and the university, which will influence the choices to be made.

PATTERNS OF ECONOMIC AND TECHNOLOGICAL CHANGE

The American economy has become increasingly effective in producing the commodities needed to assure a life of comfort and dignity for all members of society.

In this century

> *. . . productivity in the American economy has moved from roughly 2 percent a year before World War II to between 2.5 and 3 percent since the end of the war. . . . growth at 2 percent a year doubles in 36 years; growth at 2.5 percent doubles in 28 years; growth at 3 percent doubles in about 24 years. The notion that a product of an hour of work can double in 24 years . . . contributes to the sense of dynamic change which is so much a part of the economic environment.*[2]

One factor responsible for this dynamism pertains to the reduction of the time required for recognizing the value of innovations and for integrating them into specific industrial processes. One study of twenty important technological innovations during the past seventy years found that the time required for development and application has been shortened. The pace of utilizing inventions has increased.

> *. . . The typical time between a technical discovery and recognition of its commercial potential had fallen from about 30 years before the First World War to 16 years between the wars and 9 years after the Second World War. The additional time required to convert these basic technical discoveries to initial commercial application had decreased from about 7 to 5 years.*[3]

The main direction of the total economy has shifted from production and distribution of goods to the availability of services. These include, among others, medical, educational, financial, legal, retail and wholesale. The magnitude of the shift from production to services is indicated by the fact that since 1947, most of the increase in employment has taken place in the service sector, while that in production has been stable.[4] One economist, Victor Fuchs, sums up this economic trend by declaring that America has a "service economy." The magnitude of the forces responsible for this change is suggested by the prediction that, in the next few decades, services for service industries, or quarternary economic activities, will grow steadily in importance.[5]

The greater demands which service activities make of employees are reflected in the trend since the fifties of increasing college enrollment. Between 1957 and 1967, the number of persons between 18 and 25 attending college more than doubled, from 2.2 million to 5.1 million.[6] College enrollment should reach 7 million by 1975.

The proportion of young people who have attended college also has doubled in recent years. In 1947, 16 percent of men and 13.7 percent of women between the ages of 25 and 29 either had finished or had attended college. The corresponding figures for 1967 were 32.2 percent for men and 25.6 percent for women.[7] One social scientist predicts that by 1980, roughly two-thirds of the residents of cities will be college-trained.[8]

The growing productivity of the American economy, the upgrading of the labor force and the steady reduction in the proportion of the population living in poverty brings Marshall's prediction of every man a gentleman close to reality. Other technological changes and the inadequacies of political institutions may turn the dream into a nightmare.

The two major world powers have stockpiled large numbers of nuclear weapons.

> *. . . as of October 1968 the U.S. could deliver approximately 4,200 nuclear warheads compared to the Soviet's delivery capacity of 1,200.*[9]

The destructive capacity of these weapons is beyond belief.

> *. . . Secretary McNamara estimated that 400 one-megaton warheads would kill about 74,000,000 Russians, and would destroy about 76 percent of Soviety industry. . . .*[10]

If current trends of innovation and diffusion of weaponry continue unchecked, possession of increasingly destructive weapons will spread throughout the world, increasing the probability that a major military conflict will occur. One prediction of the weapons in existence by the end of this century include the following: death rays, effective techniques for chemical and biological warfare, climate changers, earth scorchers and inexpensive nuclear weapons which will be widely available.[11]

The institutions of science and the economy, the efficiency of bureaucracy and government policies have brought America to the verge of eliminating poverty and deprivation. The passing of the "underclass" soon will become an historic landmark. At the same time, destructive capabilities now threaten all of civilization and mankind, and greatly increase the urgency of changing the customary relations between nations. Such changes also will require major changes within nations and within America.

THE TRANSITION

It might seem obvious that the talents and resources which had concentrated for so many years on production of goods and of armaments could readily be redistributed to the agencies concerned with international affairs. Even if this were possible, it would not suffice to accomplish the control of destructive weapons and to establish peaceful methods of resolving international conflicts. The leaders of the nations must first decide on the type of international order which could limit the production and distribution of destructive weapons, and which could compel disputing nations to accept the rule of law. This conception of the desired state of relationships between nations could properly be called an "image" or "vision" of the future. Its adoption will help determine the agenda for national action, select the goals and priorities for which the resources of the country will be allocated.

The elements of this "image" will play a crucial role in directing the future movement of American and of other socieites. Kenneth Boulding described this state of affairs when he wrote:

> *. . . it is the image which in fact determines what might be called the current behavior of any organism or organization. The image acts as a field. The behavior consists in gravitating toward the most highly valued part of the field. . . .*[12]

This view implies that men and their organizations can rationally and purposefully control processes of change, that all important social processes can be aligned with the "image." If this is true, utopias become self-fulfilling, "the future *is* the cause of the present in substantial degree."[13]

Some scholars dispute this view. They regard certain basic features of society to be beyond man's control. Tillich, for example, sees man trapped by the industrial order which he has created, and stripped of personal autonomy.

> *. . . Man is supposed to be the master of his world and of himself. But actually he has become part of the reality he has created, an object among objects, a thing among things, . . . a cog within a universal machine to which he must adapt himself in order not to be smashed by it. . . .*[14]

This view implies the existence of powerful and parochial interests which will oppose and prevent purposeful efforts at social change, especially those seeking to establish an effective rule of law throughout the world. These interests are committed to the present and long-standing pattern of sovereign nations, each of which is the sole arbiter of its national interests, with national security dependent upon military preparedness. Whether men and nations can make the change from this orthodox conception of international relations to one emphasizing orderly transactions between countries depends on several factors. These include the types of groups participating in the processes of selecting an image of the future, and their relative strengths and weaknesses. Theologians can play an especially creative part in this process of image creation.

WEBER'S ANALYSIS OF RELIGION

Max Weber's analysis of the world religions offers valuable insights into the factors influencing the content of beliefs. Each major stratum in society may create or embrace an ideology which provides plausible and acceptable justifications for those activities which enhance the place of the group in society. Since the ideology or religious doctrines tend to vary with the place of the stratum in the class and power hierarchies, a diversity of beliefs is inescapable. The competition among these groups to influence basic policy decisions includes ideological and doctrinal conflicts. From a succession of such conflicts, certain strata emerge triumphant, and the corresponding belief system provides the basis of defining major goals, specifying priorities and appropriate strategies for action. Social structures may be modified in ways which strengthen the position of the bearers of the dominant traditions and beliefs.

Bendix summarized these features of Weber's approach when he said:

> *Status groups may be—and frequently are—the fountain-head of moral ideas that shape the conduct and the world view of the individuals belonging to them. . . . However, the world view of a status group is never solely a response to material conditions. . . . It is also the product of ideas that are the result of human inspiration in response to a spiritual challenge. . . .*[15]

Although the material interests of a stratum and the character of its beliefs were closely connected, Weber differed with Marx by rejecting the view that the former determined the latter. Ideas, for Weber, defined the goals of a class, shaped its interests and directed its energies. Weber also realized that the beliefs accepted by a class seldom demeaned the activities responsible for its wealth and power, nor belittled the conditions responsible for the stability of its place in the social order.

In the analysis of world religions, Weber offered many examples of the links between the material interests and the beliefs of a stratum. He says, for example, of the warrior class:

> *As a rule, the warrior nobles, and indeed feudal powers generally, have not readily become the carriers of a rational religious ethic. The life pattern of a warrior has very little affinity with the notion of a beneficient providence. . . . Concepts like sin, salvation, and religious humility have not only seemed remote from all ruling*

> *strata, particularly the warrior nobles, but have indeed appeared reprehensible to its sense of honor. . . .*[16]

Bureaucratic officials advocate religions characterized by rationality, orderliness and which engender disciplined activity. They favor religions which approve the procedures for assigning positions and determining advancement in the bureaucracy and disapprove of magic and irrationality.[17] Merchants, traders and financiers, especially those engaged in political and booty capitalism, incline toward religions which are this-worldly and non-prophetic.[18]

Intellectuals from privileged strata can decisively influence the orientation of a religion, when such strata have been ousted from top government positions. The withdrawal of a ruling class from politics favors development of salvationist religion. Apparently such groups seek a new meaning for their lives in less mundane activities, and their superior education adds enjoyment and importance to mental activity. The activities of the intellectuals are crucial for religion since

> *. . . It is the intellectual who conceives of the "world" as a problem of meaning. . . . there is a growing demand that the world and the total pattern of life be subject to an order that is significant and meaningful.*[19]

The intellectual may seek absolute withdrawal from the world, a contemplative life, individual salvation or the reconstruction of society in accordance with ethical standards.

In the contemporary period, where literacy is becoming universal and the proportion of the citizenry with a college education is climbing, various intellectual groups, and particulary those located in the university, will compete with one another and with elites in government, business and the military for the opportunity of redefining the "meaning" of the human condition in the twenty-first century.

THE ALTERNATIVES

A number of alternatives are available for responding to these functional problems. A combination of military, political and defense industry leaders might embrace the thesis of a continuing and growing threat of communist subversion and aggression. Meaning in life, at least for young men, could be found in the collectivist pursuit of dedicating the prime years of manhood to the defense of the nation. Government would continue to expend huge amounts of national resources for the development and production of increasingly powerful weapons. America would retain characteristics of a "mobilized polity" for the energies of many scientists and engineers would be devoted to military activities.[20] The nation would remain the basic unit of societal and political organization.

A second group of industry leaders, those engaged in mass communication and entertainment, might advocate a more individualistic and hedonistic ethos, an "amusement-entertainment-vacation" style of life for the masses. This ethos would be anchored in the gadgetry of mass production and consumption. Its participants would find meaning in travel, hobbies, outdoor activities and entertainment. Citizens would accept the social order as "given," and manifest dissatisfaction, not in movements for social change but in private pursuits, encouraged by officials of the industries which would benefit from increased use of these outlets.

A third approach would combine individualistic, achievement orientation with collective needs in a renewed emphasis on improving the "quality of life" in America Individuals would seek intellectual development and psychological fulfillment in joining with one another in efforts to overcome social problems: pollution, poverty, discrimination, hunger, malnutrition, and related social ills. The Peace Corps and VISTA represent prototypes of the future organizations, along with many voluntary associations traditionally committed to social reform. Members of various academic groups, from both the social and biological sciences, would be deeply involved in such movements. These specialists would be concerned with constructive use of science's new capabilities for modifying human heredity. They also would be concerned with using the computer in the development of information systems capable of improving the planning functions associated with decision making.

A fourth approach would be supranational, concerned with developing global institutions for regulating the use of military force. Here theologians could play a critical and possibly indispensable role. Transcendental beliefs and ethos of the Judaic-Christian creed, its universalistic commitment to the brotherhood of man would seem to be a prerequisite for developing an international society to which all nation states would be subordinated.

The main direction of development would require a reinterpretation and adjustment of ancient Christian beliefs to contemporary conditions of increased contact between nations with widely different cultural and religious traditions. These beliefs concern

> *. . . The univeralism of Christianity . . . a conception of a moral order for Christendom as a whole, with Christendom ideally expected eventually to comprise all mankind. This matched and was without doubt greatly influenced by the Roman conception of a universal socio-political order governed by a single universal system of law, a natural law coming to be institutionalized as the law of a politically organized society.*[21]

The central task concerns establishment of a common framework of sacred values and beliefs which outlaws war, justifies a universal rule of law and legal processes of conflict resolution. The belief system must not legitimize expansionist tactics by any nation-state. In some way the leaders and theologians of the major religions of the world must find the common ethical standards which would legitimize, motivate and sanctify efforts to create the institutional framework for an international, pluralistic society.

America and the world require the emergence of a value system which can function in a manner comparable to that of the Protestant Ethic in the seventeenth and eighteenth centuries. In that era, as analyzed by Weber, stubborn resistance to the role behavior and activities necessary for the rise of capitalism was overcome by a this-worldly religious ethic which defined the systematic and rational accumulation of wealth as a sign of other-worldly success. At present the western world needs an ethic to legitimize and motivate the development of institutions for peaceful resolution of conflict anywhere in the world, which can effectively subordinate national to the global interests of mankind.

Why should religion and its leaders become concerned with complex secular matters which will bring them into conflict with leaders of government and industry? Daniel Callahan offers one reason when he states

> . . . *Since all of the churches claim a special, overriding interest in moral values and the dignity of man, society can rightfully ask them to make a contribution where moral values and human dignity are pertinent to social problems. . . .*[22]

If religious leaders ignore the moral dimension of international relations, theology will have no relevance for the most urgent issues confronting mankind. Other strata, committed to narrower interests, will determine the ultimate issues of peace or war, anarchy or order on the international level.

Theologians in the western world are strategically situated for launching and continuing this movement. Many hold positions in the institution which some analysts regard as the dominant organization of the post-industrial society, the university.[23] This institutional anchorage has several advantages. As members of academic institutions, either in universities or in seminaries, theologians need have far fewer concerns with the organizational imperatives of the church, with fund raising, competition for members, gaining and maintaining support from influential patrons. Religious scholars can place first priority on adapting theology to urgent social problems. Insulated from the various pressure groups within the church and denomination, these scholars can exercise more fully their creative and innovative powers.

Discourse between scholars of religion in various nations and cultures would seem to be a prerequisite for developing agreement on values and priorities. Theologians, as members of learned professions, can freely arrange regional and international conferences on matters of importance to theology and world affairs. They can circulate among universities in foreign lands giving lectures, consulting and serving as visiting professors. Not to be overlooked is the exchange of ideas in scholarly journals and in books.

As members of the academic community, theologians have access to the experts among the faculty on problems of disarmament, control of nuclear weapons, international relations, and related matters. They can, if they choose, seek out the social and biological scientists, the historians and the humanists, whose expertise would assist them in relating their ideas to the realities of political and social affairs.

To suggest that religious ethics and theologians may have a decisive role to play in assisting America and all civilized nations in the reorganization of international relations and in developing institutional controls over armed conflict may appear unrealistic. As Stalin recognized when he inquired into the number of divisions which the Pope controlled, the influence of religion does not rest on military force. Its role in the future depends on access to the minds of an expanding segment of the population, those who are educated. The steady growth in the educational level of the citizenry gives theology professors, and intellectuals in general, a growing audience, one which consists to a large degree of the opinion leaders of the community, the men and women who help to shape public opinion and influence the preferences of decision makers.

If theologians and leaders of religious organizations become more actively engaged in the question of international order as a prerequisite in the modern era for the attainment of human dignity, intense conflict with opposing interest groups must be expected. The nation-state has been a powerful influence for many centuries; it has captured the loyalty of citizens. To identify with a supranational political entity has been synonymous with disloyalty to one's native land. Unless mankind can come to recognize the significance of higher loyalties, to the international community of man under God, controlling the proliferation and use of increasingly destructive weapons would appear to be impossible. If religion cannot contribute significantly to meeting this most urgent challenge, then it might truly become nonfunctional.

NOTES
TOWARD AN INTERNATIONAL COMMUNITY OF MAN UNDER GOD

1. T. H. Marshall, "Citizenship and Social Class," in *Class, Citizenship and Social Development* (Garden City, N.Y. Doubleday, Anchor Book, 1965), p. 74.
2. "Technology and Change," *The Public Interest,* 3 (Spring, 1966), p. 125.

3. *Ibid.,* p. 126.
4. Victor R. Fuchs, "The First Service Economy," *The Public Interest,* 2 (Winter, 1966), pp. 7–9.
5. Herman Kahn and Anthony J. Wiener, *The Year 2000* (New York: MacMillan, 1967), pp. 62–63.
6. Lawrence A. Mayer, "Young America: By the Numbers," *Fortune* (January, 1969), p. 73.
7. *Ibid.*
8. Zbigniew Brzezinski, "The Search For Meaning Amid Change," *The New York Times* (January 6, 1969).
9. Hubert H. Humphrey, "'Safeguard': A Question of Priorities," *Saturday Review* (April 5, 1969), p. 28.
10. *Ibid.*
11. Herman Kahn and Anthony J. Wiener, *op.cit.,* p. 85.
12. Kenneth E. Boulding, *The Image* (Ann Arbor, Mich.: The University of Michigan Press, paperback, 1961), p. 115.
13. Wilbert E. Moore, "The Utility of Utopias," *American Sociological Review,* 31 (December, 1966), p. 770.
14. Paul Tillich, *Theology of Culture* (New York: Oxford University Press, Galaxy Book, 1964, originally published in 1959), p. 46.
15. Reinhard Bendix, *Max Weber: An Intellectual Portrait* (Garden City, N.Y.: Doubleday, 1960), p. 268.
16. Max Weber, *Economy and Society,* Vol. 2, Guenther Roth and Claus Wittich, eds., (New York: Bedminister Press, 1968), p. 472.
17. *Ibid.,* pp. 476–77.
18. *Ibid.,* pp. 477–80.
19. *Ibid.,* p. 506.
20. Daniel Bell, "Notes on the Post-Industrial Society, (I)," *The Public Interest,* 6 (Winter, 1967), p. 33.
21. Talcott Parsons, "Christianity and Modern Industrial Society," *Sociological Theory and Modern Society, op.cit.,* p. 399.
22. Daniel Callahan, "The Quest for Social Relevance," *Daedalus,* 96 (Winter, 1967), p. 161.
23. Daniel Bell, "Notes on the Post-Industrial Society, (II)," *The Public Interest,* 7 (Spring, 1967), p. 102.

Hubert G. Locke heads Wayne State University's religious affairs office located in the recently-dedicated Charles Grosberg Religious Center and serves as research associate in the WSU Center for Urban Studies. A life-long Detroiter, active in both church and civic affairs, Mr. Locke's recent book, THE DETROIT RIOT OF 1967 (Wayne State University Press, 1969) views "his city" as paradigmatic of every other city in America—"in a race with time—and thus far losing the battle."

University Cities and the City of God: Looking Toward the Year 2000

Hubert G. Locke

Any attempt to anticipate or project the shape or style of those peculiar American twins, the city and the university, in the second millennium, represents a strong act of courage. American college campuses are in the throes of student upheavals and American cities are disintegrating. Both institutions are under severe assault; both deserve the attack; and, if either or both survive to the year 2000, it will be, hopefully, in a radically new and different form. These institutions reflect clearly the larger trauma of American society itself; therefore, in understanding why the university and the city are in deep trouble, how their problems have become so massive and unwieldy, and in attempting to define what can be done to resolve those problems, we may discover a clue to the survival and the future—if any—of the nation.

Cities and universities have been deliberately separated both physically and philosophically until relatively recent times. Their histories have kept them apart, but the times have driven them together and their destinies are now indivisible. Universities in America have, for the most part, been the result of conscious planning and clear objectives. Cities, on the other hand, have been regarded as ad hoc conglomerates, turning this way and that to serve the immediate needs of its citizens. Particular pains have been taken to isolate institutions of higher learning, physically and intellectually, away from the corrupting influence of urban environments. The colleges and universities have benefited—or suffered—from something that American cities have, generally, never had—something that is called, in popular jargon, a self-image. That self-image began in the seventeenth and eighteenth centuries with the establishment of Harvard, Yale and Princeton for the training of the clergy. It was re-directed in the mid-nineteenth century toward the demands of an agrarian-industrial society, and the institutions continue today as the primary training ground for America's growing middle-class, professional elite. It is, however, precisely that process of grinding out hundreds of thousands of technocrats to run the machinery of American society, while the society itself slips deeper and faster into the cauldron of social chaos, that has created the widespread discontent on American college campuses today There may still be some dispute about whether American society is sick, but there is little question that it is in serious trouble; it should not surprise us, therefore, to find increasing attention being turned toward that institution which has traditionally prepared the personnel to make the society function.

The troubles of the cities become clearer when we realize that they suffer not from a self-image that has shifted or been re-directed, but from the lack of having any self-image in the first place. The modern city was launched after the Civil War by the forces of immigration and industrialization, and has been allowed to drift, enlarge, expand, periodically explode, and to decay at random for more than a century. Its problems—physical, social, economic, cultural, and educational—have churned beneath the surface of urban society for so many generations that their explosion into public consciousness in the past decade has had every appearance of an urban Armegeddon. The colleges and universities were oriented, physically and financially, toward rural America, and did not sense this impending explosion any sooner than the rest of American society. When the explosion came, the scholarly world responded in typical academic fashion with a plethora of urban study centers and institutes, most of which have opted for post-facto assessments of the urban crisis. They have, in other words, chosen to find out what happened and to investigate the past with typical scholarly patience. These urban centers in colleges and universities are creations of the past decade; in the minds of man, they represent far too little response from the academic world and may prove to be far too late to make any significant contribution.

Separate though they have been in history and perspective, the fate of both city and university are now inextricably intertwined. For those institutions of higher education that are physically located in metropolitan communities, the interrelatedness of their destinies is obvious. But those magnificent citadels of learning which arise, phoenix-like, out of the cornfields of the midwest or which form the nucleus of college towns on the eastern seaboard or throughout the south, are also not immune from the failures or fortunes of the American metropolis. As is widely known, though not fully appreciated, America is for all practical purposes an urban nation; as the cities of America go, so will every institution in American society, as well as the nation itself.

Viewed historically, religion in America has played a significant role in the rise of both the American city and the American university. At times, as in the founding of the University of Chicago or during the Social Gospel Era, the contribution of religion—scholarly, socially and financially, has been a brilliant one. In other periods and circumstances, which good taste forbids mentioning, religion's role has been both pompous and paltry, if not stifling! In both cases, however, religion, as a life-style and as an institutional force, has shared the grandeur and the misery of its efforts with every other discipline or institutional way of life in American culture. Its search for knowledge and devotion to truth has been no less than those conducted in medicine, law, and the sciences. Its failures to apply its knowledge and insights to the problems of urban society have been no greater than those of the American Bar Association or the American Academy of Sciences. The present urban predicament and future hopes may force upon religion and university alike a reassessment of their time-honored positions in society as they both seek to grapple with an anti-intellectual, dehumanizing undercurrent in American urban culture which threatens to engulf them all.

Ironically, such a reassessment may reopen the ancient debate between Athens and Jerusalem that, for the past several decades at least, has been virtually at a standstill in American society. Colleges and universities which managed a century ago, rather painfully in some instances, to wrench themselves free of ecclesiastical control, have also outgrown their deep-seated and at times immature suspicions about religion and its adherents. During this same period, religion for the most part has come to accept the fact that it no longer has a monopoly on knowledge and truth, if it ever did. Currently, both enterprises seem content to live in a state of relatively peaceful coexistence. Indeed, in some academic-religious quarters recently, there have been signs of growing reapproachment between these two arenas of human endeavor, especially as both have been forced to confront a new life-style in the modern era which seems in its premises and achievements inimical to the best interests of both religion and the university.

This new life-style has arisen in large measure from what Daniel Bell terms "the bewitchment of technology and the way it has transformed the world."[1] And it is the city which has been the focus of this technological transformation and, at the same time, the principal setting transformed by technology. Cities have become simultaneously the arena and the reflection of technological change. If one looks at the city from this perspective, the transformation has been a mixed blessing. Yet, most academicians and ecclesiastiarchs alike are cautious of being hypercritical of this development, partly because wisdom dictates that both attempt to direct its potential rather than deny or fight its existence, and partly because common sense forces the recognition that all the really valid criticisms of the machine age were made by

Huxley, Orwell and others a generation ago. But current circumstances may well change the ancient question of "what has Athens to do with Jerusalem" to the more pressing issue of what has Athens or Jerusalem to do with Detroit, Chicago, Houston, San Francisco or a dozen other symbols of burgeoning technopolitan complexes.

THE ANCIENT FEUD AND ITS MODERN IMPLICATIONS

It is one of the tragedies of Western intellectual history that theology in the Middle Ages took it upon itself to become the queen of the sciences. That era represented, however, a relatively orderly arrangement of the interests of both mind and spirit. But the alliance was a fragile one, as the infamous Galileo heresy trial demonstrated. And when the alliance crumbled completely during the Enlightenment Era, it resulted in an unfortunate bifurcation of the arenas of mind and spirit. A lengthy period of competition developed, and when it climaxed in the 1850's with the publication of Darwin's *Origin of Species,* the die had been cast and the break was completed. Science as we know it today began then to hold full sway over the "house of intellect" while religion was relegated to the sphere of human emotions—only to find that even here, in the last niche of its claim to be taken seriously, its insights, methods and presuppositions became challenged by the most recent arrival in the scientific camp—the discipline of psychiatry.

Thus, the result of a centuries-long process was that religion and theology, once thought to reign supreme over all of man's activity and being, was successively and successfully challenged—on its physical presuppositions by biology and medicine, in its cultural claims by anthropology and sociology, and its mental insights by psychology and psychiatry. Even basic theological premises, not to mention some rather crystallized Christian dogmas, were brought into grave question by the new knowledge: biology and geology combined to take issue with the traditional Judaeo-Christian interpretation of creation, while historical research began to cast methodological doubts on the premises of the religious view of history. Finally, as universities broke free in America from their religious roots, and ventured forth in a new intellectual atmosphere, imbued with the spirit and methodology of the scientific approach, religion's claim to have any valid knowledge at all, in the scientific sense, came under suspicion, if not open attack. In American higher education at the beginning of this century, therefore, religion retreated to the realm of seminary concerns and on state college campuses was relegated to the role of a student activity. In both places, it was assumed that no one would take religion seriously.

Such a development does not imply nor should it suggest that religion stood helplessly by while higher education moved to center stage. Faculties of theological schools did not abandon their scholarly search for, nor their contributions to, the new insights concerning man and society, and student religious movements led by courageous and skilled chaplains often formed the vanguard of religion's most pioneering and successful efforts to creatively penetrate the social and cultural entanglements of the 20th century. But in general it can be observed that the period between the turn of the 20th century and its midpoint was marked by a cold war between religion and higher education, and that the thaw of the past two decades has been a welcomed and beneficial development for both combatants.

During this same period, the city in America was emerging in a style and form which attributed little practical value to either endeavor. Universities were taken for granted as the preparation point for the teachers, doctors, engineers, lawyers, social workers and businessmen who made the machinery of the city hum, while religious institutions were expected to provide a symbol of and a setting for the urban dweller's more decent instincts. But the real thrust of the city's aims and the significance of its efforts were clearly in other directions. The city in this era was fast becoming the foremost economic stage from which the careers of hundreds of thousands of petite bourgeoisie—miniature Horatio Algers—would be launched. For the first two decades after 1900, they were the European immigrants and for the next three, southern dream seekers. The hopes of all these people were identical. They were drawn to the city because it was the place to make money—and universities were important primarily to the extent that they enabled the second or third generation of these urban pioneers to pursue their goal professionally, while religion was valuable insofar as it made them spiritually comfortable in the pursuit. Currently, because the city no longer provides this economic utopia, both it and its institutions have become focal points of anger and frustration, instead of vehicles of optimism.

THE CURRENT SITUATION AND THE NEW DILEMMA

There was much more than just intellectual disagreement involved in the family feud—or perhaps we should call it a lover's quarrel—which erupted between churches and institutions of higher education one hundred years ago, and which, a century later, both disputants are trying to patch up. The disagreement also had its roots, as most family fights do, in the fact that the offspring which the church had so carefully nurtured in this nation for 200 years (i.e. since the founding of Harvard), suddenly grew up—came of age—and like every rebellious youth, decided to test its own wings and escape the antiquated outlook and authoritarian posture of its spiritual parent. Amply aided by its new-found friends in business and government, colleges and universities struck out on a new path of what they deemed to be greater intellectual freedom and scholarly respectability. Their progenitor, the church, was left at home in its parishes and cathedrals dismayed and perplexed over the brashness and ingratitude of its academic upstart for which it had done so much.

The debate over Charles Darwin, therefore, and whether his biological insights could be squared with the church's traditional doctrine of creation, which raged in the 1860's and 70's, was for all practical purposes a kind of watershed in American church history and American higher education. From that time forward, American philosophy began to chart a clear course away from the concerns of theology and Christian ethics and toward pragmatism, while sociology began to emerge as a discipline distinct from the benevolent concerns of church leadership, and the professions of teaching and social work began to develop as vocational interests quite apart from any religious motivations.

For the next fifty years or so, this divorce of higher education from the domination of religion seemed extraordinarily advantageous. American business and industry took up the philanthropic slack left by the splitting off of American colleges and universities from their religious sources. The Rockefellers, the Carnegies, the Vanderbilts, the DuPonts, along with the companies they founded and the foundations they controlled, began to make heavy financial investments in institutions of higher education. They built buildings, endowed chairs, created scholarship programs, established libraries, and underwrote centers and institutes. Although here and there they also built chapels, created theological libraries, and paid for the salaries of professors of religion, their primary interests were elsewhere and were reflective of that well known comment of Calvin Coolidge, that "the business of America is business." Clearly, business and industry was outgrowing the situation of a generation earlier in which a tycoon and his sons plus several good accountants and a man of unskilled labor ran the nation's factories and giant industrial complexes. For as the complexity of American business increased, American businesses turned more and more to colleges and universities for the lawyers, tax experts, engineers, personnel directors, physicists, chemists, management executives, labor relations directors and a dozen other occupational positions that were needed to make American industry and by extension, America itself, progress. Religion was simply no longer a priority in this scheme of things.

Simultaneously, American government got into this new romance, first with its large grants of land to states for the creation of agricultural colleges, and then slowly but perceptively, with increasingly significant amounts of money, in support of government research interests. Curiously, up until World War II, when the government wanted to avail itself of the university's brain trust, it simply co-opted or literally bought off whatever skills it needed. The famous Manhattan Project was a classic and horrible example of such tactics. But after the War, the government seduced, and the universities succumbed, to the persuasive notion that universities themselves should conduct research and develop programs in the national interest. Out of this strange and, for many, illicit romance has come a welter of academic abortions, like government-sponsored Ph.D. programs in glass blowing and the Institute for Defense Analysis at Columbia.

Which brings us to the chaotic present and a curious, almost ironic observation, namely that it is today's student generation which is decrying these clandestine alliances and, from their perspective, immoral affairs. It is today's students who are raising the religious questions of our time. Although we may curdle at the way in which some of them ask the questions and get turned off by the choice of language students use to frame their queries, we nevertheless miss what's happening in large measure on today's campuses if we do not hear students asking some profound, probing, indelicate but extremely pertinent questions about the structure, nature, purpose and direction of American society in the second half of the 20th Century.

Such an observation is not meant to be an endorsement of, or a rationale for, student sit-ins, the free speech movement, the underground press, pot parties or campus riots. Nevertheless, these are simply the more glaring and jarring manifestations of a much larger student sentiment which is asking questions about justice in America, about abject poverty in the midst of an affluent society, about the values of a nation which gets in an uproar about four-letter words but is indifferent to the obscenity of slums, chronic unemployment and war. And these, whatever else we may wish to call them, are profoundly *religious* questions—the same questions the ancient prophets of Israel confronted the people and leaders of that nation with 2500 years ago; the same relentless issues which Jesus of Nazareth continually raised and which made him so extremely unpopular. The concerns of serious-minded students today are no longer goldfish swallowing or panty raids or how many frat members can be crammed into a phone booth; instead our best students are asking questions about how this nation got into the mess it is in and why we continue to wallow deeper and deeper in our own mistakes. Both church and university should be grateful that someone finally is raising just such questions!

It is by no means clear or convincing that students have substantive workable answers for these questions. Their rhetoric gets at times just as pompous and dogmatic, just as doctrinaire and irrational as past generations have been in consecrating the status quo. But if this nation or its universities or the church or any other institution thinks that students can be legislated back into respectful silence, or that police officers can be used to restore the calm of the campus, while ignoring what students are saying—indeed in their language, demanding what this nation do and be—such institutions are not only sadly mistaken, but they simply court further and continual disaster.

Perhaps, therefore, the church should look upon the present campus turmoil as something of a blessing in disguise—an enormous, perhaps even weird, disguise, but a blessing nevertheless—for out of it may come some new and imaginative ways for the noblest concerns and the best wishes of the church to be harnessed with the tremendous resources, skills and insights of the university in the building of a better, more just, more humane nation.

Of this, we can be certain. If we can bring together the church's concerns, not for, but *with* most of its students, and tap the resources of our universities, we may build a new and exciting life-style for the people of this nation that will give us all cause for pride and satisfaction. If we cannot or will not do this, not only our churches, colleges and universities, but our nation may well not have a future—and certainly will not deserve one.

TOWARD THE YEAR 2000: THE CITY AS MODEL FOR RELIGION AND THE UNIVERSITY

Historical records tell us that the occasion which prompted St. Augustine to write his celebrated *Civitate Dei,* was the sack of Rome by the Goths in 410 A.D., a situation frightfully similar to our contemporary urban predicament. His task, although it took him thirteen years, was infinitely easier and certainly more realistic than the one that now faces us. Rome already lay in ashes and Augustine's initial chore, as he took it upon himself, was to dispel any suspicions that Rome's downfall was the result of Christian influence. *Civitate Dei,* of course, became much more than a Christian apology; it grew into a classic statement of the Christian philosophy of history and the proper—in Augustine's understanding—relationship between the Church and the State.

In contrast, the current task is not quite as simple. American cities have not fallen—yet; and the pressures are not from barbarians beating on our gates, they are exploding from within the walls. To anticipate the future, therefore, requires faith that the present afflictions of urban American are not fatal but perhaps only the dying of an old order so that a new and more abiding cultural form can arise. It is this task to which religion and the university must turn with increased commitment in the present era.

Throughout the history of culture, the prophetic mood of anticipating the future, which at times has often become an eschatological hope, has traditionally been a significant aspect of the religious enterprise, but like so many religious manifestations it has slowly passed into the domain of the academic world. In our own nation, this creative endeavor has recently become enshrined in that unique of all-American institutions—a committee, which under the distinguished auspices of the American Academy of Arts and Sciences, is at work defining the priorities, examining alternatives and proposing solutions for the shape and style of our society in the year 2000.

The membership of the "Commission on the Year 2000" reads like a Harvard-MIT "Who's Who."[2] However, although it identifies "Negro rights" as one of the major problems of the future, the Commission is noticeably lacking any black members. Still, the working papers issued by this body have so far proven exciting in scope and imagination. They reflect a new process which was both feared and scorned a generation ago but one which now has the highest priority in governmental and scholarly circles. This process consists not only of anticipating the future but also of planning for its shape and style. If nothing else emerges as consensus from the efforts of the Commission, this one central theme does: that without careful and intensive planning over the next three decades, American society certainly will not have a viable future and, for many Commission members, it is apparently questionable whether it will deserve one.

On all three institutions—city, religion and the university—the Commission has some perceptive observations and imaginative proposals, all of which either clearly state or intuitively presume some common concern and effort on the part of this triumvirate. The comments on religion and university, however, betray a stance which takes the urban thrust of culture in the second millenium for granted, almost as a necessary evil. Both spokesmen for religion and the university seem more concerned with the question of how best to guarantee their own institutional futures than with the more central issue of how their respective endeavors can contribute to the shaping and humanizing of the larger, societal future.

That contribution can best be made if both religion and the university return to what has been their traditional roles in society—roles which neither has played consistently and effectively, but which represent what both can do best in their respective spheres. Universities can best assure that society will reach the year 2000, and that life in that new epoch will be worth anticipating and living, if they become primarily centers of diligent, rigorous, politically and economically uncommitted intellectual endeavor. If they would be true to themselves and their tradition, universities cannot and should not be centers of social action or platforms for economic reform; instead they should produce the policies, programs and the people who can enter these processes armed with the best insights, the most creative spirits and the firmest convictions possible. To do this, universities must somehow manage to free themselves from the limited, ideologically oriented confines of serving as the handmaidens of the Pentagon or other governmental interests, no matter in what intellectual jargon universities would choose to disguise this role. At the same time, the thought and research and planning of the university will and should have, in many instances, practical applicability; this will save institutions of higher education from continuing exercises in irrelevancy. Basically, however, universities must be unencumbered from any and all influences—especially political ones—which would judge its value to the social process exclusively on the extent to which its efforts are "in the national interest" or pertinent to the urban crisis or any other dominant concern of the times. It is to ask of the university what may appear to be obvious and contradictory, but what is not always easy to accomplish or maintain consistently, that its constituents muster the courage and the integrity to keep a clear distinction between their scholarly tasks and their personal commitments. To ask such is not to encourage either duplicity or hypocrisy, but only to underscore the fact that when the university ceases to be an arena of independent thought and study and becomes instead a promoter of causes, a platform for political crusades or a tool of public or private policy, it has therewith and thereby ceased to be a university.

At the same time, religion must do what in American society is particularly difficult for an institution which is so at one with the "American way of life"; it must cease to be a consecrator of and become instead a critic of that culture of which it is part, in the name and for the sake of what Paul Tillich would call the ultimate concerns and questions which man and society face in every age. If there is one common fault which underlies both religion and university in contemporary American culture, it is that both face the temptation to become too comfortable, too identified with the way things are rather than what they ought to be. To this extent, Krister Stendahl is right in observing that "the church is no longer the religious dimension of a national or regional culture. It is an institution placed in or against that culture."[3] This also means that religion cannot merely opt for being a plaintive and pathetic cry of moralistic denunciation against prevailing cultural forms; too often this is the stance and perspective which religious institutions currently portray. Society should expect religious institutions and leadership in the future, along with every other major institution, to translate the best thought, insights, and experiences of the university into workable programs of economic reform and social action. By respecting each other's unique role and contribution and by each taking advantage of what the other can give, Athens and Jerusalem together may save Megalopolis from itself and for a far brighter future.

This latter theme of salvation, which is primarily a religious concept but which has its academic counterparts, should not be taken lightly. No matter what terminology one uses, the desire and necessity of survival for urban culture in America is real, and with it goes the hope that such survival will be in a more elegant form and style than currently appears. For over a thousand years, the idea prevailed that the salvation of culture, or its survival if one prefers, rested with the strength of religion. For the past two hundred years, society has placed its faith in science. Neither endeavor alone has brought in the millennium. Perhaps we stand on the threshold of discovering that both together might possibly insure a decent future for our posterity.

Considerable progress toward laying the foundation for a more humane future might be made by both religion and the university if they begin to look upon the city, not as an occasion for anguish and despair, but as a model around which our highest hopes and best achievements can be focused. The city in history has traditionally (i.e. until the emergence of the modern American metropolis) been just such a model. It has been the arena for and the symbol of man's most fruitful endeavors, in art and architecture, literature and learning, music, science and technology. The great cathedrals, libraries, museums, symphony orchestras and universities, together with the centers of trade and commerce, manufacturing processes, hospitals and research institutions have all been primarily located in the cities of Western civilization.[4]

The irony in American society is that a nation which has an abundance of resources—natural, intellectual, technological and spiritual—has made such an enormous mess of its urban areas. As discussed earlier, this problem has occured in large measure because cities in America have been centers of commerical and industrial exploitation rather than arenas of cultural, scientific, and spiritual achievement. The primary and most basic need therefore is for a new view of and mood toward the city—one which dramatically reverses the American urban mentality of the past two centuries and begins to focus upon the city in all of its creative potential rather than its past failures or present plight.

With this new mental orientation toward the city must come also the recognition that cities in America are physically too large to be manageable, that the continual process of trying to accommodate seventy percent of this nation's populace on ten percent of its land area, is courting continual disaster. New towns can and should be planned away from existing cities where the opportunity presents itself to start afresh, avoiding the mistakes of our urban past and taking advantage of all the social and technological insights we now have in urban planning. Existing cities also can be physically decentralized politically, educationally and socially into sub-urban communities, incorporating the best features of smaller, more cohesive social units and avoiding the worst aspects of suburbia.

If the city, decentralized and restructured into more cohesive and manageable components, becomes the socio-cultural model for the future, then religious institutions and those of higher education can become both contributors to this new model and themselves models for this new lifestyle. The intellectual and technological resources of the university should be able to offer the insights, planning and skills needed to construct and reconstruct new and existing cities in America, while churches and synagogues, together with other urban institutions, can become focal points for and implementors of community change. But universities especially, and to some extent religious institutions as well, can also serve as models for the city of the future.

University communities today, for all practical purposes are American cities in microcosm; in their enrollments they rival the populations of many towns. In the diversity of their populations—ethnic, cultural and economic—they reflect the heterogeneous mix of the larger society. Most universities today are involved in massive housing projects, have their own internal police systems, operate lab schools, run profit-making enterprises from book stores to computer installations and generally are engaged in the same processes in miniature which are a part of the larger urban scene.

Universities as cities therefore have the potential and the resources to develop as present-day laboratories for the cities of the future. We should be able to look to institutions of higher education not only for answers to technological problems, but also as settings in which problems of the dynamics of politics, human relations, participatory democracy, social justice, war and peace, racism and the myriad other difficulties of contemporary society can be tackled and resolved in a manner that will provide clues and techniques for their resolution in the larger social framework. What is basically needed both for religion and for the university as well, is not only to plan for the future but to demonstrate in the present, the shape and style of our future hopes. Rather than simply react to the current urban crisis or respond to pressures to become relevant to urban problems, universities and colleges especially are in a unique position to take the city as the social-environmental model of the future and to transform the present dynamics of their institutional life into representations of what that future setting should be—to make indeed university cities, symbols of the city of God.

NOTES
UNIVERSITY CITIES AND THE CITY OF GOD: LOOKING TOWARD THE YEAR 2000

1. Daniel Bell, "The Trajectory of an Idea," *Daedalus,* Vol. 96, No. 3, Summer, 1967.
2. Twelve of the 38 members of the Commission as of the summer of 1967 were either Harvard or MIT faculty members; another four were from Yale and two were from Columbia.
3. Krister Stendahl, "Religion, Mysticism and the Institutional Church," *Daedalus,* Vol. 96, No. 3, Summer, 1967.
4. It is of more than passing interest that the word "city" and the word "civilization" share the same Latin root!

Index